"This beautifully written and lavishly illustrated volume is a collective portrait of those Jews who served the Russian Tsars, from the converts Vice Chancellor Pyotr Shafirov and Oberpolitseimeister Anton Devier in the reign of Peter the Great to the late nineteenth-century banker Evzel Ginzburg. It sheds fascinating new light on the history of Jews under the Tsarist monarchy."
– Antony Polonsky, Albert Abramson Professor of Holocaust Studies at the United States Holocaust Museum and Brandeis University

"This fascinating book tells the curious story of courtiers of Jewish heritage who worked within and alongside the Tsarist court for centuries. The interconnections between individual Jews and the imperial court demonstrate remarkable continuities between the Russian and European experiences, where so-called court Jews were a regular feature of life in the capital."
–Jeffrey Veidlinger
Director and Alvin H. Rosenfeld Chair, Jewish Studies Program, Indiana University Bloomington

"*Jews in Service to the Tsar* is a weighty document of historical truth. Especially for those who are interested in the positive side of Jewish history in Russia. And there can be no doubt that such a side exists..."
– Mikhail Davidson, OKNA

"This book is very attractive because of its calm impartiality, protecting the author from any sort of prejudice toward the people and events herein, such that the portrait of Jews is not idealized and the portrait of Russians is not seen through the prism of Russophobia. This is history as it was, and not as someone wants to see it... Lev Berdnikov has managed to write a book which, with its not-overly-long essays, can be read in the metro or in a comfortable chair by the fire, transporting the reader back in time; one could also sit with it at a desk with pencil in hand, turning a book written for many into a book written for one. This book should be taken not merely as a fact of literature, but as a fact of circumspect historical enlightenment that leaves it to the reader to think and then draw his or her own conclusions."
– Viktor Kagan, *Notes on Jewish History*

"Oh, how Lev Berdnikov's book deserves a mass printing! It encompasses such a breadth of strengths. There is modernity – as if one is wandering the internet – and the most subtle flair for poeticisms. I was amazed when the author noted how Leon Mandelstam in the nineteenth century made a bold discovery: "the fragrance of colors," something worthy of the most exquisite poet of the Silver Age. It is a lively account, with vivid portraits of its protagonists and a massive foundation of research. In a rarity for popular literature, there are nine pages listing "primary sources," from "Memoirs of Empress Catherine II," to Olearius and Tatishchev… and including books in English, French and Portuguese… And, most importantly, there is the drama of destiny. The moral charge, journalistic pathos. My conclusion: Jews made an invaluable contribution to Russian government and culture."

– Edvarda Kuzmina, *Storony Sveta*

"The twenty-eight men portrayed in this book are specifically the Jews who did not shy away from contact with power, which is why they were able to become eminent or even preeminent figures in Russian culture, in Russian society, and even in the Russian government. Their portraits are based on little-known material. How could it have been otherwise? (During the Soviet era they tried to forget them not because they were Jews, but because they cavorted with tsarist governments). These portraits are convincing not just because they are grounded in fact, but also because of the sincerity of the author's voice."

– Lev Anninsky, *Rodina* (2010, #4)

"There was an amazing breadth of professional activity among Russian Jews: not only were the Jews merchants, entrepreneurs, jewelers, bankers and doctors, but they were also diplomats, chiefs of police, postmasters, court tutors, writers, public figures and even jesters. The reader meets characters who are paradoxical in their polarity… But one should not go looking here for footprints of Judeo-Masonicism – that child of recent times. The focus here is on the real contributions of Jews in the formation of the Russian empire… The author is faithful to historical accuracy and to the realities of each period under study: he does not over-inflate the role of prominent representatives of the Jewish people in the history of Russia, nor does he deflate it. *Jews in Service to the Tsar* does not present an itinerant people, tumbleweed, but rather patriots of the Fatherland, those deeply rooted in Russian life."

– Lena Zinovieva, *Neva* (2010, #4)

Jews in *Service* to the Tsar

Lev Berdnikov

Translated by Nora Seligman Favorov

Russian Life
BOOKS

The publication was effected under the auspices of the Mikhail Prokhorov Foundation
TRANSCRIPT Programme to Support Translations of Russian Literature

Cover: *Red Square in Moscow* (1801),
by Fyodor Alexeyev (1753-1824)

This book is an original translation of
Евреи в ливреях (**Человек**) © 2009, Lev Berdnikov.

English translation copyright © 2011, Russian Information Services.
Translator Preface copyright © 2011, Nora Seligman Favorov.
All rights reserved.

Copyright to all work in this volume is governed by U.S. and international copyright laws. Work may not be reproduced in any manner without the expressed, written permission of the copyright holder. For permission to reproduce selections from this book, contact the publisher at the address below.

ISBN 978-1-880100-65-3

Library of Congress Control Number: 2011934019

Russian Information Services, Inc.
PO Box 567
Montpelier, VT 05601-0567
www.russianlife.com
orders@russianlife.com
phone 802-223-4955

To my beloved mother Anna

Contents

In Service to the Empire 9
Translator Preface 13

A Long-Distance Friendship HOSEA KOKOS 21
Intrigue Dooms a Doctor LEON OF VENICE 27
A Pivotal Moment for Religious Inquiry ZACHARIAH AND THE JUDAIZERS 32
The Multifaceted Diplomat ALMAZ IVANOV 42
A Seventeenth-Century "Doctors' Plot" STEPHEN VON GADEN 51
A Humble Teacher NIKITA ZOTOV 59
The Baron's Finest Hour PYOTR SHAFIROV 71
Russia's First Police Chief ANTON DEVIER 84
The Jewish King of the Samoyed JAN D'ACOSTA 94
The Diplomatic Clan ABRAHAM, ISAAC AND FYODOR VESELOVSKY 105
The Scrupulous Postal Director FRIEDRICH GEORGE ASH 122
Doctor to the Empress ANTONIO NUNES RIBEIRO SANCHEZ 129
The Romanovs' Singular Court Jew LEVY LIPMAN 140
Catherine's Right-Hand Judeophile GRIGORY POTEMKIN 155
The Advisor From Shklov NOTA KHAIMOVICH NOTKIN 165
Hot Pepper ABRAHAM PERETZ 174
Russian Literature's First Jew LEV NEVAKHOVICH 183
The Banker Barons NICHOLAS AND LUDWIG STIEGLITZ 196
The Dissident Jester ALEXEI KOPIEV 203
The Enduring Finance Minister GEORG VON CANCRIN 212
The Learned Jew LEON MANDELSTAM 224
The Bibliophile Barons JOSEPH, HORACE AND DAVID GINZBURG 238

Brief Chronology of Jewish-Russian History 271
Bibliography 274
Index 280
About the Author and Translator 289

Предостережение

Ой, не шейте вы, евреи, ливреи,
Не ходить вам в камергерах, евреи!
Не горюйте вы зазря, не стенайте, —
Не сидеть вам ни в Синоде, ни в Сенате.

А сидеть вам в Соловках да в Бутырках,
И ходить вам без шнурков на ботинках,
И не делать по субботам леха́им,
А таскаться на допрос с вертуха́ем.

Если ж будешь торговать ты елеем,
Если станешь ты полезным евреем,
Называться разрешат Рос…сина́нтом
И украсят лапсерда́к аксельба́нтом.

Но и ставши в ремесле этом первым,
Всё равно тебе не быть камергером
И не выйти на еле́е в Орфе́и…
Так не шейте ж вы ливреи, евреи!

Александр Га́лич, 1964

Admonition

Don't sew yourselves livery, Jews,
You'll never be chamberlains!
So don't groan or worry yourselves,
There'll be no Synod or Senate seat for your pains.

You'll sit instead in Solovki and Butyrki,[1]
And your shoes will have no laces,
On the Sabbath you won't do a "L'Chaim,"
But be dragged by guards to interrogations.

If you become a useful Jew,
By making holy oil your trade,
They'll let you be called Ros…inante[2]
And hang your kapote with gold braid.

Yet even if you master the craft,
And pay a chamberlain's dues,
Oil will never make you an Orpheus…
So, don't sew yourselves livery, Jews!

Alexander Galich, 1964

---

1. Soviet prison camp and prison.
2. Don Quixote's horse; nickname for a worn-out, emaciated horse; also a play on the word *Rosiyanin*, meaning "Russian," as in the nationality.

INTRODUCTION

In Service to the Empire

"Don't sew yourselves livery, Jews!"

This line, from a well-known song by Russian-Jewish bard Alexander Galich, is a bitter admonition to Jews of all eras, warning them to maintain a safe distance from power. Yet the men profiled by Lev Berdnikov in this book entered history precisely *because* they made themselves visible (and vulnerable), mingling in tsarist Russia's highest circles of state and court power. What Berdnikov offers here is a rich and original gallery of outstanding Russian Jews who rose to prominence during a period that spans the fifteenth to nineteenth centuries.

People do not have the luxury of choosing when to be born. Russia's "Jews in service to the Tsar" lived and worked in times of governmental and social anti-Semitism. As a result, the majority of them had to convert to Christianity – as did the Spanish and Portuguese Marranos – if they wanted to settle in Russia, let alone enter the corridors of power. Those suspected of a secret adherence to the Law of Moses were ostracized, as in the case of the remarkable scholar and court doctor Antonio Nunes Ribeiro Sanchez, who loyally served Empresses Anna Ioannovna and Elizabeth Petrovna only to be expelled from the St. Petersburg Academy of Sciences.

All Russian Jews had to adapt to local mores and circumstances, but some went further than others. At one end of the spectrum we have Nota Notkin, a founder of the St. Petersburg Jewish community who fought for Jewish rights and supported the assimilation of Jews to Russian language and culture. At the other were men like Almaz Ivanov, a Jew by birth alone and a fierce zealot of Russian Orthodoxy who was promoted to the rank of Duma Secretary and put in charge of the Diplomatic Department.

Any understanding of Russian history that does not take into account the connection to Judaism of men like Ivanov – to say nothing of Peter the Great's teacher Nikita Zotov, Baron Shafirov, Kopiev the Jester, or Minister of Finance Count Cancrin – would not only be incomplete, but misleading. To eliminate such people from our field of vision is to ignore the mark Jews have left on Russian history. Indeed, as Berdnikov shows, even during the fifteenth-century reign of Tsar Alexei, Almaz Ivanov was far from the only Christianized Jew in state service. The list included the Russian ambassador to the Kingdom of Kakhetia, V.S. Zhidovin; departmental secretary Vasily Yudin; head of the Moscow Streltsy (palace guards) Ivan Zhidovin; and court physician Daniel Gaden, to name just a few. These men are so distant from us in time that we can only speculate about their thinking and the logic of their actions. History is silent, for example, on what Almaz Ivanov felt as he stood in the Kremlin receiving "Chmiel the Wicked," as Jewish chroniclers dubbed the infamous Bohdan Khmelnitsky, at whose hands tens of thousands of innocent Jews perished. Surely such an encounter must have stirred thoughts of his own Jewish roots?

This book is also filled with stories about men who used their privileged position to intervene with the Russian monarch on behalf of their fellow ethnic Jews. The Kremlin physician Daniel Gaden obtained permission for Jewish merchants to trade in Moscow, procured commissions for them from court, and received them in his home. The Russian ambassador to Vienna, Abraham Veselovsky, convinced Peter the Great, far from well-disposed toward Jews, of the professional expertise that could be found among Jewish specialists. And Abraham's brother Isaac, teacher of Grand Duke Peter Fyodorovich (the future Peter III), did not shy away from trying to convince Empress Elizabeth Petrovna, imperial Judeophobe though she was, to allow Jews to settle unhindered in Russia.

In relating the stories contained in this book – and this is crucial – Berdnikov remains faithful to historical truth and to the *realia* of the eras examined. This sets his work apart from some treatments of the subject that present all "Jews in service to the Tsar" as unwavering adherents of Judaism. For example, one well-known Israeli writer depicts the following fantastic scene: Jews at the court of Peter the Great, including the Hasid Baruch Leibov (who had come to St. Petersburg from Smolensk), assemble for a Passover Seder and manage to convince the Russian emperor to don a yarmulke, which he does without hesitation. "Not only is this particular scene unimaginable," Berdnikov writes, "but it is unrealistic to suggest that a special Jewish cohort existed in early eighteenth-century St. Petersburg, united by communal or religious interests and offering protection to its members." In fact, Jews at court, living as they did in a non-Jewish milieu, had little in common with the rest of Russia's Jewish community. The interests of their new homeland came first, and their sense of themselves as Jews had to be reconciled with this perspective. They did, however, often use their blood ties to advance Russian interests. For example, Vice Chancellor Pyotr Shafirov borrowed substantial sums for Russia from European Jewish bankers. And later, when Shafirov found himself a prisoner of the Turks, he allied with the influential physician, the Marrano Daniel de Fonseca, who helped him achieve Russian diplomatic objectives and lobby Russian interests.

These "Jews in service to the Tsar" were not "itinerants." Many sincerely saw Russia as their home and made significant contributions to its wellbeing. The many accomplishments of St. Petersburg's first Chief of Police, Anton Devier, paved the way for the creation of the Ministry of Internal Affairs. It was Devier's efforts that led to the country's first police and fire departments, as well as the system of internal passports. The first director of the St. Petersburg post office, Fyodor Ash, who held the post for 67 years, played an important part in shaping Russia's postal and cryptographic services. And when the Russian army was completely surrounded by soldiers of the Ottoman Empire, it was in large part Shafirov's brilliant maneuvering that saved Russia from a humiliating defeat.

Incidentally, it was Shafirov who introduced the foreign term "patriot" into the Russian lexicon. He defined the word to mean "a son of the Fatherland."[1] These were not empty words for the men portrayed here. Many were zealous patriots. The first Russian-language Jewish writer, Lev Nevakhovich, author of *Lament of the Daughter of Judah* (1803), wrote works extolling Russia that foreshadow Slavophilism. The Ministry of Education's "Learned Jew," Leon Mandelstam, who dedicated his life to broadening educational opportunities for Russia's Jews, was also a fierce advocate of Russian culture and became the first Jewish poet to write in Russian. The remarkable Jewish social activist and patron of the arts Baron Joseph (Evzel) Ginzburg urged his descendants to preserve both their Russian citizenship and their Jewish faith. His son, Baron Horace Ginzburg, earned recognition and admiration through his philanthropy and the defense of the rights of Jews and, despite witnessing pogroms and

---

1. The word derives from Modern French and came into use in English in the 1600s, but by the mid-eighteenth century began to have an ironic, derogatory meaning, as in one who is a "factious disturber of the government."

persecutions in his old age, still believed in the future of the Russian Jewish community.

So does this mean that the warning "Don't sew yourselves livery, Jews!" was baseless? Alas, it does not. As Berdnikov shows, many "Jews in service to the Tsar" suffered tragic fates. Under Ivan III, the doctor Maestro Leon perished on the scaffold, victim of a cruel conspiracy. And another doctor, Daniel Gaden, was falsely accused of black magic and tortured to death in 1682 by rebellious Streltsy. The brothers Abraham and Fyodor Veselovsky were forced to flee the country, becoming Russia's first defecting diplomats. Chief of Police Anton Devier was exiled to Siberia. Abraham Peretz, who went bankrupt after the Russian government failed to reimburse him for supplying the army in 1812, died in poverty. Even those whose services to the country were truly enormous were vulnerable to persecution. Pyotr Shafirov was ultimately stripped of his ranks and medals, with the Senate alluding to his "Yiddish breed."

Abuses pursued some of the individuals profiled here beyond the grave. Xenophobic historians, while remaining silent about Jewish contributions to Russian history, have contrived links between "Yid Masons" and some of Russian history's most dismal episodes. Such accounts outrageously exaggerate the power and influence of court Jews. According to the logic of such writers, the dark period of terror under Empress Anna Ioannovna known as the "Bironovshchina" (a reference to the abuses of Anna's favorite Ernst Johann von Biron) should have in fact been labeled the "Lipmanovshchina," after Biron's close associate, the Jewish banker Levy Lipman, who they allege was the true power behind the throne. (Berdnikov addresses the absurdity of this assertion.)

But it is not all darkness and intrigue. Berdnikov also shows some well-known Russian political figures in a new and unexpected light. For example, Catherine the Great's favorite Prince Grigory Potemkin is found to be a convinced Judeophile and the first state figure in Russian history to support the Zionist idea. In 1786, this charismatic figure armed Jews to form the Israelite Calvary Regiment, which he proposed be sent to Palestine after the expulsion of the Turks, as part of an effort to settle Jews in the Holy Land.

Instead, for the next two hundred years, a huge number of Jews continued to live and be absorbed into the Russian Empire. Among them were those who distinguished themselves as "Jews in service to the Tsar." They left an indelible mark on history and deserve our interest and attention.

Alexander Lokshin
Doctor of Historical Sciences
Institute of Oriental Studies, Russian Academy of Sciences

Translator Preface

For translators, any opportunity to work with a living author who is able to read and understand the translation of his or her work is a blessing. *Jews in Service to the Tsar* was originally written for an audience that grew up speaking Russian and breathing in Russian culture and history, whether within the borders of Russia itself or as a child of the far-flung Russophone diaspora. This readership would have had a different set of facts, attitudes, and historical and cultural reference points to guide its understanding as compared with the readership of this English edition. Lev Berdnikov and I collaborated to slightly adapt the original to this new audience. Nevertheless, although information has been "slipped into" the text to assist the English-speaking reader, there are still a number of terms and phenomena about which some readers may appreciate additional background.

The readership of *Jews in Service to the Tsar* will likely be drawn from two different, but overlapping, worlds: devotees of Russian studies and of Jewish studies. As a result, there will be some who will need a helping hand with Russian historical realia, while for others Jewish terms might need elucidation. The following glossary attempts to anticipate the terminological questions of both groups. For many of the Russian terms there is no generally accepted translation.[1]

---

1. This glossary was compiled using multiple sources. The primary source for Russian terms was the invaluable *Dictionary of Russian Historical Terms from the Eleventh Century to 1917*, comp. Sergei G. Pushkarev (New Haven, Yale University Press: 1970). The Russian-language internet is rich in historical references. Where possible, I relied on the on-line versions of the Brockhaus and Efron encyclopedic dictionary and the *Bol'shaia Sovetskaia Entsiklopediia* [Comprehensive Soviet Encyclopedia], among other sites. For Jewish terms my primary, but not exclusive, source was JewishEncyclopedia.com.

Chancellor (Канцлер)
A term used for the head of Russia's eighteenth- and nineteenth-century equivalent of the ministry of foreign affairs and the highest rank in the Russian civil service.

Chancery (Канцелярия)
Sometimes translated as "chancellery" or simply "office." In eighteenth- and nineteenth-century Russia, agencies of the central government had two divisions: one where policy was made and another that handled the clerical side of policy implementation. This clerical office was referred to in Russian as a *kantselyariya*. In the case of the *Blizhnyaya kantselyariya* (Close Chancery) under Peter the Great, the term was used for the council of boyars.

Collegium (Коллегия)
Sometimes translated as "college," sometimes simply as "department" or even "ministry," the collegia of eighteenth century Russia were simply agencies of the central government. The term was first introduced under Peter the Great in conjunction with organizational changes. According to Pushkarev, the collegia, "consisted of a president, a vice-president (Russian or foreigner in Russian service), four councillors (sovetniki), four assessors, and a [chancery]; one councillor or assessor in each was to be a foreigner."[2]

Department or *Prikaz* (Приказ)
Russian into English translators and Anglophone historians of Russia have yet to reach any sort of consensus on to how best to deal with the various names used to designate the agencies of Russian government over time. *Prikaz*, for example, is usually rendered as "office" or "department," but so too, often, are *kantselyariya* (chancery or chancellery) and *kollegiya* (collegium). The primary meaning of the word *prikaz* is "order" or "command." According to Pushkarev:

> In the early period of Muscovite history *prikaz* meant also a temporary responsibility given by the grand prince to one of his boyars. It was *prikazano* [ordered] that the *boyar* administer some branch of the large palace household, some group of the palace servitors, or some territory attached to the palace. From the beginning of the 16th century, with the growth of the state territory and its administrative apparatus, those personal and temporary commissions

---

2. Pushkarev, *Dictionary of Russian Historical Terms*, p. 40.

developed gradually into permanent government departments – offices, bureaus, or agencies – within a fixed organization.[3]

Thus the term came to be synonymous with "department" or "office." It must be admitted that the rather colorful terminology of Russian history loses something in translation. For example, the "Treasury Department" to which Almaz Ivanov was appointed *dyak* (see entry below) was, in the original Russian, the *Kazyonny prikaz*, from the words *kazna* (storehouse, including of valuables such as money) and *prikaz* (order).

Estates (Сословия)
Over the course of its prerevolutionary history, Russian society was increasingly organized into *sosloviya* or social estates assigned special legal status, the main ones being the nobility, the clergy, and urban and rural commoners (the bourgeoisie and peasantry, respectively). During the eighteenth century the merchant estate emerged from within the category of "urban dwellers" and was further subdivided into "guilds" (thus, the reference to Ludwig Stieglitz being a "First Guild merchant"). The most advantageous estate, the nobility, was not entirely closed to men of ability who performed extraordinary services to the state, and a number of the men described in this book were granted hereditary nobility (Ash, Ginzburg, Shafirov, Stieglitz). (See entry for Hereditary Honorable Citizen below.)

Gostinaya sotnya (Гостиная сотня)
Dating back to the earliest days of Rus, foreign traders engaging in wholesale trade in Russia were called *gosti*, literally "guests." The term *Gostinaya sotnya* refers to a special merchant estate in sixteenth- and seventh-century Russia and is based on the adjectival form of the word *gost* and the word *sotnya*, a noun signifying 100 people, although in fact the number within a *sotnya* was rarely precisely 100.

Grand Duke and Grand Prince (Великий князь)
Before the term "tsar" began to be used in Russia (during the reign of Ivan the Terrible), Muscovy was ruled by a *veliky knyaz*, which is sometimes translated as "grand prince" and sometimes as "grand duke." Scholars and translators appear not to have reached a consensus on whether to call the medieval polity of Muscovy a duchy or a principality, and one finds both terms in usage, or

---
3. Ibid., p. 103.

even references to grand princes ruling the "duchy of Moscow" and grand dukes ruling the "principality of Moscow." Later in Russian history, *veliky knyaz* was used to refer to members of the royal family close to the direct line for the throne, usually the children or grandchildren of monarchs. Here too the term is not translated consistently, but generally "grand duke" is favored. On the advice of a historian of medieval Russia, I used the following rule of thumb: the *veliky knyazes* predating Peter the Great were "grand princes," while those coming later were "grand dukes."

Haskalah (הלכשה)
Hebrew for "enlightenment" or "education," in the context of this work the term refers to the Jewish Enlightenment that took place in Europe in the eighteenth and nineteenth centuries. The movement's inspiration was the German Jew Moses Mendelssohn, who promoted Jewish rights as well as Jewish acceptance of European culture and languages and their greater integration into European society. According to JewishEncyclopedia.com, *Haskalah* generally indicates:

> an eighteenth century movement among Eastern European Jews toward abandoning their exclusiveness and acquiring the knowledge, manners, and aspirations of the nations among whom they dwell. In a more restricted sense it denotes the study of Biblical Hebrew and of the poetical, scientific, and critical parts of Hebrew literature. It is identified with the substitution of the study of modern subjects for the study of the Talmud; with opposition to fanaticism, superstition, and Hasidism; with the adoption by Jews of agriculture and handicrafts; and with a desire to keep in touch with the times. Its adherents are commonly called *maskilim*.[4]

Hereditary Honorable Citizen (Потомственный почетный гражданин)
This term comes up only once in the book (in reference to the father of Joseph Ginzburg), but since the name carries so little meaning in English and such rich significance in Russian it is worth elucidating. According to the complex system of estate and class that existed in imperial Russia, anyone who was not a member of the nobility or clergy had to belong to some specific privileged class to be exempted from many of the hardships, restrictions, and taxes that were part of Russian life. A decree issued under Alexander I stating that merchants were no longer eligible to belong to one of these classes (*Imenity* or distinguished citizens) meant that members of the merchant estate who were not presently members of a guild would, no matter how rich and successful they were, lose the privileges generally accorded their estate. Georg Cancrin proposed the

---
4. http://bit.ly/JISTS1

establishment of this category of urban commoner in the interest of greater class stability and in order to generally encourage education and enterprise. Its adoption through a manifesto dated April 10, 1832, was seen as a compromise between traditionalists and reformers. Among those who could petition to be granted this status were businessmen with a long record of success and guild membership and individuals who had successfully completed certain courses of higher education.[5]

Marrano
A term for Christianized Jews of the Iberian peninsula who converted under duress in the Middle Ages and were a major target of the Inquisition.

Maskil (משכיל)
Hebrew for "scholar" or "enlightened man," the term indicates a follower of the *Haskalah*.

Misnagdim (מתנגדים)
Hebrew for "opponents," the term is sometimes spelled "mitnaggedim" or "mitnagdim" in English. It refers to opponents of Hasidism or simply someone who is non-Hasid.

Orders (Ордена)
Several of the men whose stories are told in this book were recipients of "orders." Translators often stumble over references to orders for two reasons. First, whereas in English we generally talk about "awarding" medals but being "admitted into" orders, Russians "award" orders. (This is not to say that Russian orders did not represent admission into an extraordinary fraternity of honor and privilege.) The second reason it is awkward to translate references to orders is that we Americans have so little awareness of their attributes, both physical and symbolic. Whether earned through military or civil service, the award of an order was a life-changing experience that, for non-nobles, often came with elevation into the nobility and numerous privileges, as well as a life-long pension in the case of the highest orders. They were also simply exquisite works of jewelry, often made of diamond and gold and usually worn on an elaborate ribbon or collar. Russia's highest order, St. Andrew the First-Called (so named in honor of Christ's first apostle) was awarded to Vice Chancellor Pyotr

---
5. A. Belokrys, *Moskovskii zhurnal*, no. 3, 2005 http://bit.ly/JISTS2.

Shafirov only 20 years after Peter the Great first introduced Western-style orders to Russia and later to Georg Cancrin (earlier, Cancrin had been awarded the Order of St. Anna). Both Anton Devier and Fyodor Veselovsky were awarded the somewhat less exalted but still highly prized Order of St. Alexander Nevsky. Sometimes medals were created to reward those who contributed to a particular cause, such as the bronze medal awarded to Ludwig Stieglitz for his services in supplying the army during the Napoleonic invasion. The decree that ordered the manufacture of this medal specifically states that it should be given on the "Anna ribbon," i.e., the red and yellow ribbon on which the Order of St. Anna was traditionally hung, but did not provide for any pecuniary award.

Patronymic (Отчество)
In Russia, the patronymic is a "middle name" with a very specific function. It is constructed by adding –ovich, -yevich, or –yich (in the case of men) or –ovna, -yevna, or –ichna (in the case of women) to the father's first name. A man named Igor whose father was named Ivan would therefore be addressed as Igor Ivanovich, while a woman named Sophia whose father was Nikolai would be Sophia Nikolayevna. Although I have used their original names in my translation, foreign-born servants of the Russian state such as Georg Cancrin were known in Russian by a Russified first name and patronymic, Yegor Frantsevich in Cancrin's case, for example.

Peyos (תאופ)
The sidelocks or sidecurls worn by some Orthodox Jewish men and boys. Alternative English spellings include *payot*, *peyot*, and *payos*.

Pochvenniks (Почвенники)
The original nineteenth-century *pochvennik* movement embodied an anti-Westernizing "back to the soil" ideology (the term is based on the Russian word for soil – *pochva*). The movement emphasized the idea that Slavic culture is unique and not necessarily well-suited to the ideals embodied by the European enlightenment. Some adherents of the nineteenth-century movement embraced anti-Semitism. According to an article posted on the Russian Academy of Sciences Institute of Philosophy's website:

> A touchstone of the [contemporary] *pochvennik* ideology is the thesis: state policy must reflect the interests of the Russian people. Within the country this means limiting the access of non-Russian groups to power and social resources and, correspondingly, creating conditions for the domination of

Russians in economic, political, and cultural-symbolic spheres. In the foreign policy sphere it means rejecting a course leading to closer relations with the West.⁶

Secretary or *Dyak* (Дьяк)

Almaz Ivanov, Nikita Zotov, and Abraham Veselovsky all held the position of *dyak* within the Russian government. I have consistently translated this term as "secretary." Pushkarev describes the *dyak* as:

> the mainspring of the Moscow bureaucratic apparatus in the 15th to 17th centuries. In the 17th century the [*dyaks*] numbered about 100…They were assistants or associates to the [*boyars*] and other heads of central government departments (PRIKAZY), and sometimes were themselves department heads… In general, they played a very important role in Muscovite administrative, judicial, and financial institutions, as well as in diplomatic relations with other countries.⁷

Shtadlan

A representative of the Jewish community in Germany and Eastern Europe who interceded with gentile authorities to advocate for Jewish rights and lobby against measures harmful to Jews and on behalf of measures that benefited them.

Streltsy (Стрельцы)

A Strelets (the singular form of Streltsy) is literally a "shooter." English-language works on Russian history often use the original Russian term to denote these musketeers, who guarded the Kremlin in the sixteenth and seventeenth centuries (there were also units of Streltsy outside Moscow, but it is the Moscow Streltsy who are specifically mentioned in this book). When, in 1682, a dispute broke out between the families of Tsar Alexei's first and second wives as to who would succeed his son Fyodor, his daughter Sophia turned to the *Streltsy* to support her effort to put her younger brother Ivan on the throne, with her as regent. The Streltsy, among whom rebellion was already brewing, took her side, as a result of which she ruled as regent for Ivan and her half-brother Peter from 1682-1689, at which point her half-brother, the 17-year-old future Peter the Great, managed to garner sufficient support from some Streltsy and boyars to take power and confine Sophia to a convent. The initial rebellion that launched Sophia's regency is known as the Streltsy Uprising. A second rebellion took place in 1698, while Peter was on his "Great Embassy" across Western Europe.

6. http://bit.ly/JITSS3
7. Ibid., p. 12.

He returned ahead of schedule, and, as the chapter on Nikita Zotov describes, dealt brutally with the Streltsy and, ultimately, abolished this institution.

Table of Ranks (Табель о рангах)

While this term is only mentioned once in the book (in reference to Isaac Veselovsky), it is an important part of the framework of Russian history. Instituted by Peter the Great in 1722, it organized those in military and civil service into 14 hierarchical classes. To the meritocratic Peter, it was important than everyone start at the bottom and work their way up. In this sense, the Table of Ranks, with its emphasis on service rather than birth, was a friend to the ethnic Jew. Promotion to even the lowest rank of civil servant, Collegiate Registrar, brought with it personal nobility, and those who managed to reach the rank of Collegiate Assessor (Grade VIII) were able to pass nobility on to their heirs. Among Berdnikov's subjects, the highest rank was attained by Pyotr Shafirov, who in 1722 was elevated to Acting Privy Councillor, second within the hierarchy. The Table of Ranks, with a few revisions, remained in force until 1917.

Tax Farming or *Otkup* (Откуп)

Until the reform of 1863, the largest portion of the empire's tax revenues came from the vodka trade. As Finance Minister Georg Cancrin put it, "How and from what source can we find a sum equal to the vast revenues from liquor, when alcoholic drinks constitute, with us, the only possible object of taxation for the vast majority of the people?"[8] This revenue was "farmed" by "tax farmers" (*otkupshchiki*), who purchased a license to manage the taverns within an area called a tax farm. The tax farmers were in charge of purchasing vodka from distillers, managing tavern keepers (which included hiring them and paying their salaries, but also fining them if they violated government regulations), and ultimately delivering a percentage of sales to the treasury. As noted by historian David Christian, in the empire's western provinces (including Vitebsk Province, where the Ginzburg family made its initial fortune), "the profession had become a specialty of the Jewish population, a fact that did much to sustain the anti-Semitism of the region."[9]

Nora Seligman Favorov
Chapel Hill, NC

---

8. Quoted from David Christian, *Living Water: Vodka and Russian Society on the Eve of Emancipation* (Clarendon Press, Oxford: 1990), p. 211.
9. Ibid., p. 112.

HOSEA KOKOS

A LONG-DISTANCE FRIENDSHIP

During the reign of Grand Prince Ivan III (who ruled between 1462 and 1505), especially during its early years, Jews felt at home in Muscovy. They were allowed to engage in commerce and travel the length and breadth of the land unhindered. Canvas-covered carts belonging to Jewish traders could be seen throughout the principality. In his historical novel *Basurman*,[1] Ivan Lazhechnikov writes:

> Tall, scrawny horses of a non-Russian breed, appearing even taller than they actually were because of the huge hames covered with bronze crescents, stars, and apples sticking up out of their collars, could be heard a long way off due to an odd contrivance of trinkets made out of that same metal. Those sitting up front were primarily Yids…Back then there was no lucrative position that the descendants of the Judeans did not undertake. They were skilled with the whip and the caduceus [the practice of medicine], the head and the tongue… Especially in Rus…in Pskov, Novgorod and Moscow, Jewish cloth merchants, draymen, interpreters, sectarians, and ambassadors crisscrossed the land… their arrival heralded by pointed beards that stuck out like weathervanes from beneath frayed fur caps and greasy sheepskin coats and peyos powdered with frost fluttering in the wind.

"Useful Jews" could be found not only on the streets of Moscow, but also within the immediate circle of Ivan III who, as historian George Vernadsky points out, was accepting and tolerant of Jews.

---

1. The title is a rather derogatory distortion of the word "Muslim" that is applied to any non-Orthodox "infidel."

The ruler of Muscovy was not alone in his Judeophilia, for the institution of the court Jew existed in most of the countries of Europe and Asia. It was a time-honored tradition that could be traced back to Joseph's service to Pharaoh described in the Book of Genesis. The biographies of court Jews who continued to practice the religion of their forefathers and used their influence to help their fellow tribesmen appear in the Books of Daniel and Esther, as well as in the apocryphal Book of Tobias. In the Middle Ages, certain Muslim rulers invited Jewish doctors and financiers to serve at their courts, and many of these Jews made significant contributions to the lives of these countries: Hasdai ibn Shaprut, Jacob ibn Jau, and Solomon Ibn Yaish, among others. The rulers of medieval Europe also made use of Jews' financial expertise. For example, great influence was exerted in Christian Spain by Joseph Hanasi Ferrusiel, a twelfth century doctor and diplomat, and his nephew, Solomon Ibn Ferrusiel. The same could be said of Joseph ben Ephraim Ibn-Benveniste Halevi of Ecija, who served as royal councillor to King Alfonso IX of Castile in the early fourteenth century. In the second half of the thirteenth century in the kingdom of Aragon, a number of members of the Jewish families de la Caballería and Abravanel gained prominence, followed somewhat later by the al-Constantinis. The astrologer Ibn Yahya, the tax collector Gedaliah, and the treasurer Isaac Abravanel all gained wide renown while serving at the Portuguese court.

In short, Jews serving at the courts of Europe are too numerous to mention, but in Muscovy the court Jew was a much rarer phenomenon, although Jewish expertise was called upon when it came to issues of credit, commerce, and diplomacy. The fact that the traditional anti-Jewish attitude of the Russian Orthodox church prevented the institution of the court Jew from becoming a regular phenomenon in Russia only makes what historians have called the earliest experience of "Russian-Jewish friendship" all the more fascinating. We are referring to the remarkable commercial and diplomatic intermediary between Ivan III and the Crimean Khan Mengli (Meñli) I Giray. His name was Hosea (Khozia) Kokos and he came from the Crimean city of Kaffa (present day Theodosia).

A few words about Kokos' native town of Kaffa are called for here. As early as 909 it was the site of a large synagogue engraved with the words: "By wisdom a house is built and by joy it is established. May the Almighty send the Deliverer for the Gathering of Israel!" Kaffa was primarily a Jewish city. It had two additional synagogues and a multitude of Jewish houses. The main trade route from Italy to the Caucasus passed through Kaffa.

A wealthy merchant, Hosea Kokos was one of the Crimean peninsula's most successful businessmen. One contemporary wrote, "This Hebrewite is wise both in matters of trade and state. Very cunning. Now he is the most prominent of Kaffa's wealthy merchants." Hosea began dealing with Moscow's grand prince in the 1470s, at first in the sphere of commerce, selling him diamonds and other valuables through an intermediary. The prince was impressed by the Jew's honesty and reliability and saw that he could be trusted. As a result of this confidence, when Kokos sent his brother-in-law Joseph to Moscow with a request that Ivan aid Mengli-Giray in his quest to take over the khanate, the prince listened. Joseph was able to return with the necessary sum and thereby earn Moscow a vital ally.

Ivan III

Kokos was ideally suited to act as an intermediary, having already developed a relationship with Mengli-Giray. It appears that the merchant understood early on the advantages for Moscow of an ally whose domain shared borders with Moscow's greatest enemies: the Great Horde centered in Kazan to the east and Poland and Lithuania to the west. Surely an alliance with Crimea, and thereby with the sultan of Turkey, could prove extremely beneficial to Moscow. Furthermore, the problem of subduing the independent city of Novgorod, a pressing concern at the time, could not be addressed so long as there was strife along Rus' southern border. Mengli-Giray succeeded in ascending to the throne and proved a vital ally to Moscow.

It was not self-interest that motivated the merchant but rather concern for the fate of all Crimea, which was so in need of Ivan III's friendship. Kokos dreamt of a strong khanate, infusion into its treasury, an alliance with the Turkish sultan, an end to the countless incursions from bellicose Kazan, and, finally, of opening a line of communication with Moscow's protégé Kasim, the heir to the ruler of the Golden Horde. Whatever Kokos' initial motivation, it must have been gratifying when, upon taking the throne, Mengli-Giray freed Kokos' home town of Kaffa from taxes for three years in a gesture of thankfulness to the merchant.

In 1474 Grand Prince Ivan III asked the Russian ambassador Nikita Beklemishev, who was visiting Crimea, to pay his respects to Kokos and request his assistance in bringing about a rapprochement between the two sides. He also promised the Jew "his remuneration" in the case of success. The historical record contains correspondence between them that for a long time was conducted in Hebrew, which the grand prince evidently had trouble translating. A lack of access to skilled Russian-Hebrew translators is probably the reason behind the request that henceforth "he not compose missives in Jewish, but rather compose them in Russian or *Bessermen* writing," the latter (again, a corruption of the word for "Muslim") presumably being a reference to the Tatar language. Ivan also asked his ambassador to "Tell Kokos the Jew from the Grand Prince…as you have in the past served us and looked out for our welfare, should you now serve us once again, we would wish to reward you, God willing!"

In general, it was Kokos' brother-in-law Joseph who traveled to Moscow on Kokos' behalf. History leaves us a glimpse into one of these meetings between Ivan and Kokos' emissary, who appeared before His Majesty in a yarmulke and with distinctive Jewish peyos. He bowed down to the prince and wished him success.

"Why does he not kiss my hand and prostrate himself at my feet? Or does he not know how to conduct himself with the sovereign?" the Muscovite prince asked with rising fury.

"Do not punish him, sovereign, it is forbidden to them," the secretary interceded on the Jew's behalf. "Such is their faith. They have but one ruler – God – and the rest are all equal before him. They are prepared to die for their faith; be not angry, sovereign!"

"If they go to their death for their faith, this is praiseworthy. Faith is a serious matter!" Ivan replied amicably.

"Kokos writes that all the Khan wishes is a strong union with Moscow. If you call him to war with Kazan, or with the Polish King Casimir, he will be with you. Mengli-Giray believes that both kingdoms can only benefit from such a friendship!"

Hosea Kokos proved himself to be a devoted friend to the Russians at a difficult time in Muscovy's history. In 1479, Akhmat, khan of the Great Horde, trumpeted his preparations to march on Rus with a mighty army. Kokos hastened to Sultan Bayezid II of Turkey asking for peace, friendship, and mutual assistance on behalf of their northern neighbor. The document he brought back and delivered to the Russian ambassador in Crimea was of inestimable value.

> Sultan Bayezid, son of Sultan Mehmed, by the mercy of God sovereign of Asia and Europe, to the Grand Prince of Moscow Ivan Vasilyevich.
>
> We send our wholehearted salutations and hasten to inform the Grand Prince that it is with great joy and heartfelt consolation that we learned from Hosea Kokos the Jew of Your desire to have peace and friendship with us. Among that which the aforementioned Kokos conveyed was that Prince Akhmat will launch a campaign against You.
>
> Upon reflection…, we have found a way out that will be a wonderful guarantee of Your tranquility. We have advised the Crimean khan Mengli-Giray to help You and, for our part, we shall threaten the Polish King Casimir. Furthermore, so that You may rest utterly assured, I pledge that I will stand with You in peace and friendship…So that You harbor no doubts as to the firmness of these pledges, we truly vow in the name of Allah and the Holy Books and in the presence of our courtiers and ambassadors that we will fulfill this promise.

As a result of the array of alliances assembled to stand against the enemies of Rus, the Great Horde of Kazan was repulsed, never again to threaten Moscow. Although Prince Akhmat did defeat the Crimeans (Mengli-Giray fled to Turkey and Kokos to Venice), he did not celebrate his victory for long; a year later he was killed by the Nogai khan. With funds that Kokos managed to raise in Venice and the support of Ivan III, Mengli-Giray assembled an army and again took the Crimean throne.

Ivan III entrusted Kokos with matters of the most delicate nature. For example, he gave Kokos the job of arranging a marriage between his son, Ivan the Younger, and Maria, the daughter of the Mangup Prince Isaika. Although the matchmaker was cordially received, Hosea could not in good conscience vouch for the bride, whom he found to be excessively haughty. In any event, the marriage would not have taken place, as Maria died unexpectedly.

Kokos did everything he could to assist Russian merchants in Crimea and managed to convince Khan Mengli-Giray to grant them privileges. He also sent Ivan III splendid gifts, including rubies, pearls, Ypres fabrics, and velvet.

Kokos played an invaluable role in negotiating the release of Russian prisoners – first and foremost, the Muscovite statesman Fyodor Kuritsyn in 1487. Kuritsyn had many flattering things to say to the prince about Hosea's actions, about the lively impression the Jew had made on him, and asked Ivan to reward him generously. However, Hosea Kokos never did manage to travel to the Kremlin and meet the prince in person. The friendship and collaboration between the Jewish merchant and the prince continued through most of their lives, but was never crowned by a meeting.

The last selfless act that Hosea performed for Ivan III was the return of sacred objects that had been taken by Mengli-Giray from Kiev's Pechersk Monastery. Kokos bought all the objects that the khan had plundered and that were so precious to Orthodox Christians and sent them to the prince in Moscow. He was not motivated by the expectation of a reward. Raised on the Torah and with a deeply ingrained respect for the holy places and objects of his own religion, he simply saw this as a way to rectify an injustice done to another faith.

In 1502, the sovereign ruler of All Rus, Ivan Vasilyevich, celebrated complete victory: the Crimean Khan Mengli-Giray utterly defeated the Golden Horde and wiped its capital, Saray, from the face of the earth. The Jew Kokos was unable to share this victory with the Muscovite Grand Prince; he had passed away the previous year in Kaffa. Ivan did not outlive him by long.

The whims of fate had brought together these two men and endowed them with a true friendship that endured, despite the fact that they were never able to look one another in the eye.

INTRIGUE DOOMS A DOCTOR

A dramatic episode that took place at the court of Grand Prince Ivan III has been passed down through history. The Grand Prince's firstborn son, heir to the throne and co-ruler Ivan the Young (1458-1490), had fallen ill. His deteriorating condition caused great alarm, especially as Ivan the Young had earned the genuine affection of the people through a reputation for bravery and decisiveness on the field of battle. A search began for someone who could cure him. Thoughts turned to a group of skilled professionals and artists that had been recently brought to the Kremlin from Italy on the initiative of the Grand Prince's second wife, Sophia Paleologue, who was the niece of the Byzantine emperor. The group included a young Jew, "the physician Maestro Leon of Venice." This was one of the first visits to Muscovy by a foreign doctor of Jewish descent. At the time (up until the sixteenth century), the science of medicine in Europe was predominated by Semites, and almost every Jewish theologian was also a skilled physician.

Leon was assigned the task of curing the heir to the throne, who was said to be ailing from *"kamchuga"* (gout or rheumatism) of the legs. According to a chronicler:

> And the doctor Mister Leon the Jew, boasting, said to the Grand Prince Ivan Vasilyevich, the father, "I will heal your son, the Grand Prince, of this ailment, and if I fail to heal his ailment, you should command that I be put to death"; and the Grand Prince Ivan Vasilyevich, accepting the truth of his words, ordered him to heal his son, the Grand Prince. And the doctor began to treat him, and gave him herbs to drink, and began to apply burning-hot glass jars to his body and poured on hot water.

However, the treatment turned out to be unsuccessful, and on March 7, 1490, the heir to the throne breathed his last. A calamitous fate awaited the Jewish physician as well. At the conclusion of the forty-day period of mourning, Leon was taken to Bolvanovka, a neighborhood on the Yauza River where foreigners resided. He was beheaded in front of a large crowd.

While researching Leon's fate I happened upon an internet site with the rather innocuous title, "Words for Days of Remembrance for Especially Revered Saints." Imagine my amazement, therefore, when in the entry for Ivan the Young I came upon a truly stunning allegation. The site featured the statement that, since nobody dies of gout and rheumatism of the legs, the son of the Grand Prince was obviously sent to the world beyond by some potion slipped to him by Leon, who was characterized as a medical malfeasant and "fanatical Judaist willing to sacrifice his own life in order to perpetrate an act of anti-Russian sabotage."

No other historian or writer of historical fiction (some of whom were hardly Judeophiles) had ever concocted such a delusional, it appears safe to say, interpretation of this incident as to cast Leon as a Jewish kamikaze. He was invariably described as an arrogant charlatan undeserving of any sympathy, and his execution was viewed by contemporaries as the legitimate consequence of unforgiveable medical error. Back then there was a belief in the infallibility of medicine and the "incompetent" doctor alone took the blame for a treatment's failure. "In what for us is a cruel affair," wrote Nikolai Karamzin of the Jew's harsh treatment in his *History of the Russian State*, "the people saw only justice, since Leon had betrayed the sovereign and doomed himself to execution." The writer Ivan Lazhechnikov, well-known for his Judeophobia, also said nothing about poison, commenting merely, "This meister treated and did in Ivan the Young and for this was executed before the people…There were no regrets: it served him right."

There is a grain of truth to speculation that Ivan the Young was poisoned, but the finger is being pointed at the wrong culprit. Prince Andrei Kurbsky, someone who certainly had his sources, wrote on this matter to Ivan the Terrible, attesting that "the most kind Ivan," "the bravest and most glorious in knightly endeavors," was done in by "lethal poison" by his stepmother (Ivan the Terrible's grandmother), Sophia Paleologue. This is the version repeated by the authoritative Russian historians Vladimir Savva and George Vernadsky.

One need not be an expert in Russian court life of the late fifteenth century to discern a thinly veiled dynastic struggle for the throne in which Sophia

Paleologue, who bore Ivan III ten children, was quite successful. Even apologists for the Byzantine tsarevna recognize the extraordinary, truly inquisitorial refinement with which she devised her cunning schemes. And this was hardly surprising. After all, she grew up, according to Vsevolod Ivanov, amidst "webs of intrigue, in a fog of devious conspiracies where every glass of fragrant drink was a danger, where any minute a stab in the back from a steel dagger, drawn from a narrow sleeve, could come from behind!" He continues, "When it came to the struggle for power in the shadow of the throne, the Byzantines were in their element. They knew all its sly tricks and rituals, and they spared no one." Sophia's relentless efforts are also noted by historian Natalia Pushkareva: "From the early 1480s, there was barely a single major event or conflict in the Muscovite Principality in which Sophia Fominichna was not involved."

Vsevolod Ivanov discussed at length the constant threat hanging over Ivan the Young from Sophia. Indeed, between stepmother and stepson there was a longstanding and unflagging antagonism. Young Ivan was particularly upset by the fact that Paleologue treated the royal treasury as her personal property. We know, for example, that priceless family jewels belonging to Ivan's deceased mother, Princess Maria Borisovna Tverskaya, were secretly sent abroad to Sophia's Italian niece, which infuriated the tsarevich (the Grand Prince clearly intended his first wife's jewels to go to his son's wife, Yelena). Historians agree that had Ivan III died before 1490 and been succeeded by Ivan the Young, Sophia Paleologue would have vanished into some out-of-the-way convent and her grandson would probably never have been fated to become Ivan IV or earn the moniker "Terrible." There is copious evidence that Sophia passionately wanted the throne to pass to her son Vasily (the future Vasily III, father of "the Terrible") and had a vital interest in eliminating her hateful stepson. Apparently, she succeeded.

Sophia Paleologue

Prince Andrei Kurbsky has called Sophia Paleologue "the Greek sorceress," an "evil" wife, and the ultimate "wizard." In Russian folklore, sorcery and wizardry are closely associated with various potions and poisons. It should also be noted that aching and numbness in the legs (the symptoms from which Ivan was suffering) could indicate poisoning by snake venom. Sophia was born and grew up in a part of the world where the properties of snake venom were well known.

If the heir to the throne was poisoned, another possibility is extract of aconite (also known as monkshood or wolfsbane). This herb was applied to the tips of arrows and swords by the ancient Gauls and Germans during wolf hunting. In some countries, simple possession of aconite was punishable by death, and in Sophia's native Greece, this poison was used, along with hemlock, to execute criminals. Since ancient times, 75 varieties of aconite have been found in Russia, and it was doubtless well known in the fifteenth century. One of the symptoms of aconite poisoning is aching in the legs. Sophia was presumably in a position to have poison mixed into the tsarevich's food.

But let us return to Maestro Leon, who would have had to make a correct diagnosis in order to successfully treat his patient. If the tsarevich was indeed suffering from gout, then the consumption of alcohol would have been clearly contraindicated, since it is known to exacerbate the condition. On the other hand, if the tsarevich had been poisoned with snake venom, alcohol – in large quantities – would have been one of the most effective antidotes. In the case of poisoning by herbs, however, alcohol is useless, and in the case of mushroom poisoning, it only accelerates the absorption of toxins. Clearly, treatment based on an incorrect diagnosis could do the patient great harm.

Without a doubt, the young doctor seems to have become the victim of a conspiracy and the tool in an elaborate murder plot to do away with the heir to the Russian throne and conveniently blame his death on a Jew. For his part, Leon had no reason to suspect that Ivan could have been intentionally poisoned. In this light his assurances to Ivan III that his son would recover no longer look like overconfident boasting. Meanwhile, Sophia was working hard to ensure that Leon's diagnosis would indeed be incorrect, doing everything within her powers to keep the doctor in the dark. The very fact that Leon had been brought from abroad was extremely advantageous to Sophia's plan. He would not have been familiar with toxic herbs or venoms not native to Italy, so presumably it was just such an herb or venom that was used. If we are to find fault with him, it might be for failing to consult local Russian healers and soothsayers (they would have known all the appropriate antidotes), but since they were not graduates of medical academies, their opinions would have carried little weight at court. Furthermore, such a consultation was prevented by huge linguistic and cultural barriers.

Evidence that Sophia Paleologue was behind the elimination of the heir to the Russian throne can also be seen in her behavior toward Ivan the Young's son, Tsarevich Dmitry, who was officially made heir apparent after his father's death. A plot to poison Dmitry was uncovered that was surely instigated by Sophia. Fortunately, it was not successful. Security measures had been tightened in the Kremlin and the folk healers who obtained the poison were caught and drowned in the Moscow River. Sophia did finally manage to destroy Dmitry by other means. Before long, Dmitry and his mother, Yelena Voloshanka, were in prison, while the son of the Byzantine intriguer, Vasily, was suddenly ruling alongside his father and proclaimed heir to the throne.[1]

In his Russian-language work *A History of Anti-Semitism*, Lev Polyakov asserts that the cruel role foisted on Leon promoted the development of Judeophobia and was a factor in subsequent restrictions prohibiting Jews from living in Russia. However it does not appear that anti-Semitism had much to do with Leon's initial "frame up," since he was not the only doctor to have been put to death under Ivan III for failing to cure a prominent individual, and the other victim was an ethnic German. As Nikolai Karamzin describes it, "The same fate befell another physician in 1485, a German by the name of Anton, whose treatment killed a Tatar prince, the son of Daniyar: he was handed over to the prince's relatives and was stabbed with a knife under the Moscow River Bridge." Furthermore, historians credit Ivan III with being exceptionally tolerant in matters of religion. In the words of George Vernadsky, Ivan "was distinguished by a benevolent attitude toward Jews."

It is interesting that the Russian folk tales compiled by folklorist Alexander Afanasyev feature an Ivan Tsarevich who, like Ivan the Young, was brave in battle, married a woman by the name of Yelena (Yelena Prekrasnaya – "the Beautiful" – in his case), strove to protect the royal treasury from embezzlers, and was poisoned to death. A certain Sonka-Bogatyrka also figures in the tale who has great knowledge of poisons and antidotes and keeps vials filled with the water of life and the water of death. Could this be a reference to Sophia Paleologue? If so, perhaps Russian folk wisdom offers further support for the innocence of the unfortunate Leon of Venice.

---
1. Some details about Dmitry and Yelena's downfall can be found in the following chapter.

ZACHARIAH AND THE JUDAIZERS

A PIVOTAL MOMENT FOR RELIGIOUS INQUIRY

True Russophiles and Orthodox zealots frequently bring up a fateful day for both the Russian Orthodox Church and the plight of Jews in Mother Russia. The date in question came in December 1504, when the Church Council resolved to take violent measures against what was known as the "Judaizing sect" that had been active in Novgorod and in Moscow for more than three decades. In keeping with the "party line" that in Russia – the country of triumphant socialism – there has never been any such thing as a "Jewish question," Soviet historians timidly referred to this episode as the "Novgorod-Moscow Heresy."

Today, however, scholars do not hesitate to point to the ethnic and religious context of the heresy: back then, in 1504, the targets of persecution were "Judaizers," who were tortured, had their tongues torn out, and were burnt alive in wooden cages. All of them, together with their "advocates and accomplices," were subjected to ostracism and church anathema. This episode marks the start of growing religious intolerance and the mass renunciation of Judaism and Jews in Muscovite Russia. Words that had traditionally been used for Jews (such as *zhid* or *zhidovin*) began to take on more pejorative colorations and were hurled as insults against apostates from the Russian Orthodox faith seen as "anti-Christs," sorcerers, practitioners of black magic, and "seducers of the mind" who were regarded with a sort of morbid superstition.

The establishment of this sect is generally dated to 1470 (strictly speaking, it was not a sect, but rather a secular anti-clerical movement that shared roots with early European humanism). This is when Mikhail Olelkovich, viceroy of the Polish king, came from Kiev to "Lord Great Novgorod," a city that still enjoyed independence from Muscovy. With him, as Christian chronicles tell it, came "Jews and their haggling." The viceroy was particularly well-disposed toward his old friend, a native of Crimea and someone who was quite influential in Kiev, a merchant by the name of Zachariah (Skhariya in Russian). There are several differing accounts as to the background of this undoubtedly charismatic figure. According to one, Zachariah was a "Jew" (Sergei Solovyov), and according to others, a Karaite (*The Russian Biographical Dictionary*). There is evidence to suggest that he himself was not ethnically Jewish (his father was the wealthy Genoese prince Vincenzo de Ghisolfi, who ruled the Taman peninsula in Crimea, and his mother was a Circassian princess), but his long-term associations with the Jews of Crimea and, first and foremost, with the Jewish community in Taman's city of Matrega, which had miraculously survived the tenth-century destruction of the Khazar Khaganate and was undergoing a vibrant blossoming, led Zachariah to become a proselytizer of Judaism.

Zachariah's inclination is understandable considering the long-lasting and genuine interest taken by fourteenth- and fifteenth-century humanists in Jews and Jewish culture. For example, the German scholar Johann Reuchlin, like many other humanists, studied Hebrew and defended Jewish writings (the Talmud, the Zohar, the commentaries of Rashi, David Kimhi, Abraham ibn Ezra, Gersonides, etc.) from attacks by obscurantists.

A similar movement emerged among Jews. In the second half of the fifteenth century the Ottoman Sultan Mehmed II (who reigned from 1451 to 1481 and was also known as Fatih Sultan Mehmet or Mehmet the Conqueror) granted Jews all the same rights as his other non-Muslim subjects. News of this edict brought a large influx of Jews to Constantinople, turning the city into the center of an intellectual movement that shared many elements with humanism. Jews published books in Constantinople, opened schools, and were engaged in the practice of medicine and astrology. Among Jewish scholars of the mid-fifteenth century, one stands out: the Rabbi Mordecai ben Eliezer Comtino (also known as Kumatyano). He studied astronomy, mathematics, mechanics, and the natural sciences. Known for being particularly broadminded, Comtino was equally willing to work with Talmudists and Karaites, taught the secular sciences, and did not involve himself in the religious controversies of his time. Analogous humanistic movements existed in the fifteenth century among Lithuanian Jews, leading to numerous Christian conversions to Judaism.

Zachariah arrived in Novgorod possessing truly encyclopedic knowledge (something even his worst enemies had to admit). Accounts describe him as being extremely learned not only in the Old and New Testament, but also the works of the fathers and teachers of the Christian church. He also studied philosophy, the natural sciences, and especially astronomy (he was, for example, able to reliably predict lunar and solar eclipses). Among the languages he spoke fluently were Italian, Circassian, Russian, and Tatar, and he was able to write in Hebrew and Latin. "This Zachariah," his Orthodox critic, the Hegumen Joseph of Volotsk, wrote with indignation, "is a vessel of the bleating of devils and has studied the invention of all manner of evil, sorcery, black magic, the movement of stars, and astrology." Furthermore, Zachariah was a brilliant polemicist and dialectician, which, in combination with his excellent (by Russian standards) erudition, gave him a powerful weapon. It is interesting that this religious scholar sent to Lithuania for two helpers: the Jews Joseph Samuel Skorovey and Moses Khanush.

What views did Zachariah popularize in Novgorod? Here is how they are characterized by modern-day Judeophobic historians:

> First: the most important dogma of Orthodoxy concerning the trinity of God is nonsense, since nobody and nothing can possibly be both a unity and a trinity. Second: since the Deity cannot be a Trinity, then no Son can consist within Him; therefore, Jesus, who called himself "the Son of God," in fact was no such thing, but simply a man. Third: out of this same impossibility that God could be a Trinity is derived the absence in him not only of the second, but also the third face, that is, the Holy Ghost, which thus turns out to be a fiction, and thus the church sacraments, in which the Holy Ghost supposedly unites us with the world beyond, are also a fiction, and this world simply does not exist. Fourth: as there is no heavenly world, then the prayers of the faithful addressed to the holy beings who supposedly reside in this world are in vain, and therefore the institution of holy vows together with monasteries and convents must be abolished as parasitic and the human and financial resources that are thus made available must be used to improve our earthly development.

The modern Orthodox author Victor Trostnikov explains:

> The denial of the Trinity is rationalism, the denial of the divinity of Christ is anthropocentrism, the denial of an afterlife is materialism, the call to abolish monasticism is pragmatism…Everyone knows about the rationalism and pragmatism of Jews that, over the course of centuries, they have introduced into other cultures through their commercial activities. This assortment of

worldviews can thus be justifiably called the worldview of Jews or those who think like them, in other words – Judaizers.

To talk about these qualities as some sort of quintessence of Judaism, especially at a time when Jewish mysticism was flourishing, is too nonsensical to merit argument.

Furthermore, Trostnikov, along with others who have recently rejoined the struggle against the "Judaizers," pays Zachariah an unintended compliment, since in fact his views were nowhere near as harmonious and well-developed as they are made out to be: the visionary himself did not commit them to paper, and his persecutors, possessed by polemical ardor, at times contradict themselves in their definition of the very essence of "Judaizing." For example, they at times assert that the Judaizers deny the afterlife and at others claim that they recognize it. At times they state that Judaizers only worship the icon of Christ the Savior, but also claim that the "heretics" deny Christ's divinity and, consequently, could hardly revere his icons. It is well known that Zachariah and his comrades were actively engaged in astrology. According to their contemporaries, they merely "added ...*a bit of Judaism*" to their scholarship, but did not adhere to any set-in-stone religious beliefs. "This was a movement of free-thinkers," wrote the eminent historian Dmitry Likhachyov, "bound together by their common roots, possibly via Lithuanian Jews, in echoes of Western humanism. Individual representatives of this movement, obviously, immersed themselves in the free-thought in different ways and thereby occasioned contradictions in how they were characterized."

Just what manuscripts are associated with the Judaizers? They include the so-called *Six Wings*, a treatise on astrology by the Jew Immanuel Ben Jacob Bonfils, who lived in fourteenth century Italy. It represents the fruit of the passion for astronomy and astrology that gripped fourteenth- and fifteenth-century Italy. The language of the translation is Western Russian, with a few Hebrew terms (for example, the names of the signs of the Zodiac). A markedly humanist voice can also be heard in the *Secretum Secretorum* or *The Gates of Aristotle* (also translated from Hebrew), which gained popularity in the fifteenth century. According to tradition, the work was written by Aristotle himself and was intended to instruct Alexander the Great. *The Gates of Aristotle* remained popular with Russian readers up to the seventeenth century. It catered to a growing desire among humanists dating back to the sixteenth century for precise thought, knowledge of medicine, and an understanding of the relationship between human behavior and physical properties.

Among the texts mentioned is a translation of Moses Maimonides' *Logika* from Hebrew. The translator was not always able to surmount the challenges of the task and was forced to come up with numerous neologisms to deal with concepts that had yet to appear in the Russian language.

Other manuscripts associated with the Judaizers are the astrological book *Lopatochnik* (from the Russian word for scapula) – a guide to scapulimancy, divination using the shoulder blades of animals, translations of the *Book of Daniel* and the apocryphal *Book of Enoch* from Hebrew into Old Church Slavonic, and a collection of Jewish holiday motifs entitled *The Psalter of Fyodor Zhidovin* (translated in the late fifteenth century by a Christianized Jew).

It was claimed that Zachariah "stealthily but persistently began to acquaint prominent Novgorodians, including, of course, spiritual leaders, with these teachings, which had hitherto been unheard of here." This is, again, not quite accurate: the historical record shows that Zachariah's teachings fell on ready ground and his role was much more that of sower than ploughman. After all, as early as the mid-fourteenth century, the heretical *Strigolnik* sect had already emerged in Novgorod and Pskov. The historian M.M. Yelizarova suggests that the word *strigolnik* reflects a Jewish collocation based on the words "to render secret" and "to be expelled." Thus, in translation from Hebrew, *Strigolnik* meant "preserving revelation" or "secret outcast," which sounds very much like the lexicon of Gnostic and Manichaean secret societies. As the historian Gelian Prokhorov posits, the *Strigolnik* movement can be traced back to the first influence of Karaites in Northern Russia.

The *Strigolniks* refused to have anything to do with the Russian priesthood, believing it to be "steeped in evil" because dues and gifts were required for the consecration of priests. They united into separate groups, each of which was headed by an instructor or "simpleton." In the Russian North, religious controversy was a way of life; in Novgorod people from every class got together not only in their homes, but in public squares, to discuss spiritual problems. They often grew hoarse criticizing the church, its rituals and decrees. The *Strigolniks* were persecuted: we know that in 1375 three members of the sect were thrown from a bridge into the Volkhov River. Heretics of this sort were caught in Pskov and Novgorod and put in dungeons, but some ran away and spread their "theomachic" teachings from town to town.

Russian sources indicate that Zachariah "enticed into Judaism" two influential Novgorodian priests, Alexei and Dionysius, who were critical thinkers and, for the time, quite well-read. Furthermore, the "seducer," supposedly "out of insidiousness," forbade them to be circumcised; the heretics, meanwhile, did not resign the priesthood and continued to preside at church. They kept their Judaism a closely held secret, as well as their new names (Alexei, for example, became Abraham and his wife, Sarah). We find lists of names of converts, including Ivanka Maximov, Gridya Kloch, Father Gregory, Mishuk Sobaka, the scribe Gridya, Father Fyodor, Father Vasily, Father Jacob, Father Ivan, Deacon Makar, Father Naum, and even the Archpriest Gabriel of the Church of St. Sophia, and many, many more. Soon Zachariah and the Jews left the city, and the heresy continued to spread without them.

In 1479, Grand Prince Ivan III of Muscovy visited Novgorod after it was united with the Muscovite state. Ivan heard tell of the wisdom, eloquence, and pious life of the secret heretics Alexei and Dionysius, who, once he became well acquainted with them, made such a strong impression on the tsar that he suggested they move to Moscow. In the capital they were appointed archpriests of the main temples of the Russian church: the former, Uspensky Cathedral and the latter, the Kremlin's Cathedral of the Archangel. Both enjoyed respect as learned men of letters, which helped them to spread the "heresy" to Moscow.

Among those who accepted Zachariah's teachings were quite a few influential figures, including the head of the Diplomatic Department, Fyodor Vasilyevich Kuritsyn, who became the undisputed leader of the group and was a gifted writer fluent in German, Polish, Hungarian, and Greek; his brother, Ivan Volk Kuritsyn; the scribes Istoma and Sverchok; the daughter-in-law of the tsar, Yelena Voloshanka (the daughter of a Wallachian lord, and the wife of Ivan's son, Ivan the Younger); and certain courtiers who intended to use the new faith in their internal power struggle. Even Ivan III himself gave these teachings his ear for a while. However, as American historian Alexander Yanov convincingly argues, at the time, the tsar was confiscating monastery lands, so criticizing "money-grubbing" clerics fit nicely with his political agenda.

For 17 years the Judaizers (who grew in number, according to some accounts, to 1,500) managed to keep their teachings secret. It was not until 1487 that they were finally exposed by Archbishop Gennady (Gonzov) of Novgorod. He longed for the same renown and power possessed by the Spanish king's defenders of Christ, with their inquisitorial *autos da fé*, the necessity for which he had been signaling to Moscow. On the order of this Orthodox pastor, the heretics were "beaten with knouts" for their sacrilege. However, highly placed patrons of the "enemies" stood in the way of the sect's total destruction and some Judaizers found refuge in Moscow. In 1489, Zosimus, archimandrite of the Simonovsky Monastery in Moscow, became the new metropolitan of Rus. He was immediately christened the "second Judas" by the Orthodox "faithful" because he was not inclined to exact brutal retribution against the heretics. But at the Church Council of 1490 (which was presided over by Zosimus) the heresy was condemned and its adherents were labeled "brazen seducers and apostates."

The heretics stubbornly denied their guilt, but the Council stripped them of their ordination, consigned them to damnation, and sentenced them to imprisonment. Many of them were sent to Gennady in Novgorod, and the archbishop arranged to meet them forty versts outside the city and dress them in inside-out clothing and helmets of birch bark topped with straw crowns with the inscription, "this is Satan's host." They were sat facing backward on horses and the people were commanded to spit on them and chant, "Here are the blasphemers of Christ, the enemies of God!" Then the birch bark helmets were set afire while still atop the "heathens'" heads.

As part of the fight against the "faithless," all of the primary church books were reviewed, and anything alien to Orthodox tradition was ruthlessly cut. On the initiative of the indefatigable Gennady, the Bible was translated into Russian in its entirety (with the invention of the printing press, it would be printed at Ostrog Monastery in present-day Montenegro in 1580-1582), along with several polemical essays. A role in the ideological battle with the "heretics" was also played by the Saint's Lives of Theodore the Studite and John of Damascus – both of which openly condemned iconoclasm – composed by the venerated saint Nil Sorsky. But the most thorough criticism of the teachings of the Judaizers is spelled out in a work entitled "The Enlightener," written by Hegumen Joseph (Sanin) of the Volotsky Monastery.

> For as long as the sun of Orthodoxy has shone on our earth, there has never been such a heresy here. In homes, on the roads, in the market, everyone – monks and laymen – were doubtful in their discussions of faith and based their discussions not on the faithful teachings of the prophets, the apostles, and the holy fathers, but, on the words of heretics, apostates of Christ: they befriended them, ate and drank with them, and studied their Judaism.

Joseph of Volotsk and Archbishop Gennady of Novgorod

With the approach of 1492 – which according to the Byzantine calendar marked 7000 years from the world's creation and was thus prophesied to be apocalyptic – questions of apostasy took on a new urgency. However, the year came and went, and the anticipated end of the world for some reason did not take place, opening the door to heretical thinking, the questioning of faith, and differing interpretations of the Bible. "If Christ was the Messiah," some wondered, "Why did he not appear in his glory as expected?" The failed predictions of apocalypse lent credence to the teachings of the Judaizers.

But who here was really interested in reasoned argument? This was not a debate or a healthy discussion between advocates of different faiths, but an irreconcilable, uncompromising struggle that would have to end in death. Metropolitan Zosimus, for whose tolerance and moderation the most "vigilant"

Orthodox had little patience, was removed from his position, supposedly due to "a passion for wine and negligence toward the church" (but in fact because of what was seen as spineless pandering to the "enemy"). This might have seemed sufficient victory, but the heretics had not yet been utterly vanquished and managed to achieve the appointment of the monk Cassian, also a secret heretic, as archimandrite of the Yuryev Monastery in Novgorod. Under Cassian, the "demonic enterprise" enjoyed a sort of renewal, but not for long. Yet another hornet's nest was destroyed by Novgorod's ever-watchful Archbishop Gennady.

But "the heresy did not weaken," we read in the Russian-language *Jewish Encyclopedia*. "At one point (in 1498) it almost captured all power in Moscow, with Tsarevich Dmitry, the son of Princess Yelena, destined for the throne." But the triumph of the Judaizers was short-lived. The influential government official Fyodor Kuritsyn was no longer alive and Ivan III, due to family discord, had cooled toward his daughter-in-law Yelena and cast her and her son in a dungeon. In 1502 he made his son Vasily (by his second wife, Sophia Paleologue) heir to the throne. Vasily was supported by Joseph of Volotsk, who demanded that Ivan III immediately take the toughest possible measures against the heretics. The monarch admitted to Joseph that he "knew about the Novgorod heresy"; the tsar also said that his daughter-in-law had been seduced by Judaism and asked forgiveness for his sins. "Sovereign," Joseph replied, "move against these present heretics, and God will forgive you for those of the past." It is worth noting, however, that Ivan III was not unconditional in supporting the persecutors of Judaism. For a long time he wavered, wondering if it would be a sin to condemn the heretics to execution. The historian George Vernadsky labels him a Judeophile, and with some basis. The fact that he called Dmitry to his death bed and, in the presence of others, asked his forgiveness for the disgrace he suffered, deserves further analysis.

In Moscow and Novgorod on December 27, 1504, a public burning of heretics was held. Among the victims were Ivan Volk Kuritsyn and Cassian. In summing up this conflict, the historian and critic Vadim Kozhinov writes, "Lasting more than a decade and a half, the fight against 'heresy' was truly heroic and at the same time a genuine tragedy, since it involved in essence a fight against the very government and church hierarchy." However one can hardly consider it valorous to fight against opponents who from the very beginning were forced to conceal themselves and could offer no resistance: after all, the defamation and persecution of the Judaizers was utterly one-sided. Not a single accuser lost a hair from his head. The "heretics" suffered anathema, while their opponents were covered in glory and were later even canonized by the Orthodox Church. The only "tragedy" from the standpoint of the Josephinians (as the followers of Joseph of Volotsk were called) and their sympathizers was that the Judaizers were not immolated immediately (as their persecutors had desired), but allowed to live until 1504.

The apogee of anti-Semitic hysteria in Muscovy was reached during the reign of Ivan III's grandson, the despotic Ivan the Terrible, about whom it was written, "However cruel and violent he may have been, he did not persecute or despise anyone but the Yids, who did not wish to be christened and profess Christ: they were either burnt alive or hung and thrown in the water."

"The most dangerous threat to the very existence of Rus," "an act of ideological sabotage," "false teachings that undermined the true foundation of the centuries-old existence of the state" – this is how the "heresy" is now characterized by nationalistic Russian historians. The very question of the contribution made by the Judaizers to Russian culture is considered to be utterly blasphemous. Meanwhile, objective research has long since recognized the enlightenment and anti-feudal nature of the "heresy," as well as the idea that the Jewish thought and intellectual curiosity of the Judaizers benefited the cause of independent thinking in Russia, facilitating a spiritual renewal (as suggested by Lev and Natalya Pushkarev). The prominent scholar Sergei Platonov argues that the mood of criticism and skepticism toward dogma and the church instilled by the Judaizers has yet to die out in Russia.

In the words of Dmitry Likhachyov, "The Judaizing movement had a serious progressive significance, awakening thought, introducing new books into the sphere of erudition, and bringing a great sense of mental excitement to the late fifteenth and early sixteenth century."

ALMAZ IVANOV

THE MULTIFACETED DIPLOMAT

By the seventeenth century, there existed a type of Christianized Jew living in Muscovy that had not just adapted to the way of life there, but whose patriotism and tireless labors for the good of the state rivaled those of any ethnic Russian. One remarkable example of this phenomenon was a man known by the name Almaz (the Russian word for diamond) and, paradoxically, the surname of Ivanov (an archetypically Russian name). He started his professional life as a Moscow merchant.

"Many [Russian] tradesmen look quite a bit like Jews," Adam Olearius, secretary to the Holstein ambassador to the court of Tsar Mikhail Fyodorovich, wrote in his book, *Travels of the Ambassadors Sent by Frederic, Duke of Holstein, to the Great Duke of Muscovy and the King of Persia* (an English edition of which was published in 1662). It is not quite clear just what this foreign visitor to Moscow had in mind. Perhaps he was referring to a similarity of outward appearance, and the full beards of Russian tradesmen reminded him of Old Testament Jews? Or perhaps Olearius had discovered among the Muscovites the sort of resourcefulness and enterprise that is traditionally associated with representatives of the Jewish tribe?

In either case, he might well have been referring to Almaz Ivanov (of whose dates we know only that he died in 1669). Almaz represented a fortuitous blend of resourcefulness and enterprise, and his appearance clearly suggested his Semitic roots: a curly black beard, frizzy hair, large facial features, and a stereotypical nose. As we delve into his background, we notice that he was never referred to by name and patronymic. Patronymics were already being placed after the first name as a sign of respect. In the case of Almaz, as one contemporary points out, his very name "shows that this person is from the very lowest condition, as Muscovites in signatures and conversation add their father's name to their own name, except that men of distinction add to the latter the ending 'vich,' and men of lesser distinction are not allowed to do so." We know for certain that Almaz was descended from the family of a Vologda tradesman. As the historians Mikhail Semevsky and Nikolai Zagoskin have determined, Almaz was an ethnic Jew, an assertion confidently supported by the modern-day Israeli historian Savely Dudakov. Ivanov was, however, a practitioner of Orthodox Christianity and was baptized as Yerofei, although even in official documents he continued to be called "Almaz."

The name "Almaz" can be etymologically traced back, not to Jews, but to the Volga Tatars, in whose language the word "Almas" suggests someone who "would not touch or take anything belonging to someone else." It is difficult to say how fitting this nickname was to our Almaz, but it can be said with certainty that he did not suffer from the vice of theft (an age-old scourge of Russian life) and was not a covetous man.

He was endowed with a natural talent for finance, and in this he took after his entrepreneurial father, from whom he inherited the profession of merchant and a knack for business. At the same time Almaz was endowed with courtesy, sociability, and a striking urbanity that was rare among seventeenth-century Muscovites.

From an early age he showed an interest in trade and, according to the accounts of his contemporaries, was quite successful in this area. It is not known what commodities he sold (cloth, according to some), but evidently business was good, and Almaz traveled far and wide by land and sea as part of merchant caravans. Over the course of his travels he learned the Turkish and Persian languages, which he spoke fluently.

The historical record's first mention of Almaz dates to 1626. In Moscow's registry of residents he is listed as the owner of property in Kitai Gorod (the business district in central Moscow), specifically at the end of Voskresensky Lane. The buildings in question were stone mansions that, despite proverbial accounts to the contrary, he acquired through honest labor. These buildings were distinguished by tall "Dutch gables" that set them apart from surrounding structures. Almaz Ivanov was a member of a privileged corporation of entrepreneurs known as a *"gostinaya sotnya"* (literally, one hundred guests, since originally it was primarily foreigners who engaged in foreign trade in early Rus). The privileges of belonging to a *sotnya* came with the duty to perform services for the government in the area of trade and finance, and Ivanov was no exception.

While continuing to engage in commerce, he gradually began to devote more and more of his time to serving the state. At first, Almaz performed specific assignments for the tsar's grandees. In 1626 he replenished the state treasury with so-called "tavern monies" (tax revenue from taverns that he personally collected), for which he was rewarded with expensive furs, and in 1638 we see him charged with the collection of customs duties and tavern taxes along the Dvina River, in which capacity he was commanded to "know the men of commerce, as well as their ships and goods."

Evidently Ivanov acquitted himself well, and in 1639, still during the reign of Tsar Mikhail Fyodorovich, he left private enterprise entirely in order to focus on government service, in which he manifested both diligence and numerous talents. With extensive knowledge of valuable commodities and an ability to conduct accurate appraisals and accountings, Almaz proved himself invaluable to the government and was appointed secretary (*dyak*, in Russian) in the Treasury Department. This department was in charge of collecting and storing royal "treasure." One of the duties assigned to the newly appointed secretary was selecting the garments, jewels, and symbols of royal authority for various ceremonies, including diplomatic occasions. The authorities were especially impressed by his remarkable honesty and incorruptibility. He participated in the selection of gifts presented to distinguished foreigners and oversaw the bookkeeping for diplomatic expenditures. This was his first entry into the world of diplomacy.

Given the nature of his duties for the Treasury, Almaz Ivanov's transition to the Diplomatic Department in 1646 was natural and smooth. The seventeenth-century diplomat clerk and writer Grigory Kotoshikhin describes the duties of this office.

> They oversee dealings with neighboring states and receive foreign ambassadors and issue them papers; they also dispatch Russian ambassadors and envoys and couriers to various states as needed…And in the same Department they oversee foreigners residing in or visiting Moscow from all states, whether they are commercial or whatever rank they may be: and they administer justice in cases of foreign traders, and their punishment is meted out by Russian people.

Ivanov immediately became deeply involved in the work of the office and in essence performed the duties of deputy chief to its head. By November 1646 he began to be entrusted with negotiations with foreign envoys: first with the Polish ambassador, Yury Ilich; in October 1647, with other emissaries from the Polish-Lithuanian Commonwealth; in July 1648 with the Dutch ambassador, Conrad Berg; and in July 1648, with the Swedish resident, Karl Pomerening, among others.

In 1649 Ivanov was included in a diplomatic mission to Stockholm that resolved lingering issues concerning deserters. In appreciation of his diligent efforts "in diplomacy with the Swedes," the tsar bestowed him lands and money.

A proponent of an anti-Polish foreign policy, in the 1650s Almaz was completely immersed in diplomacy between Russia and the Polish-Lithuanian Commonwealth. In 1651 he set out for Krakow, where he attended meetings of the Sejm. There, on instructions from Moscow, he discussed the matter of the insult the Poles had inflicted on Tsar Alexei Mikhailovich (by rendering the sovereign's title incorrectly in certain documents). The Russians were steadfast in their demands that the guilty parties be put to death. Their attempts to exact retribution for the distress inflicted on the Russian tsar were met with a categorical refusal, but this is exactly the outcome they expected, and it gave the Russians an excuse to cut off relations with Poland, which they did.

In April 1653 Ivanov was again in Poland. The official object of the mission was to discuss an armistice with the Cossacks of Hetman Bohdan Khmelnytsky, who wanted to reunite with Russia, a union that was doomed to failure. The true purpose of the mission, however, was to assess whether or not the Poles were prepared for war against Russia, and what they saw firsthand reassured them that their potential foe was far too weak and unstable. After Almaz's return to Moscow, the tsar showed him particular favor. He was given property in the Rostov, Moscow, and Nizhny Novgorod districts, immediately elevated to the rank of Duma secretary, and appointed head of the Diplomatic Department. This made him the first in a short list of ethnic Jews placed in charge of implementing Russian foreign policy.[1] Our Duma secretary made subsequent trips to the Polish-Lithuanian Commonwealth in 1658, 1660, 1662, and 1666.

---

1. This list included Nicholas I's foreign minister Karl Nesselrode, who had an ethnically Jewish mother but was a practicing Protestant. The fact that Nesselrode held the number-two position in the government of an anti-Semitic tsar shows that Russian state anti-Semitism (as opposed to anti-Semitism at the popular level) had more to do with religion than race. During the Soviet period, Leon Trotsky and Maxim Litvinov headed the Soviet People's Commissariat of Foreign Affairs.

As a result of his efforts on behalf of Russia, territory that had been taken from Poland before 1658 remained in Russian hands.

As the ambassador of the Holy Roman Empire, Baron Augustin von Mayerberg, aptly wrote, "in the performance of many embassies [Almaz] exhibited so many examples of cunning, treachery, and resourcefulness that he was granted the position of caretaker of the kingdom's secret archive and of foreign ambassadors, and was charged with the responsibility of reporting on their missions."

When it came to the art of Russian diplomacy and the court etiquette that had been observed in Muscovy from time immemorial, Almaz had a reputation as an insightful expert. He was invariably present at the many audiences the monarch gave to foreign ambassadors and essentially performed the duties of master of ceremonies. Detailed descriptions of these ceremonies have survived from the seventeenth century and relate how the secretary played, if not the main role, then one that was very prominent. Of particular value is the illustration drawn from life by Johann Rudolf Storn showing Tsar Alexei Mikhailovich receiving Mayerberg on May 27, 1661. The drawing shows the secretary as a tall, stately, and still rather young man. He is dressed in a long caftan with a high collar and stands at the head of a column presenting the ambassador to the tsar, gesturing toward them with his right arm. In his left hand he holds a large sable hat.

Almaz even makes an appearance in Russian literature as an experienced negotiator and master of diplomatic ritual. In his historical novel *For Whose Sins?*, the nineteenth-century writer Daniil Mordovtsev depicts the following scene, in which Zaporozhian Cossacks representing Hetman Bryukhovetsky are received at court:

> The envoys entered the [royal] anteroom, and from there they were led into the chamber and brought before the sovereign. They were greeted by the Duma secretary Almaz Ivanov...The envoys bowed deeply and with two fingers of their right hand touched the floor. This is how etiquette required that they make obeisance to the Great Sovereign. But everyone was silent. Then Almaz Ivanov spoke up and, addressing the sovereign person, loudly proclaimed: "Your Great Sovereign Tsar and Grand Prince Alexei Mikhailovich, Autocrat of All Rus and the lord and master of many states! The envoys...of the Zaporozhian Hetman...have bowed down to you, Great Soverign, and beg your royal mercy!" The envoys again bowed...The tsar, who up to this point had been sitting

immobile in his gilded garments, like an icon in a golden chasuble, turned his head to Almaz Ivanov and quietly said, "Make Our sovereign pronouncement." And the secretary delivered a speech that had been prepared in advance and approved by the tsar and the boyars...Having made this speech, Almaz Ivanov, on a sign by the tsar, approached His Most Peacefulness [Alexei Mikhailovich's moniker], took a document from his hands and immediately gave it to the chief envoy of the Hetman, who reverently kissed it and the seal on it, and carefully placed it into his voluminous hat. Then the secretary, on another sign by the tsar, spoke again to the envoys: "His Great Sovereign Tsar and Grand Prince Alexei Mikhailovich, the Autocrat of All Rus and the lord and master of many states, permits you, envoys of the Hetman and of the entire Zaporozhian Host, to approach his hand!"

Ivanov's role in dealing with the Cossacks is inestimable. When the matter was finally resolved, we find him in the Golden Palace of the Kremlin ceremonially receiving Bohdan Khmelnytsky's delegation. A document dating back to the time reads, "And the tsar instructed the Duma diplomatic secretary Almaz Ivanov to convey to the envoy His royal favor, that he wishes the Hetman Bohdan Khmelnytsky and the Zaporozhian Host well and commands that they be admitted under His royal hand." What emotions might the Jew Almaz have experienced when expressing the tsar's good will to the pogromist Khmelnytsky, whose hands were stained with the blood of tens of thousands of his fellow tribesman? On this question, the historical record is silent.

May 27, 1661 reception in the Kremlin for the embassy of the Holy Roman Emperor. The man standing at the front of the group of boyars on the right (with hat in hand and right arm extended) is Almaz Ivanov.

In 1653 the commercial talents of the former merchant were again put to good use. Under his guidance, a new Customs Charter was introduced, replacing multiple Russian customs duties with a single rate of 5 kopeks per ruble.

The war with Poland that broke out in 1654 found the Duma secretary in Moscow, where plague was raging. According to some statistics, the pestilence took 70,000 lives. Under these difficult conditions, Almaz, together with two boyars, was entrusted with governing the capital. They had to stop pillaging, control access to the city, put out fires, organize the city's defenses, and maintain law and order. In October 1654 the Tsaritsa Maria Ilinichna, who had taken refuge far away, wrote to the capital, "Are all in Moscow or have all left Moscow or perished?" It was Ivanov himself who replied, "The prince of the tsar's entourage and I, your humble lackey Almazko, have been in Moscow and have not set foot out of Moscow." "Your humble lackey Almazko"! – what is behind such a self-deprecating signature? While in addressing the tsar and tsaritsa the word "lackey" (*kholop* in Russian) was commonly used during this period, in the case of Ivanov it had a particular resonance. Having dedicated himself and his life to the tsar, he did not demand any benefit for himself beyond the right to selflessly and disinterestedly serve the fatherland. This, however, did not by any means imply that he had been depersonalized by the tsar. Almaz always maintained a sense of his own dignity.

It was to Russia that he dedicated both his own life and his innate diplomatic, financial, and administrative gifts. In his story "Avvakum," the writer Dmitry Zhukov names him among royal subjects who were "new, strong, and cruel," but also infinitely "devoted to the tsar."

Ivanov carried out whatever task the monarch assigned him to the letter. At the same time, he had many regular responsibilities within the government: he was a secretary in the office of the Novgorod *chetvert*, a revenue agency that came under the Diplomatic Department; he was also immediately in charge of collecting revenues for the Treasury from the cities of Great Novgorod, Pskov, Nizhny Novgorod, Arkhangelsk, Vologda, and others. The secretary, for example, issued an order in 1648 that Cossacks of the Novgorod district, who were being paid in grain and monies, be given land to grow their own food. He also arranged to impose upon foreigners of low birth serving in Russia the obligation of serving as musketeers, while those of higher birth were assigned to serve with the Cossacks.

Between 1654 and 1668 he was also in charge of the Department of the Seal and beginning in 1667 held the responsible post of *pechatnik* – keeper of the tsar's seal. In a historical document dating to this period, the duties of the *pechatnik* are explained as follows: "He always wears the seal of His Royal Highness around his neck and, after examining them, seals our sovereign documents, so that there be nothing in them that violates our royal laws."

As mentioned above, Almaz was baptized and professed the Orthodox faith. The famous Croatian, anti-Western pan-Slavist Yuri Krizhanich warned Tsar Alexei about such converts:

> The Russian kingdom welcomes all who desire and even persuades, requests, compels, and forces many…to accept Christianity, and those people who are baptized for the sake of material good, and not for salvation, are accepted into the people and placed in high positions. Some conduct our important affairs, while others conclude peace treaties and commercial transactions with other nations.

In the case of Ivanov, such apprehensions were utterly groundless, due to his fierce devotion to the tsar and Orthodoxy. He became even more devout than the Russian monks of the seventeenth century. And his sons, Semyon and Dmitry, were raised to love their fatherland. Both followed in their father's footsteps: the former became a diplomat and the latter became a Moscow official.

In the words of twentieth-century writer Stepan Zlobin, "Almaz Ivanov was more pious than other Russian diplomats…He attended church more often and spoke with the priest on numerous occasions." According to Zlobin's account, the priest also considered the Jew to be one of his own, a true Russian. He depicts a scene in which a priest pours out his emotions to Ivanov: "It has become unbearable submitting to the power of Rome. I pray to God only that He deliver the triumph of the Russian state in battles of the sword and in battles of diplomatic wisdom!" to which Almaz replies, "We are triumphing, Father, we are triumphing!"

The piety of the Duma secretary is further attested to by the numerous contributions he made to monasteries (primarily donations of books). But what was much more significant was that this Jew was not only permitted but commanded to place himself right at the heart of the most sacred areas of Russian religious life. In 1659 he took part in talks with the deposed Patriarch Nikon – a critical juncture in the life of the Russian Orthodox Church. The tsar also entrusted Ivanov with such a delicate matter as negotiations with the Poles over annulment of the Union of Zborov between Catholics and Orthodox, which demanded a great deal of theological knowledge. And is it not amazing that the tsar, when he wanted to subordinate the church to his legal and civil authority, appointed Almaz of all people to head the government agency that oversaw monasteries? He was given the task of "bringing legal proceedings against metropolitans, archbishops, bishops, and their clerks and servants, and against monasteries, etc." The fate of the entire Orthodox clergy of Russia was thus placed in the hands of a Jewish convert.

Here is how Olearius characterizes Almaz Ivanov: "He was a subtle, capable man, endowed with a clear head and good memory." He served Russia, and his faith in his native land was as strong as the diamond for which he was nicknamed. Today as we contemplate this "diamond," illuminated by the rays of Russian glory, we are captivated by its many facets. In the words of the historian of Russian heraldry, Alexander Lakier:

> For now, our historians have little to say about Almaz Ivanov...and other Duma secretaries who nevertheless were so successful in concluding more than one war with a treaty that was advantageous to Russia and made more than one improvement in the laws and governance of our fatherland. The time will come when Russia will point to these men of action with pride.

STEPHEN VON GADEN

A SEVENTEENTH-CENTURY "DOCTORS' PLOT"

On May 15, 1682, a number of supporters of the 10-year-old future Peter the Great were put to a terrible, excruciating death. They were victims of the bloody Streltsy Uprising, which had been instigated by Peter's half sister, Sophia Alexeyevna. Ambitious and skilled at intrigue, the tsarevna was unwilling to accept the fact that Peter, the son of her stepmother Natalya Naryshkina, had been chosen to reign rather than her brother Ivan. But whether Peter or her feebleminded brother sat on the throne, she aspired to become an all-powerful regent and rule the country herself. On Sophia's command, supporters of the Naryshkins were rounded up and thrown onto pikes and battle axes. The bodies of the victims were literally torn to pieces and, mutilated and hacked, dragged through the mud onto Red Square and put on public display.

One of the rebels' first victims was a former associate of the late Tsar Alexei, the boyar Artamon Sergeyevich Matveyev (1625-1682), in whose house Natalya Naryshkina had grown up. Someone who had taken an interest in Peter, Matveyev had long been a thorn in Sophia's side. For this reason, in 1676, immediately after the death of Tsar Alexei and the ascent of his oldest son Fyodor, Matveyev had been dragged off to the northern wilds of Pustozersk, accused of practicing sorcery and black magic. He returned to Moscow only once Fyodor had gone to meet his maker and the Naryshkin party had triumphed. Once Peter's side was in control and the adolescent took the throne, it looked as if Matveyev would become a pillar of the new government. But then came the Streltsy Uprising. History obviously had other plans.

Everyone close to Matveyev also suffered a dreadful fate, including his friend and comrade-in-arms, Daniel von Gaden. Daniel was the name that had been given to the court doctor Stephen von Gaden, or, as the Russians dubbed him: Daniel Zhidovin or Stepan Fundaganov. An ethnic Jew who had served the Russian tsar since 1656, he gradually become the most popular doctor in Moscow. During the reign of Tsar Fyodor he had been entrusted "as the only one to go to the mansion – to the blessed sovereign tsaritsa and the Grand Duchess Natalya Kirillovna [Naryshkina] and to the blessed sovereign tsareviches and to the blessed sovereign tsarevnas – both big and little."

What accounted for the bond between Artamon Matveyev and Daniel Gaden, both of whom became the victims of enraged Streltsy (musketeers) during those fateful days? The friendship between the boyar and the doctor began to develop soon after Ukraine, where Gaden was living (it was then known as Malorossiya or "Little Russia"), came under Russian rule.

By then, the doctor, who had already lived an eventful and rich life, was a skilled medical practitioner. He was born in Breslavl in Prussian Silesia, to which the exigencies of fate had brought his family. His father – "a dokhtur of the Yiddish faith from Italian lands" – had instilled an interest in the natural sciences in Stephen from an early age. He studied medicine in Poland, first in the town of Karatyshin and later in Lvov and, it would seem, received the appropriate diploma (inasmuch as the records of the Apothecary Department refer to him as a "Bachelor of Medicine"). The youth was distinguished by ambition and, with his characteristic resourcefulness, took a practical approach to the various obstacles that appeared along his career path: in Breslavl, which was primarily populated by Lutherans, he became a Lutheran. When he lived in Poland, he became a Catholic.

His road to success, however, was filled with bumps, twists, and turns. He was appointed physician to the great Polish Hetman Nikolai Pototsky, but the Polish army suffered defeat, and Daniel wound up in Tatar captivity in Crimea. From there, he was sold into slavery to the Ottoman Turks in Constantinople, but escaped with the help of a Jewish merchant. After bypassing Wallachia, he found himself in Kamenets-Podolsk, where he served as doctor to Poles who were fighting Cossacks led by the son of Hetman Bohdan Khmelnytsky, Timofei. After living for a while in the cities of Drozhipol, Shargorod, and Satanov (in the last of which he was married), Gaden finally decided to settle down in the picturesque Chertkov, not far from Ternopol, where he also practiced medicine. This is where he was living in 1656 when Russians stormed the town. Daniel wound up in Kiev with the regiment of the *voyevoda* Vasily Buturlin, and he began to minister to the Russians and Ukrainians with the same zeal that he had earlier applied to healing the Poles. "And I treated warriors of the tsar," he later recalled, "and I cured warriors of the tsar – 125 of them."

Streltsy Uprising *(1862)*, *by Nikolai Dmitriev-Orenburgsky*

Buturlin was extremely close to the boyar Artamon Matveyev, having at one time served as head of the government department in charge of Ukraine. They had both taken part in negotiations with Khmelnytsky in 1654 and been assigned the task of bringing newly absorbed *Malorossiya* "under the hand of the Great Sovereign" (Tsar Alexei). The Ukrainian people looked up to these two Russians, calling them *batka* (father) and "the untiring supplicants of the tsar's mercy." Matveyev was a frequent visitor to Buturlin's home, and therefore it appears likely that he knew the regimental doctor serving under the *voyevoda*. It is also likely that it was Matveyev who arranged for Gaden to be transferred to Moscow.

Daniel was hired by the Apothecary Department, an institution that was established in 1620 to supervise all aspects of medical practice in Rus. Among its responsibilities were the oversight of apothecaries and the growers of medicinal herbs and plants, the recruitment of qualified medical personnel, and the operation of a medical service for the military. By the late seventeenth century the agency employed approximately 100 people: 82 physicians, 6 doctors, 4 apothecaries, and 3 alchemists, as well as students of medicine and bonesetting, clerks, and translators. At first, Gaden occupied the modest position of barber (in those days barbers performed many simple medical procedures). In Muscovite Rus, foreign diplomas were not recognized, so he had to start his career all over again.

Eventually, Daniel's intellect and abilities earned him the confidence of the tsar himself, but it took many long years to gain this trust. First, in 1659, he became a physician, and only in 1667 was he promoted to the rank of *under-doctor*, before finally reaching the highest medical rank of *doctor* in March of 1672. In a highly unusual move, the tsar presented him with a *zhalovannaya gramota* (a charter granting certain rights and privileges) that listed his professional services to the state. The document specifically stated that he, Stephen Gaden, was "a man of worth" and "sufficiently skilled in medical and medicinal teachings and worthy of the honors of a *dokhtur*." Special mention is made of his "thoroughness," "zeal," and "loyal service."

But his standing in Muscovy came at a cost: he once again converted, now to Orthodoxy. Evidently, the tsar was extremely pleased that he took this step. The list of gifts Gaden received from Tsar Alexei on this occasion runs several pages long and includes gold, silver, expensive furs, silk, velvet, and many other items. The historian Iona Berkhin suggests that Gaden's acceptance of the Greek faith was "only superficial, a common phenomenon in medieval Jewish history."

But we will not reproach Gaden for apostasy, since once he achieved his privileged position he always used it for the good of his fellow tribesmen. Although he may have anointed himself with holy water, his concern for his fellow Jews who had not converted never wavered. As Gaden's contemporary, the English doctor Samuel Collins, attested, "In recent times, there has been a growing number of Jews in the city and at Court: they enjoy the patronage of the Jewish doctor (considered a convert to Lutheranism)." Indeed this convert took under his wing not only his own relatives, but also Jews he barely knew. They often stayed in his home, and the doctor arranged for them to be provided transportation and gifts (of sable and money) upon their departure. He also arranged, despite stringent rules prohibiting it, for Jewish merchants to come to Moscow with fabrics, pearls, and other items and to receive orders from the court itself. As a result, the number of Jews in Moscow increased significantly. The phenomenon of visiting Jews in Muscovy became so common that a set of supplemental articles of laws decreed in 1669 stipulating the punishment for "seducing" Christians into other religions specifically mentions Jews: "should a Yid or Hagarene dare to corrupt Christians from the Christian faith, punishment of the culprit will be capital; and should a Yid have a Christian slave and circumcise him, he will be beheaded."

It should be noted that Gaden was not the only Christianized Jew to enjoy a place of honor at the Muscovite court. This category included the Duma secretary Almaz Ivanov, who headed the Diplomatic Department for 14 years; the Russian ambassador to the Kingdom of Kakhetia (in present day Georgia), V.S. Zhidovin; the departmental secretary Vasily Yudin; and the commander of the Moscow Streltsy (a position which, if we put it in a modern terms, would be senior to the commander of the Moscow Military District), Ivan Vasilyevich Zhidovin.

As mentioned above, the influence that the Jewish physician enjoyed at the court of Tsar Alexei was largely due to his association with the all-powerful Artamon Matveyev, who in 1672-1676 was the head of the Apothecary Department. Gaden and this extremely learned boyar, who was called "a seventeenth-century knight," were not only colleagues, but close friends. They lived rather close to one another in Moscow – Gaden on Pokrovka Street in Bely Gorod (the "White City" at the center of Moscow named for the white stone walls that encircled it) and Matveyev on what is now Armyansky Lane (back then in Matveyev's honor it was called Artamonovsky Lane).

Artamon Matveyev

The doctor was often found at his patron's palace, where an atmosphere of broadminded liberality reigned. Not only Russians, but even worldly foreigners were amazed by what they found there. The exquisite ceiling of the foyer was expertly painted with pastoral landscapes, the rooms were covered in mirrors, on the walls hung old-fashioned German paintings, and foreign clocks using a variety of mechanisms marked time with their resonant and steady ticking.

The two friends often spent time alone together in the library, where they engaged in lengthy conversations not only about matters of worldly concern, but also "of spiritual benefit," as Matveyev put it. Artamon was a bibliophile and polyglot, and his library was one of the best in Muscovy. It contained not only published works and manuscripts in Russian, but also in Latin, Polish, German, French, English, Italian, Spanish, Danish, and Czech. Although works on theology, philosophy, and geography predominated, the natural sciences and anatomy were also represented, as were such luminaries of European medicine as Huygens, Lubenetsky, Laurenberg, van den Spiegel, and others.

Medicine was a consuming passion not only for Gaden, but for Matveyev, and the latter's job of running his department was made much easier by the special trust the tsar placed in him. The verdict of history is that the actions taken by Artamon Matveyev in this area greatly advanced the cause of Russian medicine. And no small role in this great leap forward was played by Gaden. Both men ardently followed the development of the healing arts in Western Europe and saw to it that the Kremlin pharmacy contained the latest medicines. At the Diplomatic Department, which Matveyev also headed, he ordered that guides to the treatment of ailments be translated into Russian. We know that at Gaden's suggestion, Matveyev personally compiled a list of essential medications (more than 130 in all) in both Latin and Russian.

The building that housed the Apothecary Department was also utterly transformed under the leadership of these two gifted and dedicated men. Contemporaries have left accounts describing the lavishness with which this government agency was decorated. The walls and ceilings were covered in murals, the shelves and doors were lined with fine English cloth, the windows shone with stained glass of many colors, and window sills were carpeted with expensive velvet. Matveyev also took measures to ensure that even the general neighborhood remained free of "mud, stench, and vileness."

But given his ardent support of the Naryshkins, after the death of Tsar Alexei, Matveyev's fate was sealed, although the immediate pretext for the boyar's exile had to do with his medical activities. Matveyev had prepared a book on drugs and medicinal herbs for publication that the minions of Sophia's relatives (the Miloslavskys) saw as heretical. During his exile in Pustozersk he bombarded Alexei's successor, Tsar Fyodor, with letters arguing against the charges of black magic that had been leveled against him and referred often to Gaden as an authority on the scientific aspects of the controversy. The fact that Matveyev only returned to Moscow after Fyodor's death can probably be taken as an indication that his efforts were in vain. And when he did finally return, he found himself amidst an erupting rebellion.

History offers a description of the final minutes of his life. The boyar was trying to admonish the Streltsy, but they attacked him. Artamon managed to break away and run to his beloved Peter and took his arm. "The Streltsy burst in," one eyewitness relates, "and tore him from the royal arm, threw him from the steps onto spears; then they tore off his clothing, took him out of the Krim-

Gorod [the Kremlin], and cut him into pieces. Upon seeing this, the other boyars took flight in all directions."

But what became of Gaden? After surviving, by some miracle, the persecution of Jews that took place under Tsar Fyodor, as someone close to Matveyev the Jewish doctor was now among those whom Sophia's side (the Miloslavskys) regarded with suspicion. Of course the fact that he was not an ethnic Russian only made matters worse, something referred to in the account of the uprising by the eighteenth-century poet Alexander Sumarokov, who emphasized that Daniel was "of the Yiddish breed" and was dealt with out of "hatred toward foreigners."

All of Gaden's services to Rus were not enough to prevent the Miloslavskys from proclaiming this Jew a scoundrel of the first order who, they alleged, had poisoned Fyodor's food. The accusation was a strange one considering the fact that before the tsar consumed any medications or dishes, they were always tasted by both servants and doctors! But nobody was interested in the facts of the matter. Ignorant rabble was always ready to suspect whomever it saw fit of poisoning the monarch. The monstrous allegations leveled against the Jewish physician were as absurd and ridiculous as the charges that Matveyev had engaged in black magic. The band of Streltsy that came looking for the royal doctor were consumed by irrational fury.

According to a contemporary account, "That same day they went in search of the Yid doctor Daniel, but did not find him, as he had dressed himself in pilgrim's clothes and made his way to Kukui" (Kukui or Kokui being the district where Moscow's foreign population lived, also known as the German Quarter). For a while, Gaden managed to escape the Streltsy bloodbath by hiding in the woods and villages outside Moscow, including Maryina Roshcha, a small village then, but now a neighborhood of central Moscow. Eventually, hunger drove him back into the German Quarter, where he hoped to find refuge with an acquaintance. Unfortunately, he was recognized, grabbed, and taken to the palace. "Here," according to historian Sergei Solovyov, "the tsarevnas [Alexei's daughters] and Tsaritsa Marfa Matveyevna [Fyodor's widow] pleaded with the Streltsy to spare the doctor; they offered assurances that he was absolutely innocent in Fyodor's death and that in their presence he himself had tasted all the medicines that he had prepared for the ailing ruler – but all in vain!" The doctor was taken to the Konstantinovsky torture chambers and, as in the times of Stalin that lay far in the future, Gaden, unable to withstand the torment inflicted on him, broke down and implicated himself in all sorts of unspeakable crimes. He not only admitted to being a poisoner, but promised to name all his imaginary coconspirators, asking that he be given three days to do so. "Too long to wait!" the Streltsy cried out and dragged him to Red Square, where they cut him into pieces. His son Mikhail; his assistant, the foreign doctor Johann Gutmensch; and many of his servants – fifty simple folk – were also put to death.

It is symbolic that, in the end, after a life of switching from one Christian faith to another, Gaden died a Jew. We have the following account of one eyewitness:

> I arrived in Moscow three or four days after the pogrom and went to the burial along with the other Anusim[1] who were ordered by the tsar to bury those killed. Daniel had been cut into pieces: one leg and one arm had been chopped off, his body was pierced with a spear, and his head had been opened with an axe. The other Anusim and I buried Daniel and his son… in a field.

No record remains to tell us where Stephen von Gaden is buried, and his name is known primarily to those who labor in the dusty archives of Russian history.

Lest we look on this as merely a tale of medieval brutality, it is tragically instructive that, more than two and a half centuries later, the same ignorance and xenophobia that led to the brutal death of our seventeenth-century doctor was again marshaled in the fabricated Stalin era "Doctor's Plot," ending in the show trials and executions of some of the Soviet Union's most prominent doctors, accused of plotting to poison top government officials.

---

1. Jews compelled to convert.

NIKITA ZOTOV

A HUMBLE TEACHER

Nikita Moiseyevich Zotov (who lived circa 1644-1718) was selflessly devoted to the House of Romanov his entire life. As a secretary (*dyak*) in the Department of Petitions, he was entrusted with vital assignments of the most delicate nature. Tsar Alexei Mikhailovich, for example, placed him in charge of investigating allegations of embezzlement against a boyar serving in the Don region named Ivan S. Khitrovo. Under Tsar Fyodor Alexeyevich, Zotov was sent to the Crimea to negotiate a peace with the haughty Crimean Khan Murad Giray, a task that required every ounce of self-possession and resourcefulness the Muscovite could muster. Over the course of nine long months of Crimean captivity, Zotov (along with the tsar's other emissaries) was forced to endure unthinkable degradation. The "infidels" did not stand on ceremony with the Russians and kept them in the most wretched of quarters, more suitable for livestock than human beings. "We can truly attest," the hostages wrote back to the Kremlin, "that the dogs and pigs in the Muscovite State enjoy more warmth and calm than we envoys of His Royal Majesty, and the horses not only have no stable, but there is no place to tie them up; neither we nor the horses are being fed, and they compelled us to buy bread, barley, and hay, and that at the highest of prices." A true statist and patriot, Zotov stood his ground in the defense of Russia's interests, despite the Crimeans' threats (which included death). The Treaty of Bakhchisarai was finally signed by Murad Giray, but not on the most enviable of terms for Russia. It was Zotov who was held responsible for this treaty, which was considered an "insult" to Russia. Had it not been for him, however, there would have been no peace agreement at all.

Nikita Moiseyevich's return from Crimean captivity to Moscow only took him out of the frying pan and into the fire. He was subjected to bitter disgrace and placed under house arrest. Furthermore, he was avoided (literally) like the plague and forbidden from seeing friends or sending personal items to others out of a fear that he might have brought some pestilence back from the South. One day he was visited by a police official and ordered to immediately leave the capital for his country estate.

But Zotov was in no hurry to carry out this command. His intuition told him he might soon be needed in Moscow. He delayed setting out, contriving more and more reasons to delay his supposedly imminent departure. He claimed, for example, that without a written order from the tsar he was afraid to leave "lest he be accused of escape." In the end, he was indeed forced to set out for his meager estate of Donashevo, outside Kolomna, but he was not there for long.

Nikita Zotov

Soon a specially dispatched messenger arrived with orders summoning Zotov to Moscow for an urgent appearance before the tsar.

Nikita arrived at the palace without the slightest idea what he had done to merit an audience with the monarch. Little did he know, many flattering words had been spoken to Tsar Fyodor by the boyar Fyodor Sokovnin, who sang his praises as a sober, gentle, and humble man and enumerated such virtues as his mastery of the written word. This recommendation could not have come at a better time, for the tsar was just taking an interest in the education of his young brother and godchild, Tsarevich Peter (the future Peter the Great) and was seeking a suitable teacher and mentor. Zotov had all the right qualifications. As one Russian historian put it, "He was a candidate able to satisfy everyone: Tsarevna Sophia's entourage, which was anxiously following her stepbrother's progress; Tsar Fyodor Alexeyevich, who had finally begun to show concern for his godchild; and Peter's mother, who was suspicious of the Miloslavskys."[1]

---

1. The Miloslavskys: Fyodor and Sophia's family.

When one of the gentlemen of the tsar's bedchamber came to escort Zotov to the tsar, he "was gripped by fear and befuddlement such that he was rooted to the ground... After standing there for some time and recovering his breath, he made the sign of the cross and, with quiet earnestness, followed the courtier to His Majesty's quarters." Fyodor received him warmly, offered his hand to be kissed, and subjected him to a test, during which the well-known learned bishop and poet Simeon Polotsky assessed Nikita's knowledge of reading, writing and Holy Scripture. Polotsky was satisfied with the examinee's performance and reported to the tsar, "His writing and speaking are correct." Peter's mother, Natalya Naryshkina, then spoke to the bashful Zotov: "I place into your hands my only begotten son," she said, finally explaining the reason he had been called to the tsar's chambers. "Take him and convey to him the teachings of divine wisdom and fear of God; teach him to live a righteous life and to ponder the divine Scripture." Only now did Zotov understand what was going on and, his face "washed with tears," he fell to the tsaritsa's feet with the words, "I am not worthy to take possession of such a treasure," meaning, of course, Peter. Naryshkina, however, reassured the secretary and ordered him to begin lessons with the tsarevich the following day.

Nikita Moiseyevich came to the palace as commanded, now in his capacity as a teacher. The patriarch conducted a service on this occasion, sprinkled Peter with holy water, blessed him, and entrusted him to Zotov. The newly fledged mentor was immediately lavished with gifts, including one hundred rubles from the patriarch, a house in Moscow from the tsar, and expensive clothing from Natalya Naryshkina.

What did Zotov teach the royal adolescent? First of all, he gave him a basic seventeenth-century education, using a traditional primer, the *Book of Hours*, the *New Testament*, the *Psalms*, and the *Acts of the Apostles*. Nikita Moiseyevich supplemented this wisdom, however, with historical information, telling young Peter about celebrated Russian and foreign rulers and heroes of the past. Zotov turned out to be a marvelous teacher, for he made brilliant use of visual aids in his instruction. Exploiting children's characteristic eagerness to look at pictures, he, according to Peter's biographer Ivan Golikov:

> Ordered that all personages from Russian history be depicted in paintings..., as well as noble European cities, magnificent buildings, ships, et cetera; and these pictures were placed in various rooms, into which he would bring [Peter]

and explain them to him, subtly leading him to the conclusion that without knowledge of history it is impossible for a sovereign to be a worthy ruler.

Furthermore, our mentor also made use of an art form that was quite popular in the late seventeenth century, the *lubok* – prints featuring both colorful graphics and simple secular narratives (they were specially purchased for the tsarevich in the shops of Moscow's *Ovoshchnye Ryady*). A woodcut from that period depicts the bearded Zotov showing his royal pupil "amusing and instructive" pictures. It is interesting that, once he became emperor, Peter promoted the production of *lubok* in various ways, believing that these pictures could serve as a sort of graphic encyclopedia for the spread of knowledge and information.

Peter was quick to absorb Zotov's lessons. He learned the *New Testament* and *Lives of the Apostles* inside out, wrote tolerably well, knew church ritual, and was even able to sing in the choir "following the hooks" (sight reading music). And although later Peter, from the heights of his universal self-education, was not entirely flattering in his assessment of his elementary schooling ("You are fortunate, children," he would tell his daughters, "You will be taught during your early years to read useful books, while I, in my youth, was deprived both of books and of tutors"), it must be acknowledged: Nikita Moiseyevich's lessons awakened in him that amazing curiosity and thirst for novelty that later so distinguished this transformer of Russia from more typical monarchs.

The Russian historical novel, especially early works of this genre, has portrayed Zotov as a true Christian, pious and modest, strictly adhering to all Orthodox ritual. In the famous novel by Alexei Tolstoy, *Peter the Great*, we read, "Zotov, after making the sign of the cross, took a goose quill and a pen knife from his pocket, carefully sharpened the quill, and tested it against his fingernail. He again crossed himself, rolled up his sleeve with a prayer, and sat down to write out small, rounded letters." To borrow a phrase from Alexander Pushkin, the ascetic Nikita Moiseyevich was not just Russian – he was "more Russian than the Russians."

But if he was indeed so very Russian, why was he not perceived as such by Jesuits who visited the Russian court in the early eighteenth century? They had come in an effort to sway the "Muscovites" toward union with the Catholic Church. When this mission failed, they blamed the outcome, in part, on the scheming of powerful Jews. "Quite a few Jewish families who have come from neighboring Poland can be found here," they reported. "Although they are christened, they perform their rites in secret, or at times rather openly, as in the past. And some people are promoted to top positions. One of them runs the chancery of His Majesty the Tsar." Until 1718, the director of the tsar's chancery was none other than Nikita Zotov.

The Israeli historian, Savely Dudakov, takes the Jesuit's observations at face value, pointing out that "due to the specific nature of their order, they were distinguished for their exactitude and scrupulousness." Elsewhere Dudakov writes with certainty about Zotov as Russia's first Christianized Jew to hold the post of court teacher. Similar assertions are made by the St. Petersburg historian L. Ratner, who states that Peter's secretary was descended from Belarusan Jews.

Suggestions that Zotov was a secret Jew, to say nothing of an openly practicing one, should be approached with caution, however "exact" Jesuit evidence might seem to be. It seems safe to assume that these men of the cloth, in order to explain the failure of their mission to the Vatican, might have painted the picture in somewhat "darker tones" than was the actual case and exaggerated the influence of court Jews.

This is not to say that there is no basis for assuming that Zotov had Jewish roots; certainly the meticulous Catholics appear to have been convinced. It was not just a matter of his typical Jewish patronymic, Moiseyevich (son of Moses). In Russia this name was not unique to Jews and was used by Orthodox Christians as well. One need only consult the calendar of saints to find the name Moses (a name used by many Orthodox saints and ascetics). Had Zotov been named in accordance with the Calendar of Saints, we might be able to exclude the possibility of a Jewish background.

But Zotov's non-Russian descent is attested to in a 1713 document, signed by Peter the Great, stating that the ancestors of Nikita Moiseyevich were "from a noble foreign family." Setting aside for the moment the designation "noble" (a term that was tossed about rather loosely, including by Alexander Menshikov, the son of a stableman who also declared that he was descended from "nobility"), let us focus on the phrase "foreign family." Zotov's forefathers arrived in Muscovy in the late sixteenth century and might very well have been, as they were called at the time, "foreigners of Yiddish breed." There is also the fact that in an engraving of Nikita we can discern Semitic features. The historian Nikolai Chulkov points to sources suggesting that the Zotov family did not originate in Belarus, but rather in Georgia, a territory that was settled by Jews before the time of Christ. Once all the evidence is taken into account, it does appear most likely that Peter's teacher was indeed descended from Georgian

Jews. However, Zotov did grow up amidst the culture of Russian Orthodoxy and was passionate in his Christian zeal, with little sense of his Jewish heritage. Like other court Jews, he fervently served the cause of Peter I, by whose side he remained till the end of his days.

Evidence of Nikita Moiseyevich's slavish devotion to his former pupil dates from 1683, when he was serving as a secretary in the Duma. Records show that the young tsar showered Zotov with gifts for his service: money, fox fur to make a caftan, crimson fabrics, Chinese damask, gold braid and galloon. Whenever the tsar traveled to other towns or made religious pilgrimages, his former teacher was sure to be by his side, but he also shared more diverting occasions with Peter, such as the 1694 mock "Battle of Kozhukovo" outside Moscow.

In the 1689 confrontation between the tsar and his ambitious stepsister, the regent Sophia Alexeyevna, Nikita immediately took Peter's side and was the first of the Duma secretaries to join him at the Trinity Monastery, where he had taken refuge after being warned of a plot by Sophia to kill him. That same year, Nikita became actively involved in meting out retribution upon the rebel Streltsy guards, led by Fyodor Shaklovity, who had made an attempt on the tsar's life and that of his mother, Natalya Naryshkina. We find Zotov's signature on documents sentencing the mutineers to brutal executions both in the "Official List Based on Denunciations and Investigation of the Case" and the "Sentences Based on the Official List."

The historian Sergei Solovyov calls Zotov an "old hand at expounding the royal will in *ukazes*," an ability that earned him the title of Close Councillor." He particularly distinguished himself during the Azov campaign of 1695-1696, where he oversaw the sovereign's field chancery. At times he was called upon to write out imperial orders in military bivouacs or on the field of battle. "He was ever alert in his ceaseless labors of the pen, interrogations in many languages, and other matters," Peter spoke approvingly of him. After victory, Zotov sat solemnly atop the royal carriage that led the triumphal procession with shield and sword in hand. For services during the campaign, Peter gave Nikita Moiseyevich "a goblet with lid, a golden caftan of sable priced at 200 rubles, and 40 households to add to his patrimony."

Peter trusted his *dyadka* (an affectionate or familiar form of the word "uncle") implicitly, and later, when faced with another rebellion of the Streltsy guards in 1698, made him one of the investigators, thereby compelling him to conduct brutal interrogations. For the tsar's sake, the usually mild-mannered Nikita wound up torturing and interrogating the enemies of the throne, zealously carrying out his duties in the Preobrazhensky dungeon. Around the same time he also conducted a number of diplomatic missions. In 1699, for example, he negotiated with envoys of the Austrian emperor.

Zotov's career was on the rise. In 1699 he was appointed a Duma noble and *Pechatnik* (Keeper of the Seal) and in 1701 was named General President of the "Close Chancery" (*Blizhnyaya kantselyariya*, the council of boyars). In 1702-1703, while St. Petersburg was just being built, he oversaw improvements to recently-captured Shlisselburg Fortress, including the construction of a rampart that was later called the "Zotov bulwark." To the list of services Nikita performed must be added the fact that he belonged to one of the companies (*kumpanstvos*) engaged in building military and commercial ships for Russia. Little by little, he became a wealthy man; according to court registries, he owned 446 peasant households in the Vyazma, Kolomna, and Ruzha districts, as well as a lucrative coaching inn by the Kremlin's Borovitsky Gate and other profitable estates in Moscow.

It seemed that the efficient Zotov's every deed, both large and small, met with Peter's approval. All the more interesting in this light is a certain incident in which he displayed courage in the face of Peter's impulsiveness and quick temper. Once while dining, the tsar became furious at military commander Alexei Shein for having promoted officers to colonel for a price, rather than based on merit. "Rightfully indignant," one eyewitness recounts, "the tsar approached Prince Romodanovsky and the Duma secretary Nikita Moiseyevich. Having noticed that they, nonetheless, were defending the *voyevoda*, flailing his unsheathed sword in all directions, he erupted into a rage that brought all the diners to a state of terror...Nikita Moiseyevich, in an effort to ward off the tsar's blow, suffered a wound to the arm." But the tsar truly loved his former mentor, and such instances were rare.

In the early 1690s, Peter organized his notorious Most Drunken Synod of Fools and Jesters. These wild orgies, which apparently helped the tsar overcome anxieties and self-doubt, relieve stress, and burn off his reserves of unbridled destructive energy, are viewed by historians as a cultural, or, rather, anti-cultural phenomenon, intended as a means to break with the past and discredit church tradition in general and the patriarchate in particular. Outlandish spectacle and burlesque were indeed potent tools.

In the hierarchy of jesters, Zotov was given the rank of His Buffoonishness, Prince Pope, Archbishop of Preshburg, and Patriarch of the entire Yauza and all of Kokui (Preshburg was a "make-believe" fortress on the Yauza River, where

Peter trained his motley troops as a boy, before becoming tsar; Kokui was the name of the German Quarter in Moscow). Zotov's "elevation" took place during Christmas festivities in the village of Preobrazhenskoye, where this "man of the church" appeared in all his outrageous glory: his miter was adorned with a naked Bacchus and his scepter featured a fairly pornographic depiction of Venus and Eros. Behind followed a crowd of Bacchantes and Celadons with tankards and flasks filled with beer and vodka. To the tunes of church hymns they sang clownish and bawdy songs, and His Buffoonish Eminence swung a censer filled with burning tobacco.

As the French emissary to the Russian court, Francois Guillemotte de Villebois, told it, the "drunkard" Zotov, having achieved a high position, supposedly asked for such a comic role. "You will appoint cardinals who will be princes and will be obliged to delight in everything you tell them and submit to it," de Villebois has the tsar telling the supposedly power-hungry Nikita. "To this I will add a salary of two thousand rubles and will pay you in advance for the first six months, confirming you in your new position."

Nikita Moiseyevich, far from suffering a weakness for the bottle, in fact had a reputation for sobriety and for observing Orthodox fasts. As paradoxical as it may seem, it was specifically these traits that made him the ideal candidate for the "drunken patriarch." After all, the Synod, like Peter's other blasphemies, was governed by the laws of carnival culture, according to which reality is recreated in subverted "topsy-turvy" form. Everything is turned inside out: coats are worn with the fur lining on the outside and people are cast in roles that clash with their true personalities. For example, four stutterers were assigned the duty of Masters of Ceremony at Most Drunken Assemblages, and the obese, who were quickly winded, had to run around as footmen.

Shirking one's Synodal duties was as dangerous as shirking more serious service to the sovereign. We know of the following case: a young dunderhead by the name of Ivan Karamyshev, whose speech was exceptionally incoherent, was appointed to "serve under His Buffoonish Eminence [i.e., Zotov] as a reader." Appalled at the thought of such an onerous responsibility, Karamyshev ran home, informing his patron that he had come down with a "disease of the stomach and the leg." Peter, however, demanded his return, insisting that his comic service continue. The youth was forced to obey; after all, anyone could be sent to Siberia or even executed for failure to submit to the tsar.

The historical record gives us an idea of the transformation that overcame Nikita Moiseyevich in his new role. In 1690, before he assumed his position as mock religious leader, the pious Zotov was among those who reverentially accompanied the (actual) new Patriarch Adrian to his chambers after the solemn ordination ceremony in Uspensky Cathedral. Just a few years later, during an official ceremony at Major General Franz Lefort's palace:

> The Duma secretary Moiseyevich, in his capacity as mock patriarch, submitted to the tsar's command that he raise a glass in worship. At the same time as this role-player drank, mimicking a spiritual dignitary, everyone, as a prank, was supposed to kneel before him and ask for a blessing, which he administered using two chibouks, held at angles to one another so as to form a cross. This same Moiseyevich, with pastoral staff and other accoutrements of patriarchal dignity, was the first to break into fancy footwork and open the floor to dancing.

Eyewitness accounts have survived describing the sacrilegious rite of initiation into the Drunken Synod, which featured the renunciation of traditional spiritual values and affirmation of their polar opposites.

> They took me to Preobrazhenskoye, and…Nikita Zotov appointed me [make-believe] metropolitan, and they gave me a parchment roll to renounce, and I renounced this writing, and during the renunciation instead of asking "Do you believe?" they asked "Do you drink?" And through this renunciation I have doomed myself more than by merely shaving my beard, which I did not resist, but it would have been better to accept the crown of a martyr than to undergo such a renunciation.

We will dispense with detailed descriptions of the blasphemous ceremonies, orgies, celebrations, and mock weddings that took place. Suffice it to say that Zotov was not simply an indispensible participant, but one of the stars of the show. Nikita played along with all this to please the authoritarian tsar. Among his responsibilities was the Goblet of the Great Eagle, which held two liters. As a penalty, courtiers were required to drink its contents in one gulp, after which they collapsed unconscious.

Members of the assemblage asked for the blessing of His Buffoonish Eminence and engaged in correspondence with him that was replete with cynicism and blasphemy. The Prince Pope usually closed his correspondence with the words, "As far as the world of the Lord is concerned, you may be in trouble, but you have and will have our humble benediction. Signed by the authoritative hand of Humble Anikita." Peter lavished honors and rewards on his "*dyadka.*"

After victory was achieved at the Battle of Poltava (June 27, 1709), Zotov was awarded a royal "person" (that is, a portrait of the tsar in an ornate frame). But the tsar's "uncle" felt this was not enough. On July 8, 1710, the day Riga was captured, he asked Peter for a more substantial reward, and was elevated to Count of the Russian Empire with the following rescript: "At the request of and for services rendered by Mikita Moiseyevich Zotov, the title of 'count' is granted, as well as the rank of Close Councillor and General President of the Close Chancery." At the bottom of the document we see, written in Zotov's hand: "I am grateful for Your Most Generous Sovereign Favor." In 1713 the tsar approved the Zotov coat of arms: "A red heart pierced by golden arrows on a cross topped with a crown in a round field of blue and featuring other armorial symbols."

The historian Irina Gracheva gives her article about Zotov the catchy name "From Jester to Count!" which seems to imply that Zotov earned his aristocratic title purely through buffoonery. In fact (and this is attested to by the words written in Peter's hand beneath Nikita's coat of arms: Loyalty and Patience) he achieved success as a result of years of faithful and irreproachable service to his tsar in all the various positions he held, among which the position of jester represented but one facet of his demanding work. All of the honors and appointments showered on him over the years – a seat in the Senate Chancery and the status of one of the "five supreme gentlemen" or "principals" in the Russian government; the 1711 appointment as Government Inspector, having taken upon himself "this matter, so that nobody would evade detection and bring about harm"; and his ascent to the lofty rank of Privy Councillor – were the result of years of competent, diligent, and faithful service.

In 1714 something extraordinary happened. His Buffoonish Eminence, now 70 years old, came to a shocking decision: to take religious vows and enter a monastery. One can only imagine how sick all this sacrilege and incessant bacchanalia made him feel as he reached his advanced years. Perhaps Nikita recalled his youth, when, a humble mentor to the tsarevich, he had endeavored to lead Peter onto a path of righteousness and fear of God. Somehow quite the opposite had happened; Peter had diverted him from the path of sober virtue onto one of drunken debauchery, not to mention brazen mockery of all that is pious and holy.

So for the first time Nikita decided to disobey. He asked to be released to Moscow, where he hoped to take his vows. But the tsar, who saw monasteries as no more than refuges for parasites, would hear nothing of it and advised that he would do better to find himself a wife. (This was not the tsar's only matrimonial initiative. In 1712 he denied sixty-year-old Count Boris Sheremetev's request that he be allowed to enter a monastery and took it upon himself to find the count a helpmate.)

Yet again, Nikita Moiseyevich bent to the will of his royal patron. "And in connection with our [i.e., his and his wife's] arrival in Petersburg, Sire," he wrote obsequiously to Peter, "whatever company you might wish for Your Royal entertainment, I would be most joyously ready to arrange, Sire!"

Upon learning of preparations underway to carry out the tsar's plans for a mock wedding, Zotov's children by his first wife became concerned. His son, Konon, was particularly alarmed and worried that his father would become a target of ridicule. Furthermore, like his brothers, Konon was afraid of losing his inheritance. Konon wrote a tearful appeal to the tsar in which he implored Peter to cancel the shameful spectacle, citing his father's actual words: "I would be happy to give up my marriage, but I do not dare anger his royal majesty; so many aged men have been recruited for the effort and so many costumes have been tailored." The letter, however, came too late: it was written on January 14, 1715, and on January 16 Nikita Moiseyevich was to be joined in matrimony with the widow Anna Yeremeyevna Stremoukhova, neé Pashkova.

Guests arrived at the celebration in the most varied of carnivalesque costumes. There were Lutheran pastors and Catholic bishops, Bernardine monks and knights, fishermen and German shepherds, sailors and peasants. A strikingly exotic ethnic palette was also in evidence: walking together in the marriage procession were Armenians, Chinese, Eskimos, Japanese, Samoyed, Turks, Lapps, Poles, Italians, etc. And what a raucous affair it was! Drums, fifes, cymbals, flutes, pipes, rattles, pans, bugles, dog whistles, bagpipes, bells, and pea-filled gourds came together into a deafening, unimaginable cacophony.

The betrothed were on foot, supported by four distinguished monastic elders. They were wed by a ninety-year-old priest who had been specially summoned from Moscow. Tubs of wine and beer and various victuals had been set up outside for the public. Many cried out: "The patriarch has wed! The patriarch has wed!" and "Long live the patriarch and patriarchess!"

A detailed description of the mock wedding has been left to posterity by the tsar's chamberlain, Friedrich Wilhelm von Bergholtz:

The groom and his young wife, aged 60, sat at a table underneath beautiful canopies, he with the tsar and lord cardinals, she with the ladies. Above the head of the Prince Pope hung a silver Bacchus sitting atop a barrel of vodka... After the meal, they at first danced and then the tsar and tsaritsa, accompanied by a multitude of masks, escorted the newlyweds to the nuptial bed. The groom, in particular, was unimaginably drunk. The nuptial chamber was located in a ... wooden pyramid of great breadth and height that stood in front of the Senate. It was intentionally illuminated by candles, and the couple's bed was covered in hops and had casks of wine, beer, and vodka all around. Once in bed and in the presence of the tsar, the newlyweds were supposed to drink vodka from vessels in the form of partium genetalium [genital organs]..., rather large ones at that. Afterwards they were left alone; but there were holes in the pyramid through which it was possible to see what the newlyweds were doing in their drunkenness.

In 1718 His Buffoonish Eminence met his Maker. His children, who never tired of referring to their aged father's derangement, his "having entered an infantile state," or of reproaching Stremoukhova for having "worn him out with fleshly lust," were forced to sue their stepmother over their inheritance. Such was the ignominious end of Nikita Moiseyevich Zotov. Having served as the teacher of Peter the Great (already enough to earn him a place in history), he strove to please the tsar no matter the price or the obstacles in his way, even if it meant becoming a universal laughingstock. Somehow, this does not fit the characteristic Jewish mentality. After all, Jews are known for not bowing down to false idols and do not prostrate themselves before the powerful of this world. Zotov, it should be recognized, was a Jew like no other. By the end of his life he had been so depersonalized by the dictatorial Peter that it is hard to talk about his character in and of itself.

In the tsar's eyes Zotov was first and foremost an obedient plaything, even in death. The tsar issued the news of his passing in an ironic high style that rang with mockery: "Our father, the pilgrim Prince Pope, His Buffoonish Eminence Anikita, has departed this life, and our Most Lunatic Synod has been left headless."

But such a place of honor could not be vacant long. Soon a new Prince Pope was found: the nobleman Pyotr Ivanovich Buturlin. Not only did he inherit the deceased's attributes of mock power, he also inherited His Buffoonishness' wife, Anna Yeremeyevna.

PYOTR SHAFIROV

THE BARON'S FINEST HOUR

Among the events that stand out in Russian history is the sadly memorable battle against the Turks that took place on July 9-10, 1711, near Ryabaya Mogila on the Pruth River. The famous archbishop, poet, and orator Feofan Prokopovich memorialized this event in grandiloquent trochees:

> Над Могилою Рябою,
> Над рекою Прутовою
> Было войско в страшном бою.
> В день недельный ополудны
> Стался час наш велми трудный.
> Пришел турчин многолюдный.

> By Mogila Ryabaya
> By the course of River Pruth,
> Fought a force in mortal combat.
> With the sun high in the sky
> Came a time of mortal peril
> Hordes of Turks came set for battle.

Finding themselves without food or water and surrounded on all sides by the 200,000 strong infidel army of the Ottoman Porte and hordes of bellicose Crimeans, the Russians, it seemed, were doomed. Even Tsar Peter the Great lost his composure and confidence, writing an emotional letter to St. Petersburg:

> Gentlemen of the Senate! I hereby inform you that my army and I, through no fault or error of our own…are so surrounded by Turkish forces four-times greater than our own that all channels by which we might obtain provisions have been cut off, and that, without divine intervention, I foresee nothing but complete destruction, or that I will fall into Turkish captivity. If this should happen, then you must no longer consider me your sovereign and must not do anything that I, though I order it myself, demand of you until I myself appear among you in person. But if I perish and you receive reliable news of my death, then you will choose a worthy successor among yourselves.

In his book *The Jew of Peter the Great or a Chronicle from the Life of an Itinerant People* (St. Petersburg, 2001), the Israeli writer David Markish has the despairing tsar exclaim, "Scabrous hope!" Indeed the situation was perilous, but Peter's despair proved unjustified. He placed his faith in a remarkable man to conduct negotiations with the Turks, negotiations on which hung the fate of all of Orthodox Russia.

One of the most remarkable things about this man, under the circumstances, was that he – Vice Chancellor Baron Pyotr Pavlovich Shafirov (1669-1739) – was a Jew and he had the tsar's complete confidence. Peter was prepared for the most ignominious armistice, even the prospect of giving the Turks' allies, the Swedes, Livonia and even Pskov. In his instructions to Shafirov he was even more categorical: "Arrange everything as best you can, as God counsels you, and if they are genuine in their talk of peace, then agree to everything they want except bondage."

If diplomacy is the art of the possible, then the cunning vice chancellor seems to have taken things a step further and achieved the impossible. All the Turks got was the Azov Fortress and Taganrog. The Russian army, led by Peter, was allowed to leave their encirclement unscathed and with honor. "On a broader political level," wrote historian Svetlana Oreshkova, "the peace with Turkey did what Peter set out to do before the war: it gave Russia tranquility along its southern borders so that it could concentrate its forces against Sweden." But as part of the deal, the party responsible for this triumph, Shafirov, was forced to languish in Turkish captivity as a hostage. "They are holding us in such a fortress," wrote Shafirov from Turkey, "that we will perish from the stench and odor in a few days." As it turned out, he had to endure such conditions for two and a half years.

This episode alone would be enough to place Shafirov among Russian history's preeminent diplomats. Even the most anti-Semitic historians recognize this. For example, the famous literary scholar and historian Vadim Kozhinov writes of Shafirov's indisputable achievements that having "concluded a peace treaty with Turkey that was indispensible for Russia under very difficult circumstances…the Jew…Shafirov became one of the most distinguished personages in Russia."

But then there were also historians like Nikolai Molchanov, who asserted (in his 2003 book, *Peter I*) that Shafirov's role as a diplomat was greatly exaggerated and, more important, that Pyotr Pavlovich Shafirov "served Peter not so much for the glory of Russia as for his own advancement and wealth." This is utterly bewildering. After all, virtually every last one of Peter's fledglings was well-known for cupidity. As the writer Yakov Gordin aptly put it, "both the old aristocracy and the 'new people' stole… During the last 10-15 years of Peter's

Peter Shafirov

reign there was an endless stream of investigations, torture, executions… Only a handful were left untarnished." The prosecutor general, Pavel Yaguzhinsky, freely admitted to the tsar, "We all steal, everyone, it's just that some steal more flagrantly than others!" Yet today none would accuse Alexander Menshikov, for example, the most flagrant looter of Peter's treasury and the most talented of his associates, of feathering his nest without a thought for the good of the Fatherland. Why not give Shafirov, whose service to Russia was just as impressive and whose sacrifices were great, that same benefit of the doubt? The answer is obvious. In Molchanov's shameless speculation we see a tendency to diminish Shafirov's role in Russian history simply because he was a Jew.

The question of Shafirov's Jewishness is a subject worthy of attention in its own right. "Shafirov was not a foreigner, but of Jewish stock," it was written of him, "a boyar *kholop*, the son of someone by the name of Shayushka, and Shayushka's father was in Orsha, where he managed the melamed's household, and his relative, the Jew Zelman, still lives there."[1] One of his Russian biographers

---

1. In pre-Petrine Russia, a *kholop* was something between a slave and an indentured servant. "Melamed" is the teacher in a Jewish school.

describes his appearance as follows: "Although he was short, exceptionally fat, and could barely move his legs, he combined dexterity of action with a great pleasantness of face."

It should also be mentioned that some Jewish historians and writers, forgetting what life was like back then, try to present their fellow tribesmen as secret or even open practitioners of Judaism. They depict Pyotr Pavlovich holding forth in Hebrew and sitting at a Seder feast wearing a yarmulke. Such depictions are the fruit of their authors' imagination and are unsupported by the historical record. We do know that the father of our diplomat, a native of Smolensk by the name of Shaya Sapsayev, did adopt Orthodox Christianity (he served for some time as the *kholop* of the boyar B.M. Khitrovo). He was christened Pavel Filipovich Shafirov and given the rank of nobleman. Pyotr Pavlovich himself displayed an avid interest in Christianity, building an impressive collection of editions of the Bible in various languages.

Shafirov's Judaism, however, did manifest itself, and the voice of his heritage clearly held powerful sway over him. It is surely significant that he married a Jew (an unusual thing for a Christian to do in the Russia of his day) – Anna Stepanovna (Samuilovna) Kopiyeva, who was also from Smolensk. Furthermore, veneration of relatives (a typical Jewish trait) was deeply ingrained in Shafirov, to the point that his detractors accused him of breaking the law to gain advantage for his Jewish relatives. In any event, Pyotr Pavlovich took care – sometimes quite selflessly – of his non-Jewish relatives as well. For example, during the bleak years of Anna Ioannovna's reign, he was not afraid to petition for his son-in-law, Sergei Grigoryevich, a member of the disgraced Dolgoruky family.

What is important is that the statesman Shafirov also used his Jewish connections for the good of Russia, which he served devotedly. The Israeli historian Savely Dudakov points out that during his time in Turkish captivity, Pyotr Pavlovich became acquainted with the influential Jewish physician, the marrano Daniel de Fonseca, who assisted him in his difficult diplomatic mission. We know that Pyotr Pavlovich borrowed a great deal of money from Jewish bankers for the emperor. And for their part, Western European Jews used Shafirov as an intermediary in requesting permission from Peter to open commercial offices in Russia. Peter listened to Shafirov and valued his opinion highly.

How did the tsar first get to know this Christianized Jew, whom he essentially put in charge of the empire's diplomacy? The eighteenth-century historiographer Ivan Golikov offers the following story:

[Peter the Great], not long before his first trip to foreign lands, was wandering among Moscow's commercial stalls... Noticing the efficiency of one of the young salesclerks, he stopped at his shop and struck up a conversation with him, and from the answers he received he learned how intelligent he was, and as their conversation continued he found out that he knew German, French, and Polish, and he asked where he had learned them. From his father, was the response. "Who is your father?" the sovereign then asked. "A translator in the Diplomatic Department." "And who is your employer?" "The Moscow *gost* Yevreynov."[2] Finally, the monarch ordered him to tell his employer in his [Peter's] name that he should settle accounts [with the salesclerk], and, that he should take his employer's reference and come with his father to him, since, as he said, "I need you." This salesclerk went on to become the renowned gentlemen Pyotr Pavlovich Shafirov. Three days later the father and son appeared before the monarch... The Great Sovereign appointed him to the Diplomatic Department.

Golikov's account has engraved itself in history and appears in a wide range of literary and historical works. Its fundamental authenticity, however, is highly doubtful. In fact, Shafirov was hired into the diplomatic corps not by order of the tsar, but by that of the Secretary of the Duma, A.A. Vinius. He came to the tsar's attention in 1695-1696, four or five years after coming to work in the Diplomatic Department. And for some reason the list of diplomatic translators does not include his father.

The historian Dmitry Serov has expressed doubts as to the breadth of Pyotr Pavlovich's linguistic knowledge, asserting that the only foreign language he knew was German. Indeed, Shafirov was hired as a translator of German, and he translated several calendars from this language. In those days, calendars were a special sort of literature containing the most universal information in all branches of knowledge. They were popular reading in Moscow and promoted Western culture.

The title pages of the books Shafirov translated speak for themselves:

The Calendar of Rarely Found Things by Johann Heinrich Focht, Swedish Royal Mathematician, for the Year of 1695.

---

2. A *gost* was the highest level of merchant. This designation (literally "guest," as early merchants were mostly foreigners) was bestowed by the tsar on the most prosperous traders.

A Calendar of Cunning Mathematical Subtleties, for the Year of 1697 A.D., Containing Extensive Descriptions and with Annunciations of the Movement of the Sun and of Its Height, As Well As a Definitive Listing of Solar and Lunar Eclipses, Composed for the First Time by Pavel Harken.

However German was not the only language that Shafirov knew. The contents of his personal library are clear evidence that he was a polyglot, since his collection was made up entirely of foreign books. There was an evident preference for French literature (it is interesting to note that the collection includes Voltaire's tragedies), but there were also German, Latin, and Italian editions.

Sergei Luppov, a scholar who has researched the history of books and culture, writes, "Shafirov had many books on history and geography, lexicons, grammars, publications associated with diplomacy and international law, a few books about mathematics and military science, high-brow and low-brow literature, and books on religious topics... The lexicons and grammars that Shafirov kept in his library were evidently the references he used in reading foreign literature."

Although the library of the tsar's diplomat did not contain any Dutch publications, Pyotr Pavlovich did indeed know Dutch, and translated diplomatic documents from this language. Evidently it was Shafirov's energetic efficiency, keen mind, and knowledge of foreign languages that prompted Peter the Great to include him in the entourage of the Great Embassy, which traveled the European capitals during the years 1697 and 1698. It was an obvious choice, since prominent diplomats, including Secretary of the Duma Yemeliyan Ukraintsev and the Embassy's head, "first among ministers," Fyodor Golovin (it is noteworthy that Shafirov's daughter later married his son), had been privately singing Shafirov's praises to Peter. Soon enough the monarch himself became convinced of their protégé's merits. A well-informed foreigner reported that the tsar spent all his time with a "Christianized Jew" from whom he never parted. It is illustrative that when Peter needed to cut short his voyage to deal with the Streltsy Uprising, Shafirov was among the small number of close confidants he took with him.

Shafirov was gradually given greater responsibility and assigned missions critical to the fate of the empire. It took some time, however, before he was able to speak with his own voice in negotiations. At first Shafirov, enterprising as he was, was not a fully independent assistant to the great reformer. It was in the role of assiduous executor of the will of the tsar, who followed every nuance in affairs of state, that Pyotr Pavlovich laid the groundwork for the 1699 Russo-Dutch-Polish alliance and the Russo-Polish alliance of 1701, which were directed against Sweden.

That he performed his duties well is attested to by the fact that in 1703 Shafirov was appointed Privy Secretary to Chancellor Fyodor Golovin, who, after his death in 1706, was succeeded by Gavrilo Golovkin, a man of rather mediocre abilities. Shafirov was appointed Vice Chancellor, a position created specially for him. Golovkin played a purely decorative, ceremonial role. In fact, all negotiations with foreign ambassadors and the details of diplomatic projects fell to Vice Chancellor Shafirov. Here is how one historian characterizes his role: "Shafirov wound up at the pinnacle of his profession. He had the ability to inspire trust, was able to temper the tsar's harshness, and could keep track of details." The pro-Russia neutrality of England, Holland, and Germany can be attributed to his efforts. He also supported Transylvanian prince Ferenc Rákóczi's pretensions to the Polish throne over those of Stanislav Leshchinsky, who was supported by Sweden.

On the fields of battle, as well, Shafirov was always by his tsar's side. We know that he served as the truce envoy who accepted the capitulation of Sweden at Ivangorod and Narva in 1704. After the Battle of Poltava, one of the pinnacles of Russian military history, the indefatigable vice chancellor was given the rank of Privy Councillor, 300 peasant households, and the prosperous Ukrainian villages of Verba and Ponuritsa, among other gifts. On May 30, 1710, his birthday, the grateful tsar promoted Pyotr Pavlovich to baron, a title that would become a traditional sign of distinction among Jews of the European diaspora. Shafirov's services were also rewarded by other crowned heads of Europe: Friedrich of Prussia bestowed the Order of Generosity on him, and August II, King of Poland and Elector of Saxony, gave him the Order of the White Eagle.

In 1709, the entire Russian postal system was placed under the vice chancellor, with the main post office located on his estate (it burned down in 1737). The speed with which dispatches were delivered under Postmaster General Shafirov might be envied even by some modern-day postal services. The famous bird-troika (which made light work of Russia's terrible roads) managed the route from Moscow to Voronezh in 48 hours, reaching Tula in 36 and Novgorod in 52. Pyotr Pavlovich also built a model postal tract between St. Petersburg and Moscow.

Shafirov played a pivotal role in the first marriages between the dynasties of Russia and Central Europe, an endeavor he subordinated fully to the interests of the Russian state. It was he who, in 1710, arranged the marriage between the Duke of Courland, Friedrich Wilhelm, and Peter the Great's niece, the Grand Duchess Anna Ioannovna (who later became empress of Russia). The agreement provided for the return of lands that had been taken from Courland, but at the same time Courland was made a protectorate of Russia, which paved the way for its incorporation into the empire. An analogous agreement was reached in 1716 with the Duke of Mecklenburg-Schwerin, Charles Leopold, who married another of Peter's nieces, Yekaterina Ioannovna, for which Pyotr Pavlovich went so far as to arrange the divorce between this royal personage and his first wife.

Shafirov even tried his talents at private enterprise, becoming one of the first manufacturers in Russia. He advanced the fishing industry in the White Sea: the harvesting of walrus, whale, and cod oil, and the export of baleen to Europe. In 1717 he attempted to establish a silk factory, an endeavor that received approval and support from Peter (it was granted 50 years of duty-free sales). However the complexity and advanced technology involved in the enterprise proved more than Shafirov could handle, and in 1721 the factory was shut down. Apparently, this in no way diminished the esteem in which Peter held Shafirov. The tsar continued to use the vice chancellor to conduct his diplomacy.

Diplomacy is where Shafirov's talents truly lay. The vice chancellor's diplomatic career began its most impressive ascent after the 1711 treaty with Turkey, which was finalized in 1713 in Hadrianopolis (Edirne). Shafirov took part in the signing of alliances with Poland and Denmark (1715) and later with Prussia and France (1717). Pyotr Pavlovich now became the vice president of the Collegium of Foreign Affairs (1717), a knight of the highest Russian order, St. Andrew the First-Called (1719), and a senator and Actual Privy Councillor (1722).

He also played an inestimable role in the 1721 Treaty of Nystad, which put an end to the bloodshed of the Great Northern War (1700-1721). It should be noted that Shafirov brought victory over the Swedes closer not only through his work at the negotiating table, but with his own pen. His diplomatic talents were fortuitously combined with an extraordinary gift for polemics. The unprecedented tract he wrote in 1716 by order of the tsar – *A Discourse Concerning the Just Causes of His Royal Majesty Peter I, Tsar and Sovereign of All Russia, Etc.,*

Etc., In Undertaking the War against King Charles XII in 1700...[3] – was the first Russian work on international law. The importance the monarch assigned to the *Discourse* can be seen in the fact that it was published in three editions, with the third printing (1722) totaling 20,000 copies (an unprecedented number for the time). An order was issued that it should be distributed throughout every province of the vast empire and sold at a discounted price. Furthermore, this work reached international readers: it was translated into German and English (in fact it was the first Russian book to be translated in England).

The *Discourse* was an extremely topical political tract, presenting the war with the Swedish king as a necessity dictated by the vital needs of the state. The author drew on a broad range of historical sources, scrupulously researching Russian-Swedish relations dating back to the time of Ivan the Terrible. Shafirov argued the necessity of bringing the conflict to its conclusion and not making peace with Sweden until Russia had complete control over the Baltic Sea. The historian Sergei Peshtich is undoubtedly correct in saying that this well-documented work had great historical, diplomatic, publicistic, and legal significance.

The *Discourse* has also been noted for its lexical innovations, as it contains a wealth of words and terms that had not theretofore entered Russian usage. Shafirov borrowed words and terms from foreign languages, which was unavoidable for a diplomat in the Petrine era. As the linguist Alexander Gorshkov noted, "the main sphere in which Western European borrowings took place was official diplomatic and administrative correspondence." Some of Pyotr Pavlovich's neologisms – in particular the words революция (revolution) and гражданин (citizen) have been analyzed in Savely Dudakov's brilliant book, *Pyotr Shafirov* (Jerusalem: 1989). It is an irony of history that Shafirov first introduced the word "patriot" into common Russian usage, defining it as "a son of the fatherland." He considered himself to be a "true patriot." Little did he know that this word would later be deployed as a weapon by anti-Semitic Russian nationalists.

The book was prefaced with a "Dedication or Offering" from the author to the tsarevich, Peter's son. The significance of this dedication for the history of Russian letters has yet to be fully appreciated. It is important to note that Shafirov served here as the Russian progenitor of the genre of dedications, introducing into his country a tradition that had existed since antiquity and

---

3. This work is available in English translation as *A Discourse Concerning the Just Causes of the War between Sweden and Russian: 1700-1721.*

was widely practiced in Europe. Before long, the poet Vasily Trediakovsky would write, "The turn of phrase used in the panegyric epistle must be smooth, sweet, easily flowing and skillful, especially in dedications…the dedication is gentle and artful." Indeed these are the very qualities that distinguish Shafirov's dedication. Readers who immerse themselves in this text will be captivated by its author's eloquent oratory. And some of its collocations and calques sound decidedly modern, such as богом дарованный талант (God-given talent), слабая комплекция (weak constitution), фамилиарное обхождение (overly-familiar manners), неискусство пера (artlessness of the pen), великий вождь (great leader – a phrase applied to Peter the Great), etc. It should be pointed out that the lexicon, rhetorical flourishes, and even composition of this dedication would later become stock features of the genre, widely emulated in Russian dedications throughout the eighteenth and first half of the nineteenth century.

The vice chancellor often called himself a disciple of Peter the Great and tenaciously worked to put his transformative plans into practice. But perhaps the tsar's principle that Shafirov believed in most deeply was that people should not be valued based on their rank, but on their ability "to get things done" (a principle reflected in the famous 1721 Table of Ranks). Not only did Pyotr Pavlovich have a high opinion of his own ability "to get things done," but he suffered from unbounded ambition that bordered on arrogance. It was particularly hurtful to his pride that he found himself subordinate to Chancellor Golovkin, the scion of an ancient line, but, as one historian put it, "a decorative nonentity."

The vice chancellor's feelings were especially understandable inasmuch as, while he, the cunning and knowledgeable Shafirov, was devising an ingenious cipher used to encode diplomatic correspondence in a variety of European languages, his exalted patron did not know a single foreign tongue and communicated with visiting ambassadors exclusively through the use of gestures. Discord was constantly flaring up between the chancellor and his reluctant subordinate. Their competition with one another even extended to the lavishness of their households in St. Petersburg, with Shafirov always striving to outdo Golovkin and rejoicing when the number of servants in his employ finally surpassed that of the detested chancellor. Contemporaries tell us that in the Collegium of Foreign Affairs Shafirov once started yelling at the staff, calling them "oafs," "good-for-nothings," and "chancery creatures," and then, becoming enraged, he stood up, walked out, and, pausing at the door, shouted at the chancellor, "You think so highly of yourself – well, in my case, it's true." It must be admitted that Pyotr Pavlovich did not always stop at words. We know of an instance when, in May of 1719, agitated by an argument with the chancellor, he mercilessly beat the collegium's senior secretary, I.A. Gubin. The nineteenth-century writer, Alexander Kornilovich, wrote of Shafirov, "With his sweeping intellect and knowledge, he would have been a true nobleman had he been able to reign in his passions."

Pyotr Pavlovich may have lacked an aristocratic lineage, but his outstanding abilities earned him the status of one of the tsar's most eminent associates. Noblemen from the most estimable of boyar lines were happy to become his in-laws. His daughters were married into a number of princely families: Golitsyn, Dolgoruky, Gagarin, Golovin, and Khovansky. Nevertheless, these Christianized Jews were not allowed to forget their origins. One memoirist tells us that, at a gathering of the nobility, one of Shafirov's daughters tried to turn down a stoup of vodka the tsar had offered her. "I'll teach you to obey, you Jewish brat!" roared the enraged Peter, and gave the intractable young woman two heavy slaps to the face. She never turned down another offer by the tsar.

In 1722, a number of serious charges were leveled against Shafirov. And while anti-Semitism may not have predominated in the machinations of Shafirov's enemies, its presence could be felt. At the time, there was a clash in the Senate between Shafirov's interests and those of the all-powerful "semi-sovereign ruler" Alexander Menshikov (evidently there was a dispute concerning the profits from their joint White Sea Company). Menshikov's accomplice, G.G. Sornyakov-Pisarev – who accused the vice chancellor of embezzlement and the illegal payment of a salary to his brother, Mikhail Shafirov (who worked for the Collegium of Mines) – for good measure also threw in an accusation that Shafirov had concealed his Jewish ancestry. On this point Shafirov was able to defend himself, pointing out that the tsar had been acquainted with his Christianized father, who was granted nobility during the reign of Tsar Fyodor III. But when it came to his other "faults" (embezzlement, overstating postal rates, concealing escaped serfs, to name a few), Peter sternly commanded: Shafirov "will be put to death without mercy, and let no one count on whatever services they have rendered in the past, thinking this will remove their guilt."

This is how the marvelous Russian historian Sergei Solovyov describes the scene on the day of the execution:

Early in the morning on February 15 the Kremlin was already teeming with people... The convict was brought up in a simple sled from the Preobrazhensky Department;[4] during the reading of the sentence they removed his wig and old fur coat and raised him onto the scaffold, where he crossed himself several times, got onto his knees and, placed his head onto the chopping block. The executioner's axe was already sailing through the air, but it hit wood: Makarov, a privy royal secretary, declared that the emperor, out of respect for Shafirov's service, was commuting the death sentence to Siberian exile. Shafirov stood up and left the scaffold with tears in his eyes. In the Senate, where Shafirov was brought, his old comrades shook his hand and congratulated him on his pardon, but Shafirov remained gloomy; it was said that when the doctor, fearing the effect of such a strong shock, bled him, Shafirov remarked, "Better to open a major vein to free me of my torment once and for all."

The tsar showed mercy (if you can call the stripping of rank, orders, titles, and all movable and immovable property mercy): he not only granted Shafirov his life, but changed his place of exile from Siberia to Nizhny Novgorod. Shafirov lived there under "heavy guard," and his entire family was kept on 33 kopeks a day.

Pyotr Pavlovich's circumstances improved only when Catherine I, who clearly held him in favor, took the throne. Shafirov had not only his rank and regalia restored, but also a large portion of the property that had been confiscated. During 1725-1727 he held the prominent post of president of the Collegium of Commerce. Recalling his literary abilities, the empress also assigned him the task of writing a history of the reign of Peter the Great (a work that was never completed).

After being forced to retire under Peter II (1727-1730), Shafirov was again called into service by Empress Anna Ioannovna. He was asked to assemble an anti-Turkish coalition. Shafirov was posted to Persia as a plenipotentiary ambassador (1730-1732) where he signed the Treaty of Rasht, under which Russia and Persia agreed to jointly oppose the Ottoman Porte. In 1733 he was promoted to Senator and again appointed president of the Commerce Collegium, a post that he held until his death. In 1734 his talents as a diplomat were again called upon and he participated in the signing of a trade agreement with England and, in 1737, the Treaty of Nemirov.

---

4. During Peter's reign, an office in charge of investigating and punishing political crimes located in the Moscow suburb of Preobrazhenskoye.

But perhaps he always looked back on that sultry July day in 1711 when he, the son of a former *kholop*, the Jew Shafirov, saved the great Russian Empire from shame and defeat. Surely it was his finest hour.

ANTON DEVIER

RUSSIA'S FIRST POLICE CHIEF

In kaftans of cornflower blue with red cuffs worn over a long, bright-green waistcoat, the freshly minted guardians of order lined up in ranks and loudly pronounced the police oath: to be a "faithful, kind, and obedient slave" to the tsar, "not sparing my life if need be." Each in turn then approached the Chief of Police, Anton Manuilovich Devier, and kissed the Gospel and cross he held in his hands. But there was something highly unusual here – the senior policeman holding the Gospel and cross was a Jew.

Anton Devier

To be precise, he was an ethnic Jew, but a practicing Christian. His father, a Marrano who fled to Holland from the Portuguese Inquisition and took up the not terribly lucrative trade of gunsmith, had converted to Christianity. The father's name, Emanuel de Vieira, can be found in the lists of Amsterdam's Jewish community. We also know that soon after arriving in the land of tulips, the impoverished Emanuel departed this world and left his son Antonio, who had been born in 1682, an orphan without any means of support. The young de Vieira, or, as he later came to be known in Russia, Devier, pursued a livelihood not typical for a Jewish lad – seafaring – and by the age of fifteen he had ascended to the promising position of cabin boy.

The writer A.I. Sokolov very aptly called Anton the "dexterous Devier." Indeed, from an early age Anton was distinguished by agility and efficiency, which made a most advantageous impression on everyone around him. He nimbly climbed the ropes and adjusted the sails and swam without tiring. In a word, he performed his duties onboard impeccably. But in addition to his talents he also had the good fortune to be in the right place at the right time.

In 1697, the Grand Embassy of Peter the Great (in which the tsar was posing as one "Peter Mikhailov") reached Holland. Knowing the tsar's passion for maritime amusements, the authorities in Amsterdam arranged maneuvers featuring a rather realistic sea battle. Dozens of sailing ships formed two lines in the Ij Bay near the Schellingwoude promontory. As the performance reached its climax, true sea wolf that he was, Peter moved from his ship to one of the vessels involved in the maneuvers and took command. On board, a handsome and efficient cabin boy caught his eye. The boy's appearance is described by the Israeli writer David Markish in his book, *The Jew of Peter the Great or a Chronicle from the Life of an Itinerant People* (St. Petersburg, 2001):

> [He was a] well-built, muscular young man dressed in sailor's garb. In his face, which was either darkened by the sun or swarthy by birth, were set, like black stones, large, prominent eyes with childishly soft eyelashes, like whisk brooms. His wrists were narrow, strong, and also swarthy and dark. Everything about him was palpably exotic, foreign; although he carried himself with modesty, he was completely free of embarrassment.

After speaking with the cabin boy, the monarch immediately invited him to enter the service of Russia.

One thing is puzzling. Why did Peter, who put so much effort into building his fleet and was deeply troubled by the lack of experienced sailors in Russia, fail to use Devier in his original capacity, as a sailor or shipbuilder? Evidently the monarch's keen eye saw that this young whippersnapper was destined for greater things and brought him straight to court.

Markish speculates about what Devier might have been thinking: "It makes no difference how money is made, whether through piracy in the southern seas or looking after disreputable Russian ignoramuses. But one thing is clear: the closer you are to the tsar, the more money there will be...And these fellows, the Russians, are foreigners, like everyone here is foreign." We generally attribute such mercinariness to soldiers of fortune vying to sell their sword to the highest bidder. Devier, however, did not see himself as a foreigner in the country that would become his new home. Having placed himself and his life in the hands of Tsar Peter and Russia, he wanted nothing more than to put down roots in the country and become more than a mere "itinerant," more than a "tumbleweed" blowing through (a term used in Russia for the Jewish Diaspora). He wanted to become one of the zealous lords and patriots of the Russian state.

Being a Christian (like his late father), nothing prevented Devier from living in Russia and advancing up the ladder of service without converting to Orthodoxy (the tsar's friend, the Calvinist Franz Lefort, became a full admiral). Nevertheless, immediately upon his arrival in Moscow, Anton did convert to Orthodoxy. This step was a sign of his driving desire to adapt to Russian life. After all, the word "Russian" is an adjective, not a noun. Fervent service to the empire meant a lot more than the chemical makeup of one's blood in determining who was and was not deserving of this designation.

His innate intelligence, cheerful disposition, and energetic service quickly led to Anton's appointment as the tsar's orderly. This was a position of great responsibility, one that signifies the particular trust of the tsar and has often served as a springboard to future prominence (suffice it to say that the "semi-sovereign," His Most Serene Highness Prince Alexander Menshikov, also once held the post of orderly to the tsar).

"Clever, insinuating, selfless, and tireless," is how contemporaries described Devier. What enchanted the monarch most of all, however, was his incorruptibility and lack of mercenary drive, so rare in Russia at that time. Anton did not steal, take bribes, or attempt to stick his hand in the government till – these were the attributes that most strongly predisposed Peter toward him and earned him, for example, the privilege of entering the tsar's workshop without being announced. Before long, Anton was an adjutant-general, the approximate equivalent of a modern-day colonel.

What was it like being an ethnic Jew at the Russian court? Contemporaries report that at first high society regarded him, a stateless upstart, with icy reserve. According to some interpretations, Devier decided on an advantageous marriage in order to enhance his standing. "He did not dare try to ingratiate himself with the highly born boyar families," writes the historian Sergei Shubinsky. "Knowing that his Jewish origins constituted an insurmountable barrier here, he was forced to try his luck with the new aristocracy." When he was 28, Anton's choice fell on Anna Danilovna, the sister of the all-powerful Prince Menshikov, whose father had been a mere stableman. How much ink and paper has been expended on attempts to prove that Devier married solely based on cold calculation! They said that his intended was virtually an old maid (although in fact she was only 22 years old!) and was in no way distinguished by beauty. In truth, she was a remarkable and quite emancipated figure: a rakish horseback rider who, to the horror of the stodgier elements at court, was well-read (unlike her brother) and spoke several languages. At one point she was part of an intimate circle of friends close to the tsar (this circle, in addition to the Menshikovs and the Arsenyev sisters, included Yekaterina Trubacheva, the future Empress Catherine I). It was even said that Anna was one of the womanizing emperor's fleeting passions.

The haughty Menshikov, who himself had been snatched from obscurity and elevated to the heights of Russian Olympus, answered Devier with a sharp and categorical refusal. Anton then decided to seduce Anna and present her brother with a *fait accompli,* in order to then obtain his permission to "make an honest woman of her." His Serene Highness' reaction was, however, the exact opposite of what Devier was expecting. The prince was so overcome by fury that not only did he himself mercilessly beat the seducer, but, as if that were not enough, called on his henchmen to finish the job.

It was clear that his sister's matrimonial plans had only inflamed Menshikov's wrath. How could anyone call this a marriage based on cold calculation? Knowing how vindictive the tsar's favorite could be, Anton could not fail to understand that he was earning himself a powerful and cunning enemy. Rather than calculation, it must have been a sincere affinity and love for Anna Danilovna that motivated Devier. (They did, in fact, go on to have a happy marriage that produced three sons and a daughter.)

The contemporary writer Nikolai Konyayev offers a description of what happened next:

> After his beating, Devier told Peter what had happened, and the tsar immediately set out to see Menshikov. "Have you lost your mind, my friend?" he asked. "Why did you refuse Devier? What do you want me to look like to the Europeans?" And although Menshikov gave his sister to Devier in the end, the tsar never forgave His Most Serene Highness…Although under Peter I anti-Semitism was not yet much of an issue, Peter was already putting a decisive stop to it.

In truth, with the tsar backing Menshikov into a corner, he was compelled to agree to this "unequal" marriage (while continuing to feel an irrepressible animosity for Devier). As far as anti-Semitism is concerned, it can be stated unequivocally: it existed throughout the Petrine era both on the level of religion and ethnicity.

Judeophobia at court would reach its apex in 1722, when the interests of that selfsame Prince Menshikov clashed with those of the Jewish Vice Chancellor Baron Pyotr Shafirov (they had a dispute over the profit from the White

Sea Company, in which they both had an interest), a confrontation that was witnessed by Devier. Over the course of this conflict, Shafirov was accused of concealing his Jewish ancestry. Although it was not difficult for the Baron to defend himself on this count (by pointing out the friendship between the tsar and his Christianized father, as well as the hereditary nobility the family was granted under Tsar Fyodor), insulting words about the "Jewish race" hung in the air.

Peter, however, judged his subjects based not on their ethnicity, but on how valuable they were to Russia, and he therefore, in 1718, appointed Devier to the newly created and highly responsible post of St. Petersburg's Chief of Police (or rather Ober-Polizeimeister, as a German term was borrowed). It should be said that St. Petersburg, which had essentially become Russia's capital in 1710, was then a sprawling swamp with buildings grouped here and there, dirty streets, and a most heterogeneous and restive population (a significant portion of which had been forcibly moved there). Wolves roamed the streets, and drunkenness, vice, theft, and plunder were everyday occurrences.

To Peter's thinking, the man for the job of improving the daily life of the new capital, of developing its industry and commerce, of ensuring the city's "beautification and decency," etc., was Anton Devier, with his efficiency and talent for effective management. "Gentlemen of the Senate!" Peter wrote on May 27, 1718, "To improve order, we have designated that this city have a Police Master General, a position to which we have appointed Adjutant-General Devier; and we have given him points as to how this matter entrusted to him should be managed." There followed 13 "points" that enumerated the duties Devier's subordinates would be expected to perform.

In the General Regulation of 1721, the tasks of this new agency were spelled out in rather grandiloquent terms that sound more like panegyric than ordinance:

> The police uphold the law and administration of justice, promote beneficial order and morals, deliver to all security from brigands, thieves, violators, and swindlers and others of their ilk, suppress dishonorable and indecent living, compel each person to labor and honest business, ensure good inspectors, careful and good municipal servants, and use them to produce regular [straight] streets; prevent scarcity, and bring prosperity in everything needed for human life, guard against the occurrence of disease and see to the cleanliness of streets; and prohibit an excess of housing expenses in houses and all obvious offenses;

show charity to beggars, the poor, sick, crippled, and other needy people, protect the widowed, orphaned, and foreign in accordance with the commandments of God, educate the young in virtuous purity and honorable knowledge. In short, in all things the police are the soul of citizenship and of all good order and are a fundamental pillar of human security and comfort.

Every day the police chief traveled around the city and personally saw that order was upheld and laws obeyed. Friedrich Wilhelm von Bergholtz of Holstein claims that Devier's severity struck such terror in the hearts of St. Petersburg's population that people trembled at the very mention of his name. On the other hand, he achieved impressive results. Historians attest to the fact that under his leadership a 190-man police force was created – the first in Russia; a fire station was built; 600 hempseed oil street lights were installed; the main streets of the city were paved in stone; a team of wagon-drivers was organized to carry away rubbish; an inspectorate was set up to oversee the sale of foodstuffs; a system for registering the population was put in place; and swing gates were installed at the end of every street. Stringent measures were taken against beggars (they were beaten with cudgels and removed from the city). Sizeable fines were levied for violating passport rules, gambling, drunkenness, reckless riding or driving, or singing on the streets, and second offenses could mean exile to Siberia or even the death penalty. The police chief's zeal was noticed by the tsar, who on January 6, 1725, promoted him to the rank of General Major.

On January 28 of that same year, Peter the Great met his maker, and his wife, Catherine, was proclaimed empress. Despite the unbounded influence that Menshikov exercised over the new sovereign, for a while Devier was protected from his scheming by Catherine's personal regard for him. He was granted the privilege of free access to her at any time and frequently entertained her with his inexhaustible supply of stories, witty antics, and puns. The French ambassador to Russia, Jacques de Campredon, made the following notation in his diary in reference to Catherine: "Devier…is among her obvious favorites."

In 1725 the police chief received a high award – the Order of St. Alexander Nevsky – and in 1726 he was promoted to General Lieutenant and made a count. The Devier coat of arms is described by heraldists as follows:

In the middle of a shield, which is divided into four quadrants, is a green escutcheon covered by the count's crown with depiction of a single-headed eagle holding an orb and scepter in its claws. In the first and fourth quadrant, in a red field, are silver towers. In the second and third quadrants, in an azure field, are two lions standing on their hind legs. Atop the shield is a headpiece topped with the palatine crown. The shield is coated with azure and red with a silver underlay.

As the count's wife, Anna Danilovna was entered into the empress' suite as a court maid of honor.

In early 1727 Devier showed himself to be a talented diplomat, which, in combination with his incorruptibility, made him an invaluable asset to the Russian crown. The episode in question concerned the well-known Courland crisis, when the hand of the widowed Duchess Anna (who would later assume the Russian throne) was being sought by Maurice de Saxe, an opportunistic dandy and the illegitimate son of King August II of Poland. Allowing Maurice to become a duke was contrary to Russian interests. Anton Devier's task was to convince the Courlanders to reject de Saxe's candidacy. He set out for Mitau immediately after the return of Menshikov, whose mission there had proved an utter failure. Coveting the title of duke for himself, the prince had behaved in an insulting and threatening manner, which turned the entire local aristocracy against him. For this reason, Devier would have to proceed with intelligence and caution.

Maurice de Saxe offered Anton 10,000 écus to help him secure a marriage to Anna. The epistolary rebuff of this offer once again attests to Devier's incorruptibility and sense of duty:

> The letter received by me on this date caused me surprise and painful concern, all the more so in that, thank the Lord, all my past behavior should serve to prove that I am incapable – for all the treasure in the world, let alone a few thousand Reichsthaler – of making even the smallest step away from the assignment given me in the instructions of my most merciful sovereign. This is a strange proposal, and, like any other enticement that presumes foul and base feelings in those at whom it is directed, is an insult to any honorable man. In the aforementioned case, for which Her Majesty has honored me by choosing me as the instrument of her will, I shall, regardless of the aspirations of private persons and alien interests and without the remuneration of outsiders, fulfill my duties as befits an honest man.

Devier's mission to Courland ended with the triumph of Russian interests. However, Anna harbored a smoldering animosity toward the man who had separated her from her suitor. Later, when she became empress, she had an opportunity to exact her revenge.

Upon returning from Mitau to St. Petersburg, Anton found the mood at court gloomy and inauspicious. Catherine suffered bouts of illness with increasing frequency, foretelling an impending and difficult end. Menshikov was scheming: in order to stay afloat and preserve his unlimited power, he thought of placing Peter's grandson on the throne, the 12-year-old future Peter II, and marrying the boy to his daughter Maria. The prince himself would then serve as imperial regent until the boy reached the age of majority.

Menshikov's political impertinence, overreaching, and astounding wealth were a thorn in the side of many prominent courtiers, who tried to oppose the power-grabbing schemes of the former street vendor by whatever means they could. The contingent opposed to the former favorite was headed by the Duke of Holstein, Karl Friedrich, and included Pyotr Tolstoy, Ivan Buturlin, Alexander Naryshkin, Grigory Skornyakov-Pisarev, Andrei Ushakov, and Ivan Dolgoruky. After learning of his brother-in-law's intrigues, Devier not only allied himself with Menshikov's enemies, but became one of the group's most active members.

The denouement came sooner than expected. The empress fell ill with fever. Menshikov did not leave her deathbed and slipped her a last will and testament that would provide for the ascension of young Peter to the throne, putting the prince within grasp of becoming father-in-law to the emperor. His enemies' days were numbered, and the prince was only waiting for a convenient excuse to deliver his death blow.

An opportunity soon presented itself. It wound up being Devier's "loose lips" that served as a pretext for retribution. He had never been good at keeping them sealed, but in this case he was uninhibited by a surfeit of drink. Here is how the incident is described in a document evidently drafted by Menshikov and signed by the monarch:

> During the cruel paroxysms of illness that God willed upon us, when all our virtuous subjects were consumed with grief, Anton Devier, while being in our house, not only was not sad, but was reveling and instead twirled the tearful Sofya Karlusovna [the empress' niece] in dance and told her: "There is no need

to cry."…Anna Petrovna [Peter's daughter] was crying in that same chamber: Devier in his wicked audacity said, "Why are you sad? Drink a glass of wine!"

Of course, Devier's drunken boldness was just an excuse for Menshikov to fry bigger fish. This seems to be confirmed by a new decree issued in Catherine's name: "I myself have observed Devier commit reprehensible acts and know that he has had many accomplices; for this reason Devier should be told that he must name his accomplices." That very hour Anton was grabbed and placed on the rack, and after 25 lashes he confessed to everything and named all his confederates. Literally hours before the empress' death and at Menshikov's urging, she signed orders to punish the guilty:

> Devier and Tolstoy should be stripped of rank, honors, and the villages they have been given and then sent into exile: Devier to Siberia, Tolstoy and his son to Solovki; Buturlin, should be stripped of his rank and sent to his distant village; Skornyakov-Pisarev should be stripped of his rank, honors, villages, beaten with a knout, and sent into exile.

Menshikov arranged to have a notation made on the order in specific regard to his brother-in-law: "Devier, before being sent into exile, should be punished by beating with a knout." The former favorite did not spare his own sister Anna and ordered her and the couple's young children to remain confined to a remote estate.

In the spring of 1727, Devier and Skornyakov-Pisarev, to ensure that their punishment had the proper sting, were sent by Menshikov to frigid Yakutia, to the Arctic settlement of Zhigansk, along the barren banks of the Lena, 9,000 miles from St. Petersburg and 80 miles from Yakutsk. In this godforsaken wilderness, exiles often wanted for the most basic necessities and survived on bread and fish. The unfortunate prisoners were forbidden from talking to one another, a prohibition the watchful guards were sure to enforce.

Cut off from the world, it took not months but years for news to reach the outcasts. The star of the "Proud Goliath" Menshikov had already set (he breathed his last in 1729 in the taiga town of Beryozov, to which he himself had been exiled two years previous, just a few months after Devier), the young emperor Peter II had passed away, and Anna Ioannovna (the former Duchess of Courland) had ascended the throne. With the memory of the role Devier had played in separating her from her beloved still fresh in her mind, she was in no hurry to alleviate the disgraced count's suffering.

Only at the end of her reign did Anna show compassion. In April 1739 she issued a decree appointing Anton Devier commander of the Far Eastern port at Okhotsk, which was being expanded. Years of privation and hardship had done nothing to diminish the former police chief's administrative talents. He was again needed, and he answered the call with a burst of energy. Among his other accomplishments, he exposed abuses committed by former officials, was able to quickly outfit the expedition of Vitus Bering, and completed construction of the port. He was also able to return to his initial passion for seafaring and founded a nautical school, which later became the navigation college for the Siberian fleet.

Paradoxically, it was Peter the Great's daughter, Empress Elizabeth, a notorious anti-Semite, who retrieved Devier from exile and showered him with favor. (As for her anti-Semitism, she probably did not perceive the Russified and Orthodox Devier as Jewish.) By an imperial decree dated February 14, 1743, he was restored his title of Count, his rank as General Lieutenant, and the Order of St. Alexander Nevsky. Elizabeth also granted him 1,800 "souls" (peasants) from the estate of the despised Menshikov, as well as Menshikov's former village of Zigoritsa (with a total of 180 households) not far from St. Petersburg. He was also promoted to General-in-Chief.

Following in her father's footsteps, on December 27, 1744, Elizabeth reappointed Devier St. Petersburg's chief of police. Although at 63 he was no longer a young man, Anton Manuilovich again enthusiastically threw himself into his work. Now, however, the residents of St. Petersburg were not gripped with fear at the thought of the elderly general.

Devier was not to preside over the security of "Palmira of the North" for long. The suffering endured during his Arctic exile had destroyed his health. After repeated bouts of illness, he died on June 24, 1745, only six months after his reappointment. So ended the career of one of Peter the Great's most assiduous associates.

Anton Manuilovich Devier was laid to rest in the Lazarus Cemetery of St. Petersburg's Alexander Nevsky Monastery. A nineteenth century biographer confirms that he saw a cracked slab with the inscription: "General-in-Chief Count Anton Manuilovich Devier. Laid to rest June 27, 1745." But today the location of Devier's grave is forgotten. Fortunately, his story is not lost to history and serves to remind Russian nationalists of the inconvenient truth that Russia's first chief of police was an ethnic Jew.

JAN D'ACOSTA

THE JEWISH KING OF THE SAMOYED

The late Russian politician and general, Alexander Lebed, once mused that "a democratic general is as rare as a Jewish reindeer breeder." Little did the general suspect that, a few years later, the hunters and reindeer-breeders of Chukotka would elect a Jew, Roman Abramovich, as their governor. Yet Abramovich is not the only Russian Jew to rule a northern people. Two centuries ago, Peter the Great accorded his court jester, Jan d'Acosta, the title of king of another ice-bound people, the Samoyed. As with so many tales from the court of Peter the Great, the deeper you probe, the more interesting it gets.

Jan d'Acosta (known in Russia as Lakosta) was a descendant of Marranos, Christianized Jews who fled Portugal to escape the fires of the Inquisition. Born in 1665, in the city of Sale, North Africa, he lived a peripatetic existence with his family until he was 16, at which point he settled with his father and brothers in Hamburg and opened a brokerage house. As it turned out, commerce was not his strong suit, and he was plagued with losses. His true talents lay in the realm of manners, in which he exhibited all the refinement of a Versailles marquis. For a while, he considered giving lessons to all those "who desire to take part in the *grande monde* with ease, to learn the most wise art of making compliments and manifesting all sorts of polite behavior, appropriate to the specific time and place." But fine manners did not prove lucrative either. So Jan decided to set off for faraway Muscovy "in search of fame and fortune." According to one version, he received permission to go to Russia from the Russian ambassador in Hamburg. The testimony of d'Acosta's friend, the Russian court physician Antonio Nunes Ribeiro Sanchez, is perhaps more authoritative. According to Sanchez, "When Peter I, emperor of Russia, traveled through Hamburg, probably in 1712 or 1713, d'Acosta was presented to him. Peter I brought him home…along with his wife and children."

In either case, Jan – or as he came to be called in Russia, Pyotr Dorofeyevich – could only settle in Russia if he agreed to one condition: he had to convert. Peter was quite explicit on this point: "I would rather see peoples of the Mohammedan or pagan faith [in Russia] than Jews. They are rogues and deceivers. I root out evil rather than sow it; [so] in Russia there will be neither a place to live nor trade for them, however much they try and however many of my people they buy off."

Jan d'Acosta

Peter rejected a petition from Dutch Jews who wished to move to Russia. He responded angrily to Amsterdam Mayor Nicolaes Witsen, who had passed along their offer of 100,000 guilders for this privilege, a huge sum at that time.

> You know the Jews and the thoughts of my people, and so do I. It is not yet time to allow Jews to settle in my tsardom, so tell them in my name that I thank them for the proposal, but also that I greatly regret that they want to move to Russia, because although they are considered skillful swindlers in trade throughout the world, I doubt that they will be able to trick my Russians.

The tsar was expressing a view typical not only of eighteenth-century Russia, but of all "enlightened" Europe.

Yet Peter was no slave to prejudice, and when it came to selecting those best able to advance the cause of Russia, he was more concerned with merit than rank or nationality, and anyone who could bring glory to the state was welcome to become a citizen of Russia, regardless of race (consider, for example, his famous "Moor of Peter the Great," the Ethiopian Ibrahim Hannibal, great grandfather of Alexander Pushkin). Indeed, many Jews made good careers under Peter the Great: vice chancellor Pyotr Shafirov; St. Petersburg's first police chief Anton Devier; the diplomat brothers Abraham and Isaac Veselovsky; head of the secret police Vivier, the merchants Yevreynov, doctor of the Semyonovsky regiment Abraham Ens, and others. All of them, however, espoused Christianity, sincerely or not. Since he had already adopted Catholicism, nothing prevented d'Acosta from entering the tsar's service. "The Sovereign took a great liking to his humorous and amusing manners," wrote Ivan Golikov in his *Deeds of Peter the Great*, "and he was taken into the suite of court jesters."

Among the attributes that won Pyotr Dorofeyevich the tsar's favor was his broad erudition. He spoke fluent Spanish, Italian, French, German, Dutch and Portuguese, was knowledgeable on questions of religion, could recite entire passages from the Bible by heart, and held his own in endless theological debates with the tsar. Friedrich Wilhelm von Bergholtz of Holstein, who kept a detailed diary during his time at the court of Peter the Great, recorded the following incident.

> I heard an argument beween the monarch and his jester d'Acosta, who was usually lively company…Here is what they were aruging about. D'Acosta said that it is written in holy scripture "That many shall come from the east and west, and shall sit down with Abraham, and Isaac, and Jacob." The tsar was arguing with him and asked where this was written. The other replied that it was in the Bible. His Majesty immediately went running to get a Bible and soon returned with a huge book, demanding that d'Acosta find him the passage. The jester responded that he did not know where these words appear. "It's all nonsense, it doesn't say any such thing," replied His Majesty.

But it was d'Acosta who was actually right here, since he had reproduced from memory Jesus' words from Matthew 8:11. The meaning behind this prophesy is that pagan peoples would recognize the teachings of Christ, but Israel, the Jewish people, would not accept Christianity.

It is unlikely that the convert d'Acosta tried to introduce Peter to Judaism, as Israeli writer David Markish suggests in his book, *The Jew of Peter the Great or a Chronicle from the Life of an Itinerant People*. Markish invents a fantastic scene: d'Acosta, Shafirov, Devier and a Smolensk merchant by the name of Baruch Leibov are celebrating Passover together and trying to convince the Russian tsar to put on a yarmulke, which he does without hesitation.

Not only is this particular scene unimaginable, but it is unrealistic to suggest that a special Jewish cohort existed in early eighteenth-century St. Petersburg, united by communal or religious interests and offering protection to its members. Suffice it to point out that Baruch Leibov was subsequently burnt at the stake after being falsely accused of proselytizing Judaism, and it was under

Peter that Russia saw its first case of "blood libel" against Jews (in 1702 in the small town of Gorodnya in the Chernigov region).

D'Acosta looked like a Sephardic Jew and had an intelligent and determined face. "He was tall," wrote Sanchez, who was also a descendant of Marranos, "lean, dark complexioned, with a manly voice, and sharp facial features." Neither contemporaries nor later biographers failed to mention his Jewish heritage, and not necessarily in a positive light. Historian Sergei Shubinsky commented that "His characteristically Jewish ability to imitate and to get along with anyone secured him a place as court jester." More likely, Peter valued him not for these traits, but for his directness and refusal to compromise. D'Acosta was endowed with a sense of his own self-worth, called the awe-inspiring tsar his "kum" (godfather), addressed dignitaries as his equals, and impressed Russians with his delicacy and fine manners. He called a thief a thief, and ridiculed the vices and abuses of courtiers. When complaints about the jester's impudence reached the tsar, he responded calmly, "What would you have me do with him? He's a fool after all!"

In his role as jester, Pyotr Dorofeyevich often played the part of the tsar's comic double. He helped Peter cut boyar's robes and shave their Old Testament beards. When it came to unobtrusively reminding Russian subjects that their country's well-being should come first or recalling its victories and achievements, d'Acosta was second to none. The jester's inexhaustible wit was proverbial, and he became the subject of innumerable jokes and literary anecdotes, which tell of his unfailing resourcefulness in any predicament. Here are just a few examples:

> D'Acosta set off on a sea voyage, and one of those accompanying him asked, "How can you not be afraid of getting on a ship, when your father, grandfather, and great-grandfather perished at sea?"
> "And just how did your forefathers die?" d'Acosta responded.
> "They passed away in blessed fashion in their own beds."
> "So how is it, my friend, that you are not afraid to get into bed every night?"

> A courtier asks d'Acosta why he plays the fool. The jester replies, "You and I do so for different reasons: In my case it is lack of money, in yours, lack of brains."

> Once in church, d'Acosta placed two candles, one in front of an icon to Archangel Michael, and one near the demon the archangel is trampling

underfoot. A priest ran up and said to him, "My Lord! What have you done? You've placed a candle before the devil!"

"Well, we still don't know where we will end up," d'Acosta answered calmly, "so it won't hurt to have friends both in heaven and in hell."

D'Acosta lived many years with a quarrelsome wife. When the 25th year of their marriage drew near, he was told that it was time to commemorate their silver anniversary.

"Hold on, brothers," the jester said, "in just five more years we can celebrate the Thirty Year War!"

D'Acosta's wife was short. "Why did you, a rational person, take such a dwarf for a wife?" he was asked.

"When I decided to marry, I prudently decided to choose the least of all possible evils."

D'Acosta supposedly converted to Russian Orthodoxy. Six months later, his priest was told that the jester hadn't been performing any church rites. The priest summoned the new convert and started to rebuke him. "Father," d'Acosta responded, "when I became Orthodox, wasn't it you who told me that I had become pure, as if I had been reborn?"

"True, I said that. I cannot deny it."

"Well, if it's only been six months since I was reborn, what can you expect of a six-month-old child?"

In the course of a lawsuit, d'Acosta often visited one of the judges to find out how his case was faring. During one visit the judge finally said, "I honestly do not see this case ending well for you."

"Here then, my lord, are some proper eyeglasses for you." And he slipped the judge a pair of banknotes.

While many of these anecdotes are the fruit of unbridled fancy, there are others that are documented historical fact and testify to Peter the Great's relationship with his favorite jester. They tell, for example, of d'Acosta's hatred for the court surgeon, Johann Hermann Lestocq. Apparently, the jester had good reason for animosity, as the influential doctor had seduced his daughter. Where did Tsar Peter stand in this conflict? He took the side of the offended father and harshly punished the offender, sending Lestocq into exile in Kazan under heavy guard and without the right of correspondence, where he remained until the reign of Catherine I. From this the historian Sergei Solovyov concluded that d'Acosta was the monarch's main jester. Peter, it should be mentioned, had no fewer than a dozen.

For Peter I, revelry and merry-making were serious business. He promulgated the celebrated decree: "From this day forth all drunkards...are to gather on Sunday to collectively praise the Greek gods," and to proclaim health and long life "to the Hellenic god Bacchus and the goddess Venus." He thus founded the ill-reputed Most Drunken Synod of Fools and Jesters, which was made up of the dregs of high and low society: the more a nonentity a person was, the more likely he would end up in Peter's anti-clerical "Synod." The tsar himself occupied the humble position of proto-deacon in this satirical hierarchy, "fulfilling his duties with such zeal that it might seem they were not in jest." There were notorious mock-weddings where the bride was over 60, the groom 80 and funerals complete with processions of dwarfs. As one eyewitness wrote, "Prince Volkonsky was tarred and turned on his head, a candle was inserted in his backside and lit, and the assemblage formed a circle around him, dancing and singing. The nobleman Ivan Maslov died from having fur stuffed up his rear. Everyone awaited the tsar's diversions as if preparing for death."

This, rather improbably, brings us to the northern people known at that time as the Samoyed (they are now known as the Nenets).

According to eighteenth-century Russian geographer Ivan Georgi, the Samoyed inhabited the Yamal Peninsula and the Mangazeya region and led a nomadic life of fishing, hunting, and reindeer herding. As Georgi describes them:

> The Samoyed are very short, rarely shorter than four or taller than five feet. Moreover, they are thick-set, with short legs and necks, large heads, markedly flat faces and noses, with the lower portion of the face thrust somewhat forward, a large mouth and ears, small black eyes, rather long eyelids, thin lips, small feet, dark skin, with no hair anywhere except on the head, and that black and coarse. The men's facial hair is only fuzz. The women are somewhat better built, shorter in stature, but equally as unattractive as the men.

The Samoyed were pagan and worshiped idols, the geographer continued, ate raw meat, drank blood with greater relish than water, and were distinguished by their ferocity. Their winter clothing, worn on the naked body, was sewn from deer, fox, and other furs, and their summer clothing was made from fish skins. The eighteenth-century historian Vasily Tatishchev claimed that the Samoyed ate human flesh, a practice that earned them their name. In Russian, *samoyed* means "cannibal."

Clearly, this people had a unique way of looking at things. The famous Swiss ethnographer and traveler Philip Johan von Strahlenberg, who visited the Samoyed during Peter's reign, pointed out that they even had their own way of counting. "When the Samoyed bring their tribute, they tie together the ermine, squirrels, and other pelts into bunches of nine. The Russians, who found this number difficult to deal with, upon receipt retied them into groups of ten." The nomads did not understand why their system, so very convenient for counting, did not meet the Russians' approval.

As was customary among aboriginal peoples, the Samoyed had a leader whose word was law. The Great Reformer, however, had no interest in Samoyed customs and traditions. For Peter, who often compared his subjects to "little children" needing to be taught to see things his way, Russian traditions were bad enough. We can only imagine how he felt about an obscure, aboriginal people. The Samoyed should be ruled not by some primeval leader who was at the beck and call of a shaman, but by a king – a cavalier in the European style. And if he wants, let him adorn himself in those Samoyed skins, for exoticism's sake!

In 1709, three years before d'Acosta's arrival in St. Petersburg, Tsar Peter awarded the title of King of the Samoyed to their "pale-faced brother," a Western European who had been given the nickname "Vimeni." One source claims that this adventurer had actually declared himself King of the Samoyed, and Peter simply gave his approval. Be that as it may, Peter organized a jesters' coronation of Vimeni, for which were summoned 24 Samoyed, who swore loyalty to the new king and brought along a large number of reindeer.

According to one account, Vimeni came from "a good French family, but in his homeland he had suffered many reversals of fate and was confined to the Bastille for many years, which resulted in periodic insanity." When Vimeni first arrived in Muscovy, he did not understand Russian (let alone Samoyed), and a letter has been preserved in which the monarch ordered that "The Samoyed Prince, who is being sent to you from Voronezh, be taught to speak Russian, and also Slavonic grammar."

Vimeni actually learned Russian rather quickly, and soon, on Peter's orders, translated Jean Baptiste Molière's comedy, *Les précieuses ridicules*. Yet the writer

Dmitry Merezhkovsky commented (in his novel *Peter and Alexei*) that "this translation...must have been done while dead drunk, because it's impossible to understand anything in it. Poor Molière! This monstrous Samoyed writing offers all the grace of a dancing polar bear." In his *Life of M. de Molière*, Mikhail Bulgakov described Vimeni's translation as having been written "in clumsy lines."

Tsar Peter, however, was extremely fond of Vimeni, and according to Christian Friedrich Weber, representative of Braunschweig at the Russian court, he settled the Samoyed from his retinue on Petrovsky Island, near the capital. There, it was reported, a skirmish broke out between the jester-king and the Samoyed's native leader. It was said that the Samoyed leader "attacked people who came to inspect the island, bit them on the ears and face, and in general gave them a hostile welcome, with malice and violence." When the leader was harshly punished, he, as if to illustrate how his people had earned their name, "bit off a piece of flesh from his own arm." Clearly it appealed to Peter's sense of black humor to put Vimeni, a representative of European culture, whatever his failings as a translator, in charge of these savages.

A cortege of Samoyed with Vimeni at its head took part in the triumphal procession of December 19, 1709, that marked Russia's victory over Sweden in the Battle of Poltava. The Danish envoy Just Juel left a detailed account of this event.

> The Frenchman Vimeni rode on a sleigh pulled by reindeer and with a Samoyed riding the footboard; there followed 19 Samoyed sleds, with two horses or three reindeer each. On every sled lay one Samoyed...They were covered from head to toe in reindeer hides, fur side out, and each had a fur doll attached to his belt.

The Dane also commented on the spectacle's ideological subtext:

> This people is short in stature, with undersized legs, big heads and broad faces. It is easy to understand what sort of impression, and what laughter this train inspired... But without doubt it was quite galling to the Swedes that their tragedy should be marked with such absurd comedy.

Peter wanted to use the jester-king and his suite to symbolize the wild impudence of the Swedish King Charles XII, who had dared to attempt the impossible: to conquer Russia, depose Peter, and split up the empire.

Not long afterward, the French King of the Samoyed passed away. An eyewitness described the funeral that Peter staged for Vimeni: "Many important people, their clothing covered with black capes, accompanied the deceased and were seated on Samoyed sleds pulled by reindeer and with a Samoyed riding the footboard."

Nature abhors a vacuum, and someone had to be found to take Vimeni's place. The writer Alexander Rodionov, in his novel *The Khiva Campaign*, has Peter make the following comment: "He [d'Acosta] is an excellent jester, and I will soon give him a promotion. D'Acosta will be King of the Samoyed and will govern these 'pinched mugs' at my court – we should give him the title of count and master of ceremonial amusements."

Of course, Peter was not concerned with the new king's ethnic background. The important thing was that d'Acosta, like his predecessor, was a cultured and politically savvy person.

One can hardly imagine that the jester-king actually ruled the Samoyed. He apparently played a purely ornamental and symbolic role, and the tsar found this very amusing. Having the sophisticated Pyotr Dorofeyevich prance around in Samoyed native dress was a great cause for hilarity, and the jester made many an appearance at masquerades in this guise. For his excellent service as a jester, the tsar bestowed on d'Acosta the island of Sommers, in the Gulf of Finland. Peter generally kept d'Acosta by his side and took him on various outings. The historical record contains, for example, a list of those accompanying the tsar on a particular excursion compiled by Alexander Menshikov that includes our jester (plus a note that he has been ordered to prepare three horses). D'Acosta's tenure as court jester continued under Empress Anna Ioannovna (1730-1740); however, the requirements of the job changed. In her choice of jesters, male and female, the empress liked to combine the base with the gallant, the barbarous with the refined. And while under Peter jesters were encouraged to mock the vices of prejudice and ignorance (even, at times, among his followers), at Anna's court jesters were simply entertainers, without any rights, and forbidden to criticize or comment on politics. Now the makeup of the "collegiums of clowns" underscored the regal standing of its mistress and its ranks were increasingly filled by members of the titled nobility (including such eminences as Prince Mikhail Golitsyn, Prince Nikita Volkonsky and Count Alexei Apraksin), as well as by foreigners (such as the Italian Pedrillo).

The jesters' witticisms were now marked by uncommon cynicism and salaciousness. The empress was amused when her entertainers climbed onto nests filled with chicken eggs and took turns loudly crowing. The wilder the

"Jesters in the Court of Anna Iovannovna" (1872), by Valery Jacoby

antic, the better, and the court fools found themselves leapfrogging, making idiotic facial contortions, and staging fist-fights. As one memoirist wrote, "At first these jesters would just pretend to argue, and then they would start to call one another names, and in due course, hoping to better entertain their audience, began to really throw punches. The empress and the entire court enjoyed this spectacle immensely, and used to die of laughter."

D'Acosta, too, was caught up in this mayhem. In the historical novel *Word and Deed*, the writer Valentin Pikul describes a battle of jesters in which d'Acosta took part that went beyond the playful in its intensity. However, among Anna Ioannovna's assemblage of jesters, Peter's Jewish jokester stood out. As the Swedish scholar Carl Berch comments in his *Travel Notes on Russia*, of all the empress' jesters, "D'Acosta is the only smart one." It appears that Anna was entirely pleased with Pyotr Dorofeyevich, inasmuch as she awarded him the mock Order of St. Benedetto, a miniature cross on a red ribbon suggestive of the Order of St. Alexander Nevsky.

Under Anna, the whole idea of having a king of the Samoyed took on new significance. Unlike Peter, for whom the national dress of his empire's peoples was no more than a target for satire, for Anna, with her love of folklore, they had intrinsic value. After all, it was under her patronage that the St. Petersburg Academy of Sciences undertook a series of ethnographic expeditions to Russia's far corners. The empress not only reaffirmed d'Acosta's "rule" over the Samoyed, but on July 22, 1731, ordered the governor of Arkhangelsk Province to "seek out approximately 10 Samoyed, with one sled and a pair of reindeer each and another sled, made larger than is customary for them, to be drawn by six reindeer… And send them off, having supplied them and without angering them, so that they will make the journey more eagerly and take care of the reindeer." In October of 1731, the Samoyed caravan arrived in Moscow.

In the words of writer Yuri Nagibin, it was around this time that Anna was first "struck by the realization of the greatness and vastness of the land she ruled." She used the occasion of the wedding between two of her jesters, Mikhail Golitsyn and Avdotiya Buzheninova (which took place in the famous "House of Ice," a frozen palace the empress had built during the winter of 1739-40), to celebrate the diversity of her realm. For this event she "ordered the governors of all of the provinces to send to St. Petersburg several people of both sexes. Upon arrival in the capital, these people were dressed at court expense in their native dress." The costumed representatives of all the tribes inhabiting the Russian Empire rode on sleighs pulled by deer, oxen, pigs, goats, mules, dogs, and even camels. They played folk instruments, and then each ate their own national foods and danced their indigenous dances. A surviving list of participants includes: "a warrior with a spear in Samoyed dress," "d'Acosta dressed as a Samoyed chieftain," and "a male and female Samoyed."

The ethnographic variety of costumes was meant to demonstrate the huge size of the powerful empire and the prosperity of its many diverse inhabitants, including the Samoyed. In other words, it all had a very clearly expressed panegyrical purpose. As the poet Vasily Tredyakovsky put it, "Rejoice all peoples of Russia, / These are golden years for us!"

After the ice house wedding, the name of the Jewish jester does not appear again in historical sources. It is known that in the fall of 1740, when Anna Leopoldovna became regent for the infant Emperor Ivan VI (1740-1741), she dismissed all court jesters, awarding them rich severances. She angrily condemned the abuse of human dignity, "inhuman insults" and "the infliction of torments" that had been heaped on them. Indeed, she should be given her due for ending this despised occupation. Jesters no longer appeared at court in their comic dress.

And what about d'Acosta? He died that very year. Perhaps weary of the tinsel and bustle of court life, he cast off the guise of Samoyed king and lived out his final days in peace and tranquility, presaging the bitter wisdom of his fellow Jew, the writer Leon Feuchtwanger, who in one of his novels posed the rhetorical question: "Why does a Jew need a parrot?"

ABRAHAM, ISAAC, AND FYODOR VESELOVSKY

THE DIPLOMATIC CLAN

In the history of the empire, no clan has exerted as much influence over Russian foreign policy as did the Veselovsky brothers during the second decade of the eighteenth century. Three members of this remarkable family – Christianized Jews of Ashkenazi descent – have gone down in history as paragons of Russian diplomacy.

The founder of this dynasty was a man by the name of Jacob (Yakov) from the Polish shtetl of Veselovo. He performed vital services for the Russian army during the capture of Smolensk in 1654. After being baptized – something he was compelled to do if he wanted to continue supplying the Russian government – he moved to Muscovy. His son, Pavel Veselovsky, married Maria Arshenevskaya, a Christianized Jew who was related to Russia's Vice Chancellor, Pyotr Shafirov. The union produced six sons and two daughters. Very little information about Pavel Veselovsky has been passed down, although we do know that he served as *stolnik*[1] at one point and was, the evidence suggests, an educated man. Otherwise he would not have been appointed superintendent of Moscow's German schools, a post he held from 1706 to 1711. He owned a house outside the capital's Pokrovsky Gates in the Earthen City (*Zemlyanoy Gorod*), which encircled the heart of Moscow. During the final years of his life he headed the Apothecary Chancery, roughly equivalent to the Ministry of Health. He died in 1715.

In the early eighteenth century his sons, Abraham (Avraam), Isaac (Isaak), and Fyodor Veselovsky, entered – or rather, burst – onto the Russian historical

---

1. From the word for table (*stol*), since in medieval Russia *stolniks* served the tsar at festive meals. Later the term was used for high-ranking government officials.

stage. Two of them wound up leaving Russia to escape their monarch's wrath, taking refuge in England (one later returned). The third waited out the storm in his native land. This is their extraordinary story.

I. THE DISGRACED DIPLOMAT

Even more than a half century after fleeing Russia, this near-centenarian with snow-white hair maintained a lively and genuine interest in the land of his birth. "I visited Monsieur Veselovsky on Your behalf," wrote a certain prominent Frenchman to the imperial chancellor, Alexander Vorontsov, from Ferney, in the Swiss canton of Geneva: "The kindly old man ...was filled with enthusiasm by everything I told him about his native land, and his joy was reflected in his eyes and on his face." The eminent Petrine-era diplomat Abraham Veselovsky (1685-1783) had settled in Switzerland in 1730, where he lived in dignity and comfort, surrounded by a loving family; in 1741 he had married for the second time, to a French woman by the name of Marianna Fábry. The marriage added four daughters to the progeny of this doting grandfather and great-grandfather.

Abraham Veselovsky

It was Empress Elizabeth who first proposed that Abraham return to Russia. Under Catherine the Great he was finally able to do so with appropriate honors. What allowed him to resume a place of respect at the Russian court was the fact that the patriarch of Ferney – none other than Voltaire, a close friend of Abraham – had whispered many words of praise about him to Catherine. Prominent Russian travelers (including such emblematic figures as Princess Yekaterina Dashkova, President of the Russian Academy, and Count Alexei Orlov, who had been given the victory title of Chesmensky after defeating the Turks at Chesma) considered it an honor to visit Veselovsky's home in Ferney. What was it, then, that caused this imperturbable gentleman to lose his composure and begin shaking like a leaf every time he happened to lay eyes on a portrait of the historic reformer, Peter the Great?

Perhaps the thought of Peter transported the aging diplomat back to the bygone 1720s, when he was in the perilous position of Russian ambassador to the Hapsburg court in Vienna. Back then, Abraham had disobeyed an order from Peter dated April 3, 1719, commanding him to return to Russia "with due haste," supposedly to perform "certain commissions at another court." At first Veselovsky seemed to be complying with the order. Stopping in Berlin along the way, he encountered the Russian envoy Alexander Golovkin and Privy Councillor Pyotr Tolstoy, but soon thereafter Ambassador Veselovsky vanished without a trace.

The tsar immediately raised the alarm. Instructions were sent to every Russian emissary in Europe to find and arrest the fugitive Veselovsky. During the spring of 1720, a military operation was even deployed to apprehend the mutineer in one of the duchies of Germany. The operation was commanded by Prince Yuri Gagarin, who went by the name of Volsky. Volsky and his comrades were supposed to track down Abraham and deliver him to St. Petersburg. If it proved impossible to capture him alive, there was even a contingency to kill the former ambassador. Diplomatic cover for these Russian operatives was arranged by Peter's close associate, Major General Pavel Yaguzhinsky.

At first the bloodhounds thought they had picked up the scent of this "good-for-nothing Christianized Yid," as they called him. He was rumored to have been seen in the area of Frankfurt am Main, in Hesse-Kassel. Realizing that defection was not considered a crime by Western law, the tsar attempted to give their operation an aura of legitimacy by ordering Volsky to allege that Veselovsky was trying to evade a sizeable monetary debt. Veselovsky's pursuers were closing in on him, and the trap was about to snap shut. But Abraham had well-wishers. Warned of his impending ensnarement at the very last minute, he quickly took off for points unknown and vanished once again.

Before long, he surfaced in London, putting him beyond the reach of Volsky and his men. Peter, however, did not acquiesce and was furious when he received the following reply from the banks of the Thames: "The English king is unable to fulfill the request of the Tsar without infringing the right to refuge, which must remain inviolable among all peoples." The tsar was also reminded that Veselovsky had been neither convicted nor sentenced. Although the House of Commons had not approved Abraham's November 1724 petition to become a naturalized Briton, the emigrant felt safe in his new home. In 1730 he moved from Foggy Albion to scenic Switzerland, where he settled for good.

What was it that forced Veselovsky to become the first diplomatic defector in Russian history? People are not born emigrants but become them, and only the logic of their entire preceding life can lead someone to such a desperate decision. This is why we must begin our protagonist's story from the very beginning.

One might say that from an early age all doors were open to Abraham. After all, he was related to the most brilliant diplomat of the time, Vice Chancellor Baron Pyotr Shafirov (he was the baron's nephew). Veselovsky spent a portion of his childhood in his polyglot uncle's household, which is where he must have acquired the interest in foreign languages that led him to gain fluency in German, as well as a mastery of Latin. It was there that he was first noticed by the astute Peter the Great, who foretold a great future for him, even though Abraham was still just a teenager.

When the young many reached the age of 19 he attended, at government expense, Russia's first *gymnasium*, which had only just been established in Moscow. The school was headed by Johann Ernst Gluck, a Lutheran pastor from Marienburg (today, the Latvian town of Aluksne). (An interesting side note is that Marta Skowrońska, the future Empress Catherine I, worked for Gluck as a housemaid in her youth.) Gluck's encyclopedic knowledge extended to a vast number of fields, and he was the author of several works in Russian, including a short geography, a book on grammar, and a prayer book; a Slavonic-Latin-Greek dictionary; and translations from Czech of Jan Amos Komensky's *Vestibulum, Janua linguarum reserata,* and *Orbis Sensualium Pictus.*

The universality of the education Veselovsky received at the *gymnasium* is striking. Courses were offered in geography and politics, history and astronomy, Latin rhetoric and ethics, pragmatic and Cartesian philosophy, the art of dancing and "advances in French and German civility," fencing, equestrianism, and manège. Particular attention was paid to languages (which were taught by foreigners). Veselovsky studied French, German, Latin, Greek, Hebrew, and even Syrian and Chaldean.

But even this was not enough for the inquisitive young man. In order to improve his linguistic abilities, he set out in March 1705 for foreign lands, where he at first served under the Russian emissary Heinrich von Huyssen and later under Peter's eminent associate Boris Kurakin, who at the time was carrying out important missions for the tsar that were designed to enhance Russia's international standing. It was under Kurakin's tutelage that Veselovsky first learned the science of diplomacy. This must have been why, upon returning to St. Petersburg, he was immediately posted to the Diplomatic Department's Chancery, where he began working as a translator in December 1708. Assigned to serve in the department of "secret affairs," he was paid 200 rubles per year, a tremendous salary for the time.

By the time of the Battle of Poltava, Abraham had risen to secretary (*dyak*) in the Diplomatic Department. The tsar kept him close at hand, but in June 1709 sent the shrewd Jew to Denmark with a letter announcing the Russian victory over the Swedes. In 1710 Abraham was appointed to the Izhorian Chancery (set up to absorb newly conquered Ingria, where Peter would soon build his new capital) under the "Minister of State Secrets," His Highness Prince Alexander Menshikov, who assigned Veselovsky a very high position. One contemporary commented, "Now Abraham Veselovsky…is very much in the prince's good favor, and although we do not see him with His Highness, he appears to be the one who conducts business."

In 1715 Veselovsky was appointed ambassador to Vienna. Within five days of his arrival in the capital of the Habsburg monarchy he was received at the palace by Emperor Charles VI himself. Skillfully building relationships at the Viennese court, he proved to have a knack for the art of diplomacy. In the argot of the day, this art was referred to as "seeking the necessary channels," and Veselovsky's task was to ensure that these "channels" nurtured Russia. It is noteworthy that Veselovsky worked to secure the support of the influential Count Zinzendorf. A keen psychologist, he was not always scrupulous in his methods. Upon learning that the count's wife had an insatiable passion for cards, he loaned her a certain sum in exchange for important services by her husband to the Russian crown.

Veselovsky not only fulfilled his diplomatic duties, but carried out Peter's assignment to find "necessary people," since the young Russian Empire had a pressing need for qualified doctors, engineers, architects, and other educated professionals. Furthermore, he attempted to recruit his fellow Jews and was bravely prepared to intercede on their behalf with the tsar, who made it clear that he was not well-disposed toward this people. In one letter to the monarch Veselovsky writes, "Jews have always distinguished themselves in their knowledge of medical science, and only with the help of Jewish doctors has it become possible to successfully fight many dread diseases including, incidentally, leprosy" (by "leprosy" he meant syphilis). The monarch replied to this letter with the following: "For me it is of no consequence whatsoever whether a person is christened or circumcised, so long as he knows his business and is of upstanding character." This assertion was unprecedented, considering that earlier Peter had called Jews knaves and swindlers and categorically prohibited them from settling in Russia. It would appear that the impulsive tsar succumbed here to the charm and reason of his Viennese ambassador.

Russia's Viennese ambassador was indefatigable. One moment he was hunting down valuable books on jurisprudence for the tsar, while the next he was negotiating with the teachers at a Jesuit school in Prague to have encyclopedias translated into Russian, or arranging the purchase of a *caroche* for Alexander Menshikov.

Veselovsky's diplomatic star continued to rise until his productive service was interrupted by a historic turn of events: the case of Tsarevich Alexei. Under an assumed name, Peter's recalcitrant son had fled his royal duties and sought refuge in Austria. Veselovsky was responsible for tracking him down and returning him to his infuriated father. Between December 1716 and June 1717 Veselovsky was essentially in charge of the tsarevich's capture. In March 1717 he finally succeeded in learning that Alexei was hiding in Ehrenberg Castle in Tyrol. The ambassador attempted to arrange a surrender through diplomatic means (he negotiated with Prince Eugene of Savoy and even was granted an audience with Charles VI to discuss the matter), but in vain. Suddenly (possibly due to his exertions traveling by carriage in search of the tsarevich) "Veselovsky was struck with a kidney ailment, accompanied by a fierce fever the likes of which he had never before suffered." He was forced to give up his efforts, and the task of returning the tsarevich to St. Petersburg was reassigned to different emissaries, Alexander Rumyantsev and Pyotr Tolstoy, who finally succeeded.

What motives drove Veselovsky during the events surrounding Peter I's unfortunate son? It is intriguing that historians whose perspectives are polar opposites in other regards reach the same conclusion concerning the diplomat's conduct in this affair. Take, for example, the nationalistic historian Nikolai Molchanov, who in essence accuses Abraham of indulging and concealing Alexei. In his book *Peter I* (Moscow, 2003), Veselovsky appears as a dangerous schemer. Molchanov concludes, "It is clear that [Veselovsky's] intrigues were not undertaken for Peter's benefit; otherwise the former ambassasdor would not have been afraid to return to his native land." We find the same basic view expressed by the Israeli writer David Markish in his book *The Jew of Peter the Great or a Chronicle from the Life of Itinerant People* (St. Petersburg, 2001). He contrives a scene where Veselovsky slyly warns the tsarevich of danger: "Take care, Your Highness, do not leave Ehrenberg without protection and let no strangers near you! And do not return to Russia before the time is right." Abraham goes so far as to offer to use his "channels" (Markish also uses this word!) to send medicine to fortify Alexei's disgraced mother, Yevdokia Lopukhina, whom Peter had confined to a convent in Suzdal.

Some aspects of Markish's account seem rather farfetched. We see a certain Yankel showing up in Suzdal making haste to fulfill Veselovsky's assignment that he meet with Lopukhina, and there is the Viennese ambassador himself receiving a visit from a dealer in kosher meat who is carrying a secret letter from Veselovsky's relative, Pyotr Shafirov, warning of looming danger.

In fact, both Shafirov and Veselovsky became quite accustomed to life in a non-Jewish environment and had little in common with religious Jews. Suffice it to say that Abraham Veselovsky did not simply convert to Christianity; after joining the Russian Orthodox Church he converted yet again, this time to Protestantism. This, of course, did not preclude both men's sense of solidarity with other Jews – typical of members of this ethnic minority – and a desire to alleviate their plight in a fundamentally anti-Semitic country. Nevertheless, it was the interests of Russia that came first, and these two court Jews tried to reconcile their feelings of ethnic solidarity with these interests. It is therefore highly doubtful that Shafirov, the man who had essentially been put in charge of Russia's foreign policy, would call upon his subordinate, Veselovsky, to disobey Peter's orders and fail to return, which was tantamount to treason. Furthermore, Shafirov played an ominous role in the punishment meted out upon Tsarevich Alexei, for whom he had little sympathy.

Evidently, regardless of whether or not Veselovsky was guilty in the eyes of the tsar, once he heard of the many brutal executions that were carried out in connection with Alexei's betrayal, he knew a wide net would be cast and was understandably reluctant to return to St. Petersburg.

DURING HIS LONG YEARS in emigration after Peter's death, Veselovsky made do with small bits of news from Russia. Seven monarchs had ascended the throne since Peter – Catherine I, Peter II, Anna Ioannovna, Ivan VI, Elizabeth Petrovna, Peter III, and, finally, Catherine II – and Abraham had yet to venture back to the land of his birth. He had become accustomed to the role of observer from afar.

Yet why not return? This is the very question that Count Alexei Orlov-Chesmensky put to the aging Veseolvsky during their visit in Switzerland. His answer was this: "I will return to my motherland when three proverbs no longer hold true: 'Did nothing wrong, but guilty nonetheless,' 'Ready, like it or not,' and 'All belongs to God and Tsar.'" Abraham thus raised his voice against the violability of the person (did nothing wrong, but guilty nonetheless), obsequiousness (ready, like it or not), and authoritarian omnipotence (all belongs to God and Tsar). This places him among many other political refugees from Russia and shows that he had much in common with the third-wave emigrants of the Soviet era.

Out of respect for the memory of the eminent diplomat, in 1803 Emperor Alexander I granted Veselovsky's daughter an annual pension of 100 Dutch ducats. Other descendants of Abraham also received pensions from the Russian court as late as 1843 – during the reign of Nicholas I, who was clearly no friend to the Jews. Thus was our disgraced traitor posthumously rehabilitated and his services to the motherland given the credit they deserved.

II. MENTOR TO THE ROYAL HEIR

Here is a paradox: the Jew Isaac Veselovsky (1690-1754) instructed the future emperor of Orthodox Russia, Peter III, in the Russian language. In order to fully appreciate the irony of this arrangement, it must be understood that, at the time, most Jews living in the Russian Empire barely spoke Russian, if they knew it at all. Furthermore, while Isaac had great skills as a linguist (after all, he was born in Moscow and grew up speaking Russian), this outcome was also surprising because of Isaac's academic record. At Ernst Gluck's gymnasium, which his older brother Abraham had also attended, Isaac had the reputation of a negligent student and troublemaker of the first order, for which he often felt the sting of the rod. Yet, during his school years, this frolicsome boy also stood out for his savvy and subtle sense of humor. As a result, he went on to become one of the most original minds of his time, his witticisms and puns making the rounds at court with lightning speed.

A polyglot like his brother, he pursued a career in diplomacy. In 1707 he began working in the Diplomatic Department as a translator of German and Latin. By 1709 he was sent to the Russian Embassy in Prussia and, in January 1710, to Denmark. The knowledge and experience the younger Veselovsky acquired during these postings made him extremely useful during the tsar's second trip through Europe in 1716-1717, over the course of which Russia intended to form alliances with Prussia and Denmark against Sweden. Furthermore, the tsar had a high opinion of Veselovsky's mastery of French and often used him as an interpreter during his stay in Paris.

It was probably during this European journey that Isaac developed a close relationship with Peter. Otherwise it would be difficult to explain his subsequent ascent. In 1718 he was elevated to the rank of Secretary and, at the same time, appointed head of the Foreign Branch of the Diplomatic Chancery; in February 1720 he was made Secretary of the entire Collegium of Foreign Affairs.

Fortune turned her back on him, however, when news of his brother's defection reached Russia. Peter immediately demoted Isaac to the most menial of positions in the much less prestigious Collegium of Mines. However the tsar appears to have quickly realized that mining and industry were not where Veselovsky's linguistic talents could be put to best use. At this point, Peter entrusted Isaac with the task of teaching French to his regal daughters, the tsarevnas Anna and Elizabeth. Considering that the monarch was planning to marry Elizabeth to the King of France, it seems safe to assume that her knowledge of this subject was something to which he assigned primary importance and took extremely seriously. Veselovsky introduced the tsarevnas to French language and culture over the course of three years, from June 1722 to June 1725. Perhaps it is this three-year period that holds the key to the Gallomania that would later take hold of the court of Empress Elizabeth.

Peter III

In 1726 we find Isaac in the Caucasus, serving on the staff of Army Commander-in-Chief Vasily Dolgorukov, who was in charge of the Nizovy (Persian) Corps. The educated Jew performed the duty of secretary. A remarkable military leader, Dolgorukov acquired Karguerou Province, Astara, Lenkoran, and Kyzyl-Agach for Russia. That same year he was awarded Russia's highest order, St. Andrew, for his military feats (for the second time, no less), and in 1728 was promoted to Field Marshal. Meanwhile, not only did his secretary not receive any medals, he was even arrested in Kolomna, not far from Moscow, after having been granted leave from his duties in Gilan (Persia).

It turned out that Isaac had become entangled in the so-called Bestuzheva Affair, so named for Princess Anna Volkonskaya (neé Bestuzheva), who at the time presided over Russia's first high-society salon. Veselovsky had been particularly close with Volkonskaya's brother, Alexei, Russia's ambassador to Copenhagen, and through him had become friendly with the princess. The small home of "Asechka Ivanovna" (as she was called by her friends) on Admiralteysky Island's Greek Street became a refuge for all of her friends, including Veselovsky. Among the salon's habitués were the future Field Marshal Buturlin, a favorite of Peter's daughter Elizabeth; the chamberlain of Catherine I, Semyon Mavrin; the Ethiopian Ibrahim Hannibal, the famous "Moor of

Peter the Great"; and Senator Yury Neledinsky. "As frequently happens among youthful companions," wrote one historian, "the friends created their own little world of jocular relationships, with their own customs, silly ceremonies, and nonsensical words and nicknames. They liked to get together, chitchat, dance, and drink coffee, which was just coming into fashion." There was one other thing that united them. Every last one of them (each for his or her own reason) loved to hate Prince Alexander Menshikov, a favorite topic at their gatherings.

It was an excess of chitchat that doomed Volkonskaya's salon. One day Asechka brought fresh gossip from the palace: Menshikov had devised a plan to marry his daughter Maria to the heir to the throne, the future Peter II. Upon hearing this news the friends, without mincing words, unleashed a barrage of criticism about Menshikov's usurpation of power.

When news of this reached Menshikov, he immediately dealt with Asechka and her imprudent companions. Volkonskaya was ordered to leave St. Petersburg for her village outside Moscow, Hannibal was posted to the backwaters of Siberia, and Mavrin and Buturlin were demoted. Veselovsky, despite the lack of hard evidence against him, was nevertheless sent to Gilan and later, in August 1730 (after Menshikov's downfall and death), transferred to Derbent.

This is where he received an order from Empress Anna Ioannovna appointing him Secretary for Chancery Affairs for the Nizovy (Persian) Corps, now under Major General Ivan Bibikov. Isaac was elevated in rank to Collegiate Assessor before being placed at the disposal of the commander-in-chief of the Russian army in Persia, Duke Ludwig Hessen-Homburg, who, in 1733, with benefit of superior numbers, defeated rebellious hordes of Tatars and Crimeans. But before the year ended the duke was recalled to St. Petersburg, while Veselovsky remained condemned to exile, now in Astrakhan and Tsaritsyn. The historical record shows that for many years he was not paid a salary. He was only released from his exile in October 1740 and shortly thereafter, in March 1741, relieved of duty, due, as he wrote, "to debility."

Yet Isaac recovered from his "debility" as soon as Elizabeth took the throne. The ascension of Peter the Great's daughter breathed new life into Veselovsky's career, which reached dazzling heights. In addition to the empress herself, who held her former French teacher in high regard, Isaac had another friend at court, Alexei Bestuzhev, who was now one of Russia's most influential grandees.

By December 1741 Collegiate Assessor Veselovsky was promoted to Actual Councillor of State, skipping from Grade VIII to Grade IV in the Table of Ranks. "In terms of honorifics," Israeli historian Savely Dudakov commented, "this change elevated fortune's darling from the rather commonplace 'Your Nobleness' to the almost celestial 'Your Excellency.'" His diplomatic talents also proved to be in demand; Isaac was appointed head of the Secret Department of the Collegium of Foreign Affairs. A true statist, he again dove headlong into his work, actively participating in negotiations with Sweden in 1743 and with England in 1744-1745. In 1744 he was a forceful proponent for building a line of fortifications in Siberia to defend against nomad raids; and he initiated an alliance between Russia and Saxony to counterbalance the growing might of Prussia. In 1745 Veselovsky was promoted to Privy Councillor and in 1746 he was awarded the Order of St. Alexander Nevsky.

Empress Elizabeth

Another task that the empress assigned Veselovsky was instructing her nephew, the future Peter III, in Russian, a language that the heir to the throne never learned, having grown up in Schleswig-Holstein. Isaac began his mentoring task in 1742 and, apparently, did an excellent job, since the Grand Duke spoke the language of his future subjects fluently after just one year of study. Evidence of this has survived in the form of compositions dated 1743 that the royal adolescent wrote and translated from German into Russian. Of course, Peter's written Russian was far from flawless, but it must be borne in mind that even many native-born Russians (including some at court) were known to make far worse errors in their writing.

"The smartest man in Russia" (as he was labeled by one eminent foreigner), Isaac lived and breathed the progressive ideas of the era. He was an inveterate reader and a keen student of world literature. For example, historian Vladimir Lublinsky writes of Veselovsky, "The topic of the latest French literature so persistently penetrates his business correspondence that it bears special study."

Indeed, turning to the surviving letters written by Isaac, we find in almost every one a mention not only of Montaigne, but of Pierre Bayle, Voltaire, and Jean-Jacques Rousseau, as well as many other contemporary writers. Furthermore, our protagonist proved himself enviably knowledgeable when it came to current cultural events in Europe. For example, he was able to comment intelligently on Voltaire's arrest in Frankfurt in 1752, and he manifested solidarity with writers and philosophers. It is illustrative in this regard that the Westernizing Veselovsky, with the chancellor's full support, worked successfully to lift limitations on the import of foreign books into Russia. As a result, these publications began to appear regularly in the bookshops of Moscow and St. Petersburg. "We can expect books from France on the last ships of the fall season," he wrote with evident satisfaction to Count Mikhail Vorontsov in 1753.

Veselovsky was also not afraid to insistently appeal to the Judeophobic Empress Elizabeth on behalf of his fellow Jews (just as his older brother had once done to her father, Peter the Great). He introduced every conceivable argument in favor of allowing Jews to reside within the Russian Empire and even managed to bring Chancellor Bestuzhev over to his side. But the empress was implacable in her refusal to rescind her famous decree of December 13, 1742 ordering the expulsion of all "Yids" from the empire with her famous phrase, "I have no desire for profit from the enemies of Jesus Christ!" How did the Jew-hating Elizabeth react to such an "impertinent" appeal by a Christianized Jew? In any event, she did not punish him or subject him to disgrace and continued to hold him in personal favor. Perhaps she did not see and did not wish to see an enemy of Christ in her former teacher. Most likely Elizabeth interpreted his persistence as naive soft-heartedness, a trait forgivable in a Christian.

To be fair it should be mentioned that under Elizabeth Veselovsky had nothing to fear and was well protected from the intrigues of his enemies, to which he was no stranger. One revolved around the row that broke out between Count Mikhail Vorontsov and Chancellor Bestuzhev. In this instance, Isaac took Vorontsov's side (despite his close relationship with the chancellor). We will not tease apart the tangled web of conflict between these distinguished men, only noting that the infuriated chancellor demonstrated his loyalty to the crown by writing a denunciation of Veselovsky. Bestuzhev alleged that Veselovsky had refused to drink to the health of the empress at a diplomatic reception. According to his account:

> Only Veselovsky would not drink a full glass, but poured merely a spoonful and a half – and even that was water – and so stood stubbornly before everyone, although the chancellor, out of faithfulness to Her Imperial Majesty and out of shame before the ambassadors, said to him in Russian that he should drink to Her health with a full glass as a faithful servant, for Her Imperial Majesty had showed him much kindness and raised him from a low rank to such a lofty one.

Clearly Bestuzhev was hoping that Veselovsky would be charged with the criminal offense of insulting a royal personage (a transgression punishable by torture in the previous regime's Secret Chancery). If so, he was disappointed: Elizabeth completely ignored the denunciation and continued to shower Isaac with favors.

The final years of the privy councillor's life were largely spent in the quiet of his study, reading his beloved books. He read exceptionally quickly, obviously not wishing to miss any opportunity to enrich his mind and elevate his soul. Isaac Veselovsky departed this world in September 1754 and never reached the old age his brother enjoyed. No record of his place of burial has yet been found.

III. THE AMBASSADOR'S RETURN

While serving as Russia's ambassador to London, the Jew Fyodor Pavlovich Veselovsky (whose exact date of birth we do not know; he died some time before 1776) managed to have a Russian Orthodox church built in the English capital, the very first in Foggy Albion. Truly, the Lord works in strange and mysterious ways!

The historian Dmitry Serov has suggested that this adherent of Russian Orthodoxy was Isaac's twin. Like his brothers, he was educated at Ernst Gluck's *gymnasium* in Moscow (where he shared Isaac's reputation as a mischief-maker), after which he was hired by the Diplomatic Department as a translator of German and Latin. Fyodor's life was every bit as dramatic as his brothers' and, like theirs, was marked by a series of dizzying ascents and precipitous falls.

Fyodor Veselovsky's career began brilliantly. He had the opportunity of serving under the "ambassador of the Russian State," Prince Boris Kurakin. A classic Russian aristocrat and outstanding figure of his time, Kurakin was an experienced diplomat distinguished for his erudition, breadth of interests, dispassionate and ironic intellect, and fiery temperament. He immediately recognized Fyodor's talents and took him under his wing. In 1707 Fyodor traveled with his patron to Rome, to lobby Pope Clement XI to reject Stanislaus Leszczynski's candidacy as king of Poland. Young Veselovsky joined Kurakin in kissing His Holiness' shoe. Their mission proved a success, and after its completion the two Muscovites traveled across Europe, making stops in Venice, Vienna, Hamburg, and Amsterdam. Their travels were far from idle tourism; they were attempting to thwart the recruitment of mercenaries by the Swedish Army, an effort that was largely successful. In January 1710 Fyodor accompanied Kurakin, who had been appointed Plenipotentiary Minister, to Hanover, where they conducted lengthy negotiations with Prince Elector Georg Ludwig (the future George I of Great Britain). Kurakin and Veselovsky succeeded in concluding an alliance that ensured the principality's friendly neutrality toward Russia and its allies.

In 1712, Fyodor, who now held the rank of Diplomatic Secretary, was sent to the Hague, where he and Kurakin worked together to persuade Holland to ally with Russia against Sweden. While serving as secretary, Veselovsky had the opportunity not only to advance professionally as a diplomat, but to develop his ability to take a bird's-eye view of the European system of international relations. Gradually, Fyodor cultivated the necessary connections among the leaders of European states and was able to splendidly orient himself within contemporary international politics.

In 1716, Fyodor finally emerged from Kurakin's shadow and began to serve the cause of Russian diplomacy in his own right. In April of that year he set out for London, where he at first unofficially fulfilled the duties of Russia's ambassador to the English court before being officially appointed to this position in June 1717. In addition to his actual diplomatic duties, Veselovsky recruited qualified specialists to come work in Russia, negotiated commercial contracts, and was entrusted by the Holy Synod to conduct talks on merging the churches of Russia and England. On top of everything else, the ambassador was expected to keep an eye on occasionally unruly Russian students whose studies had taken them to London.

Boris Kurakin

One might have thought that his position was utterly secure, but all of a sudden the career that seemed to be gaining momentum came to a screeching halt. What happened was that Fyodor's fugitive brother Abraham had taken refuge in the residence of the Russian envoy. Once the Russian authorities learned of this, they immediately took British affairs out of Fyodor's hands and appointed a new ambassador in his place, Mikhail Bestuzhev, who was charged with conveying to Fyodor orders to "travel to the Danish court posthaste." If Veselovsky were to disobey these orders, Bestuzhev was instructed to "make every proper effort to arrange for Veselovsky's arrest in England under a charge of having possession of much of our money without having reported it."

Sensing that something suspicious was afoot, Fyodor categorically refused to travel to Denmark.

"It is plain to see," he bitterly lamented, "that my recall from this court and reassignment to Copenhagen is for no reason and reflects no intention other than that I suffer on behalf of my brother, and I can clearly see that the intention is to throw me onto a ship upon my arrival in Copenhagen and carry me off to St. Petersburg, where I will be asked about my brother under cruel and painful torture, whether I know anything or not...Fear of this apparent and ceaseless misfortune has led me to such desperation that I, having renounced all well-being in this world, have now resolved to retire to some corner so that neither memory nor rumor of me will remain, and thus to live out the last miserable days of my life, no matter how extreme my poverty and misery, but with calm conscience and without suffering.

This, however, was not the last to be heard of Fyodor Veselovsky. He still had a good five decades ahead of him, and he in fact had little desire to "retire" to a remote corner. Like his brother, he simply endured a self-imposed exile and continued to live a respectable life in London.

Tsar Peter could not forgive the English government its protection of Abraham and Fyodor. In his own hand we see written on a 1724 draft concerning the reconciliation of Russia and Great Britain a provision that "the Veselovskys be handed over to us, because both in monetary expenditures and other matters entrusted to them they did much against us that demands investigation." England, of course, did not turn over the defectors.

We may never know the extent to which Fyodor longed to see his native birch trees or granite-clad St. Petersburg, but we do know that nostalgia gnawed at him more strongly than it did his older brother. He never quite managed to accustom himself to life far from home, and he repeatedly petitioned Russian authorities for permission to return to the land of his birth. During the reign of Empress Anna, he began sending valuable communiqués to Vice Chancellor Count Andrei Osterman concerning English politics and containing bits of news from parliament and the court, among other things. He assured the count of his desire for nothing more than to "use the last days of his life to serve his fatherland...as befits any true and good subject." Historian Savely Dudakov posits that Russia was in no hurry to grant Fyodor permission to return home specifically because such an important "channel" of information "was particularly needed in London."

But Fyodor strove stubbornly to earn himself a way home. The envoy Antiochus Kantemir reported from London in January 1742:

> Today the former ambassador to the English court, F. Veselovsky, came to see me. He diligently asked that I most humbly petition for leave for him to return to his fatherland so that the remainder of his life can be used to serve his empress. He awaits such supreme mercy due to Your characteristic magnanimity toward all Your subjects. It would not be without benefit to Your affairs to summon this man from here, being someone skilled in the Russian language who at times can be used in sorting through ciphers.

Could this possibly be a reference to secret diplomatic codes?

At last the joyous news arrived. In November 1742 Fyodor finally received an imperial resolution by Elizabeth stating, "We most graciously grant [Veselovsky's] request, concerning which you shall, in a befitting manner, inform him of this permission and shall be pleased to aid his return hither."

Fyodor Veselovsky returned to Russia in early 1743. He petitioned to be taken into service "particularly in foreign affairs, to which I devoted myself for many years." But the erratic and capricious empress took it into her head to use him at court (it should be recalled that this was when his brother Isaac was charged with instructing the Grand Duke). Well-versed in European politesse, Veselovsky must have been the first Jewish master of ceremonies in the history of the Russian imperial court – not an insignificant rank, the civil equivalent of an Army Brigadier (that is, between a general and a colonel). This was the post Veselovsky still held in 1752, when he was elevated to Major General before being retired.

Little is known of his final years. Under Elizabeth, his diplomatic talents remained unutilized, unless we count the mission he was sent on in 1757 to try to convince Voltaire to write a history of the reign of Peter the Great. To this end Fyodor set out for Geneva where, incidentally, he visited his disgraced brother.

In St. Petersburg Veselovsky grew close with Elizabeth's favorite, Ivan Shuvalov, the renowned educator and patron of the arts. Shuvalov recruited Fyodor, as a man with encyclopedic knowledge, to serve as curator of the recently established Moscow University, a position he held from August 1760 to November 1762. His efforts there were noted by the empress, who in 1761 made Veselovsky a Knight of the Order of St. Alexander Nevsky. Upon his retirement he was promoted to the rank of Privy Councillor. Fyodor Veselovsky died during the reign of Catherine II, having lived almost nine decades.

THESE THREE BROTHERS were not the only members of their clan to earn themselves a place of distinction in Russian history. Among their most outstanding descendants are: Alexander Nikolayevich Veselovsky (1838-1906), a member of the St. Petersburg Academy of Sciences, scholar of comparative literature, and founder of the science of historical poetics; Professor Nikolai Ivanovich Veselovsky (1848-1918), archeologist and orientalist; Stepan Borisovich Veselovsky (1876-1952), a member of the Soviet Academy of Sciences and a prominent expert in the socio-economic history of Russia and source studies; and Professor Boris Borisovich Veselovsky (1880-1954), a historian and economist. Each bore the imprint of talent bequeathed to them by their distant ancestors.

FRIEDRICH GEORGE ASH

THE SCRUPULOUS POSTAL DIRECTOR

If the *Guinness Book of World Records* had existed in the eighteenth century, Friedrich George Ash (1683-1783) would certainly have deserved an entry. It was not just that, even by modern standards, he lived an amazingly long life (an entire century), but he held the same job for 67 years – longer than today's average life expectancy for a Russian man. This long stretch of continuous service began in St. Petersburg in 1716 where, at the behest of Peter the Great, Ash took over management of the city's post office. His tenure spanned the reigns of four emperors and four empresses.

The scion of Ashkenazi Jews, Friedrich was born in Silesia. We have no specific information about his upbringing or education, but do know that he was fluent in many European languages, something that proved extremely useful in his career.

There is evidence to suggest that Friedrich was invited to Russia by Tsar Peter himself. What we know for certain is that at the age of twenty-four, Ash was serving on the staff of Russian Cavalry Lieutenant General Baron Karl Ewald von Rönne (1663-1716), who at the time was positioned in Poland, along the Silesian border. A courageous warrior and insightful student of human nature, von Rönne quickly appreciated the abilities of the clever Silesian and made him his personal secretary. From that time forward they never parted. Friedrich George, whom his newly adopted countrymen gave the Russified name of Fyodor Yuryevich, accompanied his patron on all his military campaigns. The Baron's army acquitted itself brilliantly during the 1709 Battle of Poltava, a highpoint in Russian military history, where von Rönne himself demonstrated stunning fearlessness, rushing straight into the thick of battle. Legend has it that he came very close to taking King Charles XII of Sweden himself captive, and he was the only Russian commander wounded at Poltava. That very year he was promoted by the tsar to the rank of Cavalry General.

In 1710, von Rönne's troops distinguished themselves during the capture of Riga. But perhaps his most impressive victory took place on July 25, 1711, when the seemingly impervious Turkish fortress at Brailov was captured. On the day this bastion capitulated, the tsar awarded the general the highest Russian order of chivalry, the Order of St. Andrew.

And what about the General's secretary, Fyodor Yuryevich Ash? He also made a contribution to the success of Russian arms, but not on the field of battle. This "useful Jew" enjoyed the particular trust of top Russian officers and was put in charge of managing the army's correspondence (including top secret communications). It was specifically to Ash that reports, dispatches, communiqués, and the most urgent and vital information were channeled, the sort of intelligence that is crucial to any military endeavor. The tsar appreciated Fyodor Yuryevich's role and made him the quite extraordinary gift of one thousand rubles, a huge sum of money at the time.

After von Rönne's passing, Ash's talents were still in great demand. He was appointed aide-de-camp to one of Peter's closest military associates, General Rodion Khristianovich (Rudolf) Bauer (1667-1717), who at the time was commanding a cavalry division in Ukraine.

Remembering how successful Fyodor Yuryevich had been in his capacity as chief of army communications, in 1714 Peter made him a Secretary in the St. Petersburg Postal Authority and, when the position became vacant in 1716, Director. It was not just Ash's high level of professionalism that was so to Peter's liking, but his impeccable honesty and incorruptibility, a trait that was not easy to come by in Russia. Suffice it to say that his predecessor, Postmaster Henrik Gottlieb Krauss, was caught committing a number of improper acts and was charged with the illegal issuance of *podorozhnayas* (certificates entitling their bearers to the gratis use of post horses) and with receiving gold and jewels from overseas. According to his contemporaries, Ash was utterly immune to bribery and was distinguished by exceptional efficiency and exactitude.

To imagine what sorts of responsibilities rested on Ash's shoulders, one would have to understand a few things about life in eighteenth-century Russia. To put it in modern terms, postal work was a "high risk" profession. After all, traveling along the roads of Mother Russia was, at the time, an extremely dangerous undertaking, since the highways were the domain of gangs of runaway soldiers and hungry peasants. The authorities dispatched an armed

A 1987 postage stamp with images from the history of the Russian Postal Service.

convoy, the members of which had to sign an oath of loyalty, to accompany each postal carriage. Peter assigned the work of the postmen special importance (incidentally, rather than the home-grown word *pochtar*, he preferred the Italian *postiglione*, on which the modern Russian word почталён is based). In order to service the postal route between Moscow and St. Petersburg, the monarch ordered that coachmen be sent from every town in Russia – a total of 5000. Archival documents give us a general idea of how the postal director's employees were dressed and how they did their jobs. "In dry weather they were expected to wear green caftans with red cuffs and lapels, and when it rained, long gray cloaks with cornflower blue cuffs and lapels. On their heads they wore tricornes with red trim, and on their chest hung a bronze badge with an eagle." A courier was supposed to announce his arrival by sounding a horn (Ash invited a German postman from Memel to teach his couriers to play this instrument). Try as he might, however, even resorting to punishments and fines, Fyodor Yuryevich was not able to enforce this practice, and the appearance of Russian postal coaches was inevitably accompanied by rollicking whistles and cries.

Soon after Ash took over as director in 1716, the St. Petersburg post office moved from a run-down single-story edifice of daubed wood to a two-story stone building near what is now known as the Field of Mars (where the Marble Palace stands today). In addition to its primary function of coordinating communication, the post office became a sort of indispensible cultural center for the capital. The office's clerical work was performed on the first floor, while in the formal chambers upstairs Peter assembled various get-togethers, or simply came to dine. By invitation of the tsar, eminent foreign guests would be accommodated here. Friedrich Wilhelm von Bergholtz, gentleman of the monarch's bedchamber, commented in his diary, "All passengers usually stay in the post house until they can find themselves quarters, as there are no fashionable hotels here." Every day at twelve o'clock sharp, twelve musicians played horns and pipes in the building's courtyard.

In 1735, the building of the second St. Petersburg post office burned down. In the 1740s, a new three-story building was constructed on Millionnaya Street, next to the Winter Palace. Our postal director worked in this building until his death. To this day it is known as the Third St. Petersburg Post Office.

Ash was not at all pleased with this new facility. The postal director bombarded the relevant authorities with requests that they be given a more suitable and spacious building and offered persuasive arguments as to why moving the postal services to this location had been completely counterproductive. He steadfastly asserted that the building was unsuitable: there was no housing with apartments for the clerks, the close quarters did not allow for "the laying away of sufficient firewood for the winter," and furthermore, it was much less easily accessible. Historian of the Russian postal system Alexander Vigilev claims that "despite his positive attributes, Ash was wanting in initiative." However, Fyodor Yuryevich's reaction to the new post office building would seem to demonstrate exactly the opposite.

Unfortunately, Ash's protests, despite the compelling arguments he offered, were not supported by the powers that be. As a result, the rest of his career was spent in the much-despised Third Post Office building. As at the old facility, here too music was played in the courtyard and upstairs important visitors were wined and dined, while nearby there were stables for post horses and sheds for the carriages.

The hustle and bustle of the post office's more public operations concealed from prying eyes another aspect of its activities that was just as routine – the censorship of letters in the interest of preserving state secrets. Some historians even liken Fyodor Yuryevich to Postmaster Shpekin, a character from Gogol's *Inspector General* who abuses his position and opens other people's mail for his own purposes. Such a comparison is surely unfair to Ash, who was a faithful servant of the tsar. Reading the correspondence that passed through his post office was one of the duties assigned to him by Peter, who, as it was said, "was inclined to know everything." The postal director was merely fulfilling the tsar's 1716 decree, which stated "that nothing about military or state affairs should be contained in letters." Particular attention was given to monitoring mail going to Sweden during the Northern War (1700-1721). This measure was clearly in the interests of the young empire.

Under subsequent Russian monarchs the postal director reliably executed these same duties. For example, under Empress Elizabeth Petrovna (Peter's daughter), Chancellor Alexei Bestuzhev renewed Ash's obligation to open and copy all international correspondence to and from foreign ambassadors (even those written to members of the fair sex). This same scrutiny extended to all private letters that crossed the Russian border. The most interesting missives were copied.

Just how was this difficult task carried out? Given its sensitive nature and the secrecy it demanded, Fyodor Yuryevich personally opened the envelopes, read the dispatches, and had his subordinates copy specific passages. He then resealed the envelopes so that no one would be the wiser. However this was not always possible. One 1744 letter from Ash to Chancellor Bestuzhev survives in which the former complains about the difficulties of reading foreign mail:

> The last two letters could be unsealed without difficulty...Also an envelope to the Berlin post office was easy to unseal, however two letters in it, to the king and the cabinet, were in such a state that, although every effort was made, it was nevertheless impossible to open them. The envelopes were not only sealed with glue at the corners, but glue was everywhere, and this glue was used to affix a thread to the envelope in the form of a cross that was so hardened that the steam of boiling water, over which I held the letter for several hours, would not loosen and detach it. And the glue under the seals (which I did manage to remove), could not be loosened. Consequently, to my profound regret, I could not find any way to unseal these letters without utterly mangling the envelopes.

Ash had at his disposal exact copies of all the seals of the foreign ambassadors accredited in the northern capital (they were prepared, at his request, by master engravers at the Academy of Sciences). Archives in Moscow and St. Petersburg contain a multitude of private letters copied by the postal director. In the Russian State Archive of Ancient Acts, for example, there is a folder with an appendix labeled "the letters of various foreign Ministers (ambassadors) to the Russian court sent through the post."

The task of reading diplomatic mail was further complicated by encryption, and even when mail was successfully opened, its hidden meaning still had to be rendered comprehensible. The truly brainteasing job of codebreaking fell to the St. Petersburg postal director. It goes without saying that Fyodor Yuryevich also had to know all the major European languages, which he did. If correspondence in a new language came under his purview, he was able to master it with amazing speed.

The business of cryptanalysis reached new heights in the seventeenth century, when the first services dedicated to deciphering correspondence began to appear. In France, Cardinal Richelieu appointed Antoine Rossignol – the author of a diplomatic code consisting of a system of syllables and words with 600 components – to head such a service. In Germany, letter-based codes were replaced with numerical ones, in which numbers signified the number of steps by which a letter in the encrypted message shifted in the alphabet. Due to its simplicity, this cipher was widely used in the eighteenth century.

In Russia, encryption came into use as early as the twelfth century, but the first cryptographic service is generally considered to date to 1549 (the reign of Ivan IV), when the Diplomatic Department was established and given a special "cipher office." The same sorts of codes were used as in the West: symbols, substitutions, rearrangement. Under Peter the Great special "cipher alphabets" began to appear.

In Russian diplomatic practice, the encryption of correspondence was overseen by Vice Chancellor Pyotr Shafirov, who devised a special code for communicating with the sovereign. We find, for example, a 1706 letter from Shafirov to the Russian ambassador in Paris, Andrei Artamonovich Matveyev, that touches on this subject: "The movement of foreign mail has come to an utter halt, and this is the third week of no letters to anyone...I am herewith sending two new [cipher] alphabets, inasmuch as the Old one has already in many cases been lost among the troops and has, perhaps, fallen into enemy hands."

Peter had also placed Shafirov in charge of the deciphering of diplomatic dispatches. It is probable that Ash was taught the secrets of decryption by Shafirov, who was at one point his immediate superior (the postal service had previously come under the vice chancellor's authority). In any case, Shafirov clearly knew and valued Fyodor Yuryevich's ability to conduct secret correspondence, since in 1719 he recommended Ash as an excellent candidate for this sort of work.

The circle of individuals who knew the key to reading secret correspondence was extremely small. We are aware of only one employee who assisted Postal Director Ash in this matter: the future professor and, at the time, adjunct of the Academy of Sciences, Ivan Taubert. Beginning in 1743 they labored together to decode French, English, and Prussian dispatches.

Beyond the challenges of his career, Fyodor Yuryevich led a quiet, uneventful life, which clearly centered on his 67 years of irreproachable service. We know of only a few milestones in his professional history. In 1744 Empress Elizabeth promoted him to the rank of Colonel and granted him permanent possession of the Khotinets estate outside St. Petersburg, in the former Yamburg district. By the time of his death, he had attained the rank of State Councillor.

In 1762 he and his posterity were elevated to barons of the Holy Roman Empire by Austrian Emperor Franz I. In general, the title of baron became a traditional sign of distinction for the Jews of Europe, both those who adopted Christianity and those who continued to observe the faith of their forefathers. During Peter's reign, Shafirov and the Solovyov brothers became barons. Among prominent Jews who would later bear this title were the Polyakovs, Stieglitzes, Federikses, Velios, Feleizins, Frankels, Zacherts, Mestmachers, as well as the Ginzburgs and the world-famous Rothschilds.

A March 11, 1763, decree by Catherine the Great entitled Ash to use this title in Russia. The diploma that made this official, however, was only given to Fyodor Yuryevich's descendants after his death in 1783. The coat of arms of the barons Ash is found in Part V of the *Book of Heraldry of the Noble Families of the Russian Empire* under entry No. 126 and features the motto, "Virtute Duce" (May Virtue Be Our Guide).

Indeed, the baron was not only an honest and assiduous civil servant, but a virtuous family man and the father of four sons and three daughters. Three of his sons also earned a place in Russian history. The eldest, Ivan Fyodorovich Ash (1726-1807), was an eminent diplomat who served for a long time in Poland as a plenipotentiary minister of the Russian government. Two other sons went into medicine. Yegor Fyodorovich Ash (1727-1807) earned a doctorate in medicine and defended his dissertation at the University of Göttingen, with which he maintained a close association. Empress Elizabeth assigned him to travel Europe and research all the sources of curative mineral waters. When the Medical Collegium was established in Russia in 1763, he was its first member. The third son, Pyotr Fyodorovich Ash, lived in Moscow, where he earned a reputation as a skilled physician and was also a member of the Medical Collegium.

The line of Barons Ash came to an end in the late nineteenth century. But who knows? Perhaps the famous Ashkenazi writer Sholom Ash is related to our post office director, however distantly.

ANTONIO NUNES RIBEIRO SANCHEZ

DOCTOR TO THE EMPRESS

Standing at a writing table, a man of about thirty-five moves his pen quickly across the page. His very appearance rivets the attention and engraves itself on the memory: an intelligent, resolute face, a bald head, the narrow neck of an ascetic, prominent cheekbones, an expressive brow, and deep-set almond eyes. This man is the descendant of Portuguese Marranos, Doctor Antonio Nunes Ribeiro Sanchez (1699-1783), also known in Russia by the names Sankhetz, Sanshes, and Sanshe. He has been working in Russia for four years. He is writing a treatise on the persecution of "new Christians" (Marranos), Jews forcibly converted to Catholicism in Portugal and Spain.

Here, in frigid Muscovy, the doctor has a thriving career; it is even rumored that soon he will be appointed doctor to the Empress Anna Ioannovna. But while the Russian goddess of Fortune seems to be smiling on Sanchez for now, he is always aware that imperial favor can be replaced by oppression and disgrace at any instant. Although all is well in his own life, he never ceases to contemplate the misfortunes of his fellow tribesmen. The hardships suffered by his people, hardships that for him are not a distant abstraction, never lose their bitter intensity. He places his pen aside and gives in to reminiscence...

Perhaps he is recalling how he fled Portugal, a land that he loved but that treated him like an outcast. The Inquisition was wreaking havoc there. For the Portuguese authorities, this scion of wealthy Marranos was not a true son of his country but an unworthy stepson whose crime was being born a Jew. In 1497 the Jews of Portugal were confronted with a choice: baptism or exile. Many left, and those who remained were called "new Christians," and they were suspected (for good reason) of performing their Jewish rites in secret. The situation became particularly dire in 1536, when unbridled zealots of the Christian faith launched a violent campaign against the Marranos, a campaign that continued to escalate in brutality. The victims were hunted down in cities and villages, in forests and mountains. There was nowhere to run. The bonfires of the infamous *autos da fé* raged. Thousands of Marranos perished. Many died with Jewish prayers on their lips.

The Inquisition's sword of Damocles hung over the Sanchez family as well. Despite having achieved wealth and erudition, they had become accustomed to living in fear of reprisals, although by the eighteenth century the Catholic frenzy had somewhat abated. Antonio was taught from childhood that he, as a pariah in a world that bristled with hatred, had to be better, more educated, and more talented than others. The eternal Jewish thirst for knowledge and striving for inner perfection consumed him from an early age.

Antonio Sanchez

He did not follow in the footsteps of his father, a prominent businessman, but chose the profession of his uncle, Diego Nunes, a renowned Lisbon physician who instilled in him an early interest in medicine. At the age of seventeen Sanchez set out for the city of Coimbra, where he studied fine arts at Portugal's oldest university. Then, in 1721, he began his intensive study of medicine at the University of Salamanca, in Spain. In 1724 he graduated with a diploma in medicine and began his practice in the town of Benavente. While there he wrote his first scholarly work on the properties of medicinal waters.

In 1726 Antonio fled to England. Some historians attribute this move to the dangerous situation for Jews in Portugal and mention an event that had a direct impact on Sanchez's decision. That year, the Sanchez family had been subjected to a new round of persecution, after the Inquisition accused his cousin, Manuel Nunes, of secretly practicing Judaism. But just as compelling a reason for Antonio to move to England was his insatiable appetite for the sort of knowledge that could only be had in countries where the science of medicine was relatively advanced.

Antonio spent two years in England, where he obtained a solid grounding in disciplines essential to the practice of medicine, such as physics, natural history, chemistry, pharmacology, and anatomy. It has been suggested that, while there, he developed relationships with local Jews (one name that comes up is his colleague, Jacob de Castro Sarmento), secretly converted to Judaism, and was even circumcised. Be that as it may, he never advertised his Judaism (which was looked at askance even in "enlightened" countries); his career came first. Sanchez's further path took him to France, where in the universities and hospitals of Paris, Marseille, Montpellier, and Bordeaux, he eagerly delved into the science of healing.

In 1727 something happened to fundamentally change Sanchez's scientific thinking and, indeed, the course of this life: he became acquainted with the writings of the great Dutch doctor, botanist, and chemist, Herman Boerhaave (1668-1738), renowned as the father of what was then known as the Leiden school of medicine. He was the first to apply the ideas of the Renaissance to medicine, taking it out of the realm of medieval scholasticism and attempting to draw connections between the principles of anatomy and physiology on the one hand and practical experience on the other. In Leiden, Boerhaave established a clinic for the study of diseases that became a focal point for the era's medical thought. Antonio was among those who hastened there to further their knowledge, and within three years he was named one of the most accomplished pupils of the renowned Dutchman. In 1730, when the Russian government requested that Boerhaave recommend a learned doctor for an important medical position in Russia, he suggested Sanchez as a worthy candidate.

Our protagonist arrived in Russia in 1731 and labored for the country's well-being for more than 16 years. He imparted medical wisdom to *feldshers* (physician assistants), midwives, and pharmacists in Moscow. He then went to work for the military, where he treated the troops and even partook in more than one campaign. Later he made his way to St. Petersburg and was appointed head doctor at the Noble Cadet Corps (a privileged institution of learning for the nobility that was nicknamed the "Academy of Knights"). At the same time he served as personal doctor to Cabinet Minister Artemy Volynsky. Word of Dr. Sanchez's talent and mastery reached Empress Anna Ioannovna, who summoned him to court. He was appointed her doctor and treated her bouts of urolithiasis (painful stones in the urinary tract).

Officially a Catholic, he was supposedly immune to the persecution of Jews in Russia, as well as to Catherine I's 1727 decree prohibiting Jews from living anywhere within the Russian Empire. But as a secret Jew he must certainly have been alarmed in 1738 when Baruch Leibov, a Jew, and Captain Alexander Voznitsyn, whom he had converted to Judaism, were brought to trial. Leibov was charged, among other things, with having built a synagogue in the small town of Zverovichi, which, of course, the authorities burned down, together with its prayer books. The case was in the hands of the head of the ubiquitous Chancery of Secret Investigations, Andrei Ushakov, a man with a sinister visage, suggestive of a Grand Inquisitor. The sentence handed down was indeed inquisitorial: Leibov and Voznitsyn were to be "executed and burned." The *auto da fé* took place in St. Petersburg, on the corner of Nevsky Prospect and Bolshaya Morskaya Street before a large crowd. Although Sanchez was not directly involved in this ordeal, the incident pained him, as it did all of the empire's ethnic Jews. Among them was his friend, the empress' jester, Jan d'Acosta, also descended of Portuguese Marranos.

Although there was a saying, "a christened Jew is a forgiven Jew," Sanchez was occasionally reminded of his Jewish roots. We know what attitudes were "in the air" from private correspondence, for instance references such as the one by the eighteenth-century writer and poet Alexander Sumarokov to a foreigner "of Yiddish breed," as he put it. This particular "breed" (*poroda* – a word not generally used for humans in Russian) elicited from courtiers a certain aversion and haughty disgust. The historical novelist Valentin Pikul, well-known for his anti-Semitism, portrays the Russian empress' Judeophobia quite accurately, in his book *Word and Deed*. Pikul envisions her calling Sanchez a "betrayer of Christ":

> "Well, Yid!" Anna Ioannovna said to him, pulling her blanket up to her chin. "Take a look at my majesty." She did not, however, let him remove the blanket. "You'd better make do looking through the blanket... It's your good fortune that I'm lying here sick. Otherwise I'd teach you a lesson... Write out your prescription, you mumbler... Do you really think that I, autocrat of all the Russians, would show you, of all people, my arse? Better that I die than suffer such degradation!"

Of course it was the royal doctor who suffered the real degradation. It is not surprising that he made the excuse of some indisposition rather than attend this autocrat's state funeral.

The fleeting rule of the straightforward and charitable Anna Leopoldovna, who served as regent for her son, the young emperor Ivan VI, marked the apex of Sanchez's career. In November 1740 he was appointed Imperial Court Physician with a salary of three thousand rubles. Anna Leopoldovna so believed in the remarkable doctor that she entrusted her most august child to him. She sent the young monarch to Sanchez for examinations and had him approve any prescriptions written by other doctors.

Historians write of the sincere devotion the doctor felt for the Brunswicks (Anna Leopolodovna was married to Duke Anthony Ulrich of Brunswick), a devotion that, in their opinion, may have proved his downfall. But this point of view hardly seems justified. After all, Sanchez was in no way persecuted when Empress Elizabeth came to the throne. He remained in the post of court doctor and she often made use of his services, despite the fact that she had little love for his people.

Evidently, at the time the empress did not suspect that the Portuguese-Catholic doctor was a Jew (she was also very favorably disposed toward the sergeant of the Life Guards, the Christianized Jew Grunstein, who had helped her take over the throne and to whom she made the gift of hundreds of Christian serfs). In 1744 the doctor provided a particularly important service: he cured Grand Duke Peter's intended, the future Empress Catherine the Great, of a dangerous case of pleurisy.

When Sanchez submitted his retirement due to eye disease, he was sent off to France with ceremony and honors. The certificate (*abshid*) given to him with the imperial signature reads as follows:

> The bearer, Doctor of Medicine Antonio Ribeiro Sanchez, was summoned and hired into Our service after the capitulation of 1731, from which time, being in Our service, he acquitted himself well in accordance with the practices of medicine and being in various places, as befits a skilled doctor and honorable man; thus for his labor and art he was engaged by Our Grace and attended Her Imperial Person as the second court doctor with the rank of Actual State Councillor, and because he, the doctor, due to illnesses that he suffers, asked to be retired from service, we therefore instructed that he be given this *abshid* for Our own signature.
>
> Elizabeth, St. Petersburg, September 4, 1747

The St. Petersburg Academy of Sciences hastened to elect Sanchez an "honorary member in the class of physics, with the allotment by Her Imperial Majesty of a salary of 200 rubles per annum" so that he would be able to "send various articles and dissertations" from abroad.

Before Sanchez's departure, the Academy acquired a sizeable portion of his book collection – more than 700 volumes, which to this day can be found in the Library of the Russian Academy of Sciences in St. Petersburg. The collection's contents attest to the breadth of the doctor's interests. Here we see works in Latin, French, English, Italian, Spanish, and Portuguese. Medical literature predominates: practical handbooks, atlases, reference books, and studies in areas such as anatomy, physiology, surgery, obstetrics, pharmacology, and hygiene. He also owned works by ancient and medieval doctors (Hippocrates, Galen, Celsus, Avicenna, Vesalius, Paré, de Graaf), as well as by his contemporaries, including Boerhaave, Astruc, Haller, and Junker. But the subject matter of these books was not limited to the natural sciences. There are volumes on theology, ancient and modern history, aesthetics, law, mathematics, art, rhetoric, poetry, philology, bibliography, commerce, and many other areas. Among historical works, there are treatises by Bodin, Machiavelli, Sarpi, and Frederick II of Prussia. Of particular interest is a biography of Lucilio Vanini, a freethinking Italian who was burnt at the stake during the Inquisition. Most books in the collection feature the owner's inscription and various marginalia and notations. Sanchez's collection has yet to be systematically investigated. Such an investigation could open a window onto the creative laboratory of this encyclopedically learned man.

Russia's imperial court physician enjoyed an excellent reputation throughout Europe. Even before his arrival in France, Sanchez was already a full member of the Paris Academy of Sciences. Once there, he took a lengthy vacation and then returned to the practice of medicine and the writing of scientific treatises. He also carried out assignments given to him by the St. Petersburg Academy. Among other things, he arranged for prominent foreign scholars to enter Russian service. Given these circumstances, we can imagine how surprised and vexed he must have felt upon receiving a decree by Empress Elizabeth dated November 10, 1748, commanding that Sanchez be "excluded from honorary membership in the Academy and that his pension be discontinued." This deprived him of a learned title and an important source of income, he noted ruefully in a letter to the president of the St. Petersburg Academy, Kirill Razumovsky. Presuming that he had fallen into disfavor due to charges of political disloyalty and with a particular instance in mind that might have occasioned such charges, Sanchez argued his innocence.

The source of imperial displeasure, however, lay elsewhere. Here we have what Chancellor Alexei Bestuzhev wrote on this matter:

> Monsieur Sanchez concerns himself with a circumstance that had nothing to do with his disfavor. Her Imperial Majesty has the greatest respect for scholars and is an utmost patron of the sciences and arts. But she also desires that members of her Academy be good Christians, and she has learned that Doctor Sanchez does not belong to this category. Therefore, to the best of my knowledge, the reason he was deprived of his position was his Judaism, and not any political circumstances.

Razumovsky offered a similar explanation in his reply to Sanchez: "She became angered toward you not for any misdeed or disloyalty committed directly against Her. But She feels that it would be contrary to Her conscience to have someone in Her Academy who has thrown down the banner of Jesus Christ and decided to act under the banner of Moses and the Old Testament prophets." Why was Elizabeth, who had patronized the doctor in the past, suddenly gripped with inquisitional ardor and prompted to accuse him of betraying Christianity? Historians suggest the Russian empress may have received reports to the effect that, upon arriving in Paris, the doctor became involved in the city's Jewish community and was attending a synagogue.

In despair, Sanchez asked the prominent Swiss mathematician, Leonhard Euler, who had been a member of the St. Petersburg Academy from its very inception, to intercede.

> Her Imperial Majesty is not angry with me for some political failing, but because her conscience does not permit her to keep me in the Academy so long as I profess the Jewish faith. I responded to this with great restraint that such an accusation is false and is all the more libelous as I am of the Catholic religion, but I am not concerned with refuting this, since I was fated from birth to be seen by Christians as a Jew…, and furthermore, Providence has destined this by the blood that flows through my veins, the same blood of the first saints of the church and the holy apostles, who were humiliated, persecuted, and martyred in life and revered and worshiped in death.

This was written in the eighteenth century, but this reproof to all Judeophobes that call the Semites the descendants of the "tribe of Judah" sounds surprisingly modern. For some reason such Christians pretend not to know, and indeed do not want to know, that Jewish blood flowed in the veins not only of the prophets of the Old Testament, but those of the first Christians and evangelists. This mismatch between historical truth and modern prejudice was the fodder for humor, such as the comment about the Bible, "Back then everyone was a Jew. What could you do, such were the times!" Along the same line, there was another joke told in Russia: One pious old woman says to another, "You know, it turns out Christ was a Jew!" "Well, what of it?" the other reassured her. "After all, he did adopt our faith."

But neither the intercession of Leonhard Euler (who wrote, "I doubt very much that such shocking measures will help bring glory to the Academy of Sciences"), nor Razumovsky's evident affection for Sanchez did anything to change the situation: Elizabeth would not budge.

Deprived of his pension, and therefore in straitened circumstances, the doctor nevertheless continued to labor selflessly. He treated the poor at no charge, was actively engaged in scientific research, and conducted a lively correspondence with the luminaries of medicine. In 1750 he published (in French) his first major work, on the origins and treatment of syphilis. The book brought the author great renown and was twice translated into German. It has been considered a classic and its importance is undiminished by time.

A committed rationalist, Sanchez spoke out in support of science and experiments, advocated for secular education unfettered by the church, and insisted on the need to make education universally accessible. His treatise on pedagogy, "Letter on Educating Youth" (1760), is infused with Enlightenment ideals and is on a par with works by Voltaire, Diderot, L'Alembert, Holback, and Buffon (with all of whom the doctor was personally acquainted) and represents a monumental work on educational theory. He was also insightful in the area of economics, about which Prince Dmitry Golitsyn wrote: "This venerable old man has more knowledge in this area than one would expect to encounter in a person who has spent his entire life so remote from the management of affairs. In conversations with him we covered this subject exhaustively."

The doctor's knowledge was truly encyclopedic, in fact he was an active collaborator in the famous *Encyclopédie française* and contributed a number of entries. The name of Antonio Ribeiro Sanchez also gained renown in his native Portugal, where reforms were introduced after the Marquis of Pombal came to power (as Minister of the Kingdom, he was *de facto* ruler from 1750 to 1777) that limited the authority of the Catholic Church and the Jesuits. Essentially a dictator, Pombal implemented Enlightenment principles through harsh authoritarian measures. In 1773 he did something Sanchez had been dreaming of: he eliminated legal differences between "old" and "new" Christians, giving them equal rights. Although the Inquisition would not be completely quashed until 1821, its activity under the Marquis was drastically reduced. Pombal initiated the publication of Sanchez's works in Portugal and helped restore his fame there. The Royal Academy of Sciences in Lisbon elected him an active member.

Sanchez welcomed Russians who visited France, something we see evidence of in a report by Kirill Razumovsky to the chancery of the Academy of Sciences immediately after the death of Empress Elizabeth: "Sanchez, while living in Paris, in accordance with his customary fervor for Russia, performs various useful services for Russians who come there to acquire greater knowledge for themselves in the sciences and arts, services about which those visiting Paris cannot say enough in praise." Razumovsky proposed returning him his title and pension.

This only became possible during the reign of Empress Catherine the Great, who maintained a deep sense of gratitude toward the doctor. The monarch ordered "The payment of a pension of one thousand rubles per annum, to be taken out of palace accounts, to Doctor Sanchez, the court doctor previously in service here and currently residing in Paris, for as long as he may live, in that he saved me from death with the help of God."

There had always been close friendships between Sanchez and Russian grandees, but now they were able to conduct these relationships openly. For example, Count Mikhail Vorontsov wrote to Ivan Shuvalov from Berlin to Paris, "I ask that you convey a friendly bow to Monsieur Sanchez." It was Sanchez who designed for Shuvalov a program for teaching medicine at Moscow University and wrote "On the Importance of Science in the Civic and Political Development of Russia." The doctor also maintained close ties with the president of the Academy of Arts, the outstanding Russian pedagogue and educator, Ivan Betskoy. The doctor sent him instructions and other materials for the orphanage that was opened in Moscow in 1764. It was also to Betskoy that he sent, for translation into Russian, his manuscript treatise on Russian *banyas,* a work that later became well-known and was published twice in Russia, in 1779 and 1791. On the title page of the edition published during his lifetime appear the words:

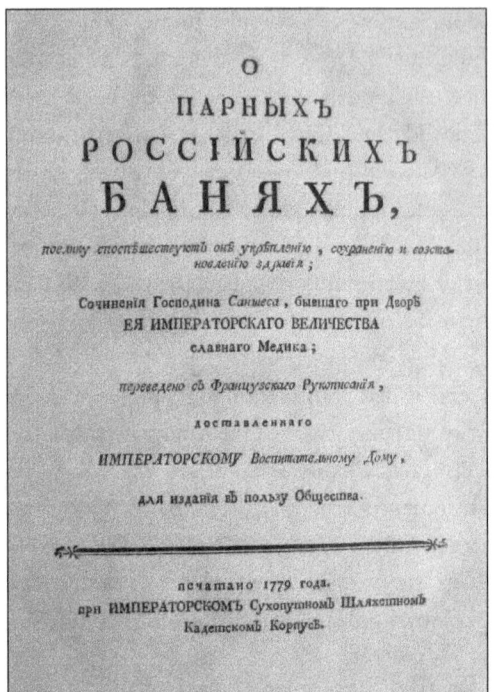

The title page for Sanchez's treatise on Russian banyas.

"Concerning Russian steam baths, inasmuch as they further the strengthening, preservation, and restoration of health; composed by Monsieur Sanchez, formerly a renowned doctor in the court of her Imperial Majesty."

This subject was particularly topical at the time since the French astronomer, Jean-Baptiste Chappe d'Auteroche, had argued the harmfulness of the Russian *banya* in his 1768 work, *Voyage en Sibérie*, to which Catherine the Great responded in the most forceful of terms. In the foreword to his book, the "renowned doctor" Sanchez writes, "My sole and sincere desire is to demonstrate the advantages of the Russian banya over those that existed in the times of the Greeks and Romans and those that exist today among the Turks, both for the preservation of health and for treating many illnesses." Incidentally, Sanchez saw the primary advantage of Russian *banyas* in that in them "the steams are renewed every five minutes. The steam produced thus relaxes the hard parts of the body, since this steam is composed of the elemental particles of fire and air...It softens the skin, but does not weaken it...It expands the respiratory apparatus, veins and other filaments, and revives and restores these parts." The author goes on to talk about Russian *banyas* as a precious good that can serve the "fortitude and health of the body" not only in Russia, but in other countries. Thus did Sanchez have a hand in the spread of Russian *banyas* to France, Germany, Switzerland, England, and the United States. His book, which was translated into several European languages and became a classic work of international medical literature, and remains influential to this day.

Antonio Ribeiro lived a long and rich professional life. He died in Paris in the calm of his office on September 11, 1783. The Paris Academy of Sciences devoted a special session to his memory.

Among the doctor's papers were found 28 completed manuscripts, two of which deserve particular attention. *Thoughts on the Inquisition: For My Personal Use* and *On the Reasons for the Persecution of Jews*. These titles speak for themselves; his concern for the fate of his fellow tribesmen endured into old age.

At the same time he seemed to recognize that the most meaningful portion of his life was spent "in service to the Russian Empire." Indeed, his best years had been given over to this cause. He not only administered medicine to Russians and helped them, but in various ways popularized Russian culture and civilization in the West. Therefore Sanchez earned the right to be called a son of Russia, for he worked assiduously on its behalf. In 2004 there was a major exhibit at St. Petersburg's Russian National Library devoted to the court doctor.

Portugal, too, claims Sanchez as one of its most distinguished sons. One Portuguese poet dedicated an ode to him that called the doctor "the new Portuguese Hippocrates." The encyclopedias of this country invariably underscore his Portuguese roots. In 1999, the 300th anniversary of the birth of Antonio Ribeiro Sanchez was commemorated in Lisbon.

The historical record paints a portrait of a man who was deeply concerned by the plight of his fellow Jews. But, like so many Jews throughout history, he was forced to choose between the faith of his fathers and the pursuit of knowledge and career. How deeply felt a sacrifice this was for Antonio Ribeiro Sanchez we will never know.

LEVY LIPMAN

THE ROMANOVS' SINGULAR COURT JEW

The period of European history between approximately 1550 and 1750 saw the overlapping of the Age of Absolutism and the Age of Mercantilism. This was the period during which Jewish courtiers came to the forefront of the historical stage. There was not a single European monarch who managed without them. In keeping with their elevated appointments, they walked around dressed like any other highly placed courtier. Endowed with analytical minds and an entrepreneurial spirit, these "Jews in livery" usually handled a broad range of financial needs for their sovereign, purveying jewels and other valuables, serving as chief quartermasters of the army, overseeing the royal mint, creating new sources of revenue, negotiating loans, and devising taxes.

Why was it that the sphere of trade and finance fell specifically to Jews? During the Middle Ages, they were prohibited from engaging in certain professions. The field of commerce, which Christians traditionally held in contempt and had no desire (and little ability) to engage in, was left open to Jews, who developed great proficiency in this area. Therefore, when entrepreneurial know-how and resourcefulness wound up being in great demand, Jews were ready. They served their king, duke, or prince faithfully and truly, demonstrating enviable initiative and efficiency. Furthermore, the low legal and social status of Jews (as members of an ethnic minority that was discriminated against due to their religion) was an added appeal to a monarch, since it allowed for less independence and made them more manageable than their Christian counterparts.

Many court Jews throughout Europe had highly successful careers. For example, in Vienna, the construction of defensive fortifications was overseen by Samuel Oppenheimer (1630-1703), who was able to assert that, in a time of war, he would be able to yearly "equip two armies for the monarch." His colleague, Germany's wealthiest Jew, Samson Wertheimer (1628-1724), who was even called the "Jewish emperor," faithfully served three Hapsburg rulers and carried out important diplomatic missions. In his palaces hung the portraits of the kings and dukes who had benefited from his services. In 1697 Behrend Lehmann (1661-1730), the court Jew of August II, prince elector of Saxony, was able to raise 10 million thalers, allowing his patron to win the "elections" and become king of the Polish-Lithuanian Commonwealth. Even the zealous Catholic, Charles V, had his own "Jew in livery," Josel of Rosheim (1476-1554), who was so powerful a Finance Minister that the emperor was utterly unable to manage without him. The financiers of Vienna, Hamburg, and Frankfurt were closely linked to bankers and agents in Amsterdam, the Hague, London, Paris, Venice, Rome, and Warsaw. Their common Jewish faith served as a pledge assuring their mutual reliability.

This was hardly the fabled "Jewish conspiracy" in action or the fulfillment of some age-old dream of the sons of Israel to take over the world. In fact, if there was an element of conspiracy and sedition in all this, its target was the foundations of the feudal world order. American historian Max I. Dimont put it well: "The Court Jew was a revolutionary figure who heralded the coming of the radical capitalist state, which would do away with the power and privileges of the nobles. In the Court Jew the nobles correctly foresaw their doom."

For Russia in the first half of the eighteenth century, however, capitalism, to say nothing of the downfall of the nobility, lay far in the future. Furthermore, unlike the more tolerant West, where most countries had their own Jewish communities, this country, in the words of one self-proclaimed Judeophobe, was "hitherto the only European state that has been safe from the terrible Jewish canker." Not only could Jews not reside within Russian borders; they were strictly prohibited from crossing them.

However, as the anti-Semitic historian Alexander Pyatkovsky once lamented, "almost every limitation placed on Jews was subject to various personal exceptions," and that was indeed the case, although we can count these exceptions on the fingers of one hand. Surviving information about these Jews is, for the most part, extremely scant and fragmentary. One example we know of is a certain Abraham Roth, who was permitted by Peter the Great to open an apothecary in Moscow. Another is the tsar's factor and commercial agent, a native of Vilna by the name of Israel Hirsh, who, in 1715, based on the signature of Alexander Menshikov (whose power under Peter earned him the moniker "semi-sovereign ruler"), was given a patent to live in Riga, a city that had traditionally been closed to Jews. His son Zundel set up his household in St. Petersburg, where, together with his companion Samson Solomon, he became supplier to the royal mint. Zundel was also engaged in procuring lumber for shipbuilding and was able to travel through Russia on business. He and his son, Moses Hirsh, remained in St. Petersburg even after the April 20, 1727, decree by Empress Catherine I expelling all Jews from the empire. In his letter, signed "Your Most Humble Slave, the Yid Zundel Hirsh," he asked that he and his family be allowed to remain in Russia, a request that was later granted by Emperor Peter II in a royal decree dated January 6, 1728. But all of these figures are of secondary importance and did not play any role in Russian history.

Of much greater interest was the prominent Jew Levy Lipman, who for two decades operated at the highest echelons of the Russian state. His life and fate are especially intriguing inasmuch as, throughout the entire history of the House of Romanov, he was the only non-Christianized Court Jew.[1] Something that was a typical phenomenon in the courts of Western Europe, for Russia was exceptional, a case of breaching the accepted order.

Fortune smiled broadly on Lipman during the gloomy years of the reign of Empress Anna Ioannovna, a period that was sometimes called the time of the "alien stranglehold." Those favoring this interpretation like to quote the prerevolutionary historian Vasily Klyuchevsky, who wrote: "Germans rained down on Russia like dross sprinkling from a threadbare sack, covering the court, encircling the throne, and finding their way into all the most lucrative positions in government." The artful pens of the nineteenth century dubbed Anna's rule the *Bironovshchina*, combining the name of her favorite Ernst Johann von Biron and a Russian suffix suggestive of some uncontrolled force reeking rampant misfortune. And although prominent Russian historians (Alexander Kamensky, Eugene Anisimov) have demonstrated that Biron's role has been greatly exaggerated and that there is no reason to believe in a "German party" at court, there are still scholars who continue to promote the idea of underhanded schemes by insidious enemies of Russia.

Reading some of these historians we might conclude that the period would have more aptly been called the *Lipmanovshchina*, since the influence of the empress' favorite was supposedly entirely surpassed by that of his close associate, the court banker Levy Lipman. In his book *Two Hundred Years Together* (which has yet to be translated into English), Aleksandr Solzhenitsyn

---

1. An aspect of his biography pointed out by Mina Kirstein Curtiss in *A Forgotten Empress: Anna Ivanovna and Her Era* (New York, 1974).

asserts that Biron "placed the management of all financial matters in his hands" and "turned to him for advice on questions of Russian governmental life." There are also memoirists and writers who explicitly state that Biron did not make a single decision himself until he had the approval of this Jew and jump to the unequivocal conclusion that Lipman was the ruler of Russia, a controversial assertion, to say the least. It remains to us to examine the historical record and clarify this murky picture.

Lipman was the court Jew of Karl Friedrich, the Duke of Holstein-Gottorp (1700-1739), a scion of Swedish kings. Although the Jewish community in Holstein was not numerous and some towns were more tolerant of Jews than others (the situation in Kiel and Lübeck, for example, was much worse than in Friedrichstadt, Glückstadt, and Rensburg), Karl Friedrich did not suffer from ethnic and religious phobias and was happy to benefit from the services of Jewish financiers.

Ernst Johann von Biron

It should be noted that Emperor Peter the Great saw the duke, a pretender to the Swedish throne, as critical to the geopolitical interests of the empire and intended to marry off his daughter to him. In the summer of 1721 Karl Friedrich was cordially received in Russia. The duke arrived in Moscow with his suite, which included followers of the Law of Moses, specially permitted (!) to enter the country as the companions of such an esteemed personage. The first reference to Levy comes from this period. In a diary entry dated June 23, 1721, Friedrich Wilhelm von Bergholtz, a member of the Duke's suite, describes his stop along the way to St. Petersburg at the famous watering hole, The Red Tavern, located 15 versts from the city. "Soon after me there arrived by post from Reval [Tallinn] our Yid Lipman, who immediately continued his journey." Karl Friedrich's visit extended to six long years. He married the emperor's eldest daughter, Anna, and became a member of the Supreme Privy Council. It was specifically thanks to his patron that Lipman acquired such useful connections.

Lipman's acquaintance with another Anna – Peter's niece and the future empress Anna Ioannovna – who at the time was the widowed Duchess of

Courland, certainly changed the course of his life. In his book, *Chapters in the History of the Latvian Jews* (available in Russian, Hebrew and Yiddish), the historian Mendel Bobe asserts that under Anna, Lipman appears to have "managed all the duchy's finances," which seems rather hard to believe. After all, while Anna lived in Courland she was chronically broke, a fact the duchess constantly bemoaned in her letters to her tightfisted "dearest uncle" Peter the Great and "dearest auntie" Catherine I. She was always drowning in debt. "I was forced to enter deeper into debt," she wrote to St. Petersburg, "And, having no means to repay it, I will not be able to obtain credit anywhere." Given this state of affairs, it would not have made sense for Lipman to become entangled in the financial affairs of Courland. For this reason the version of events proposed by historian Yuly Gessen seems to make more sense, that the duchess was in desperate need of funds and Lipman had an opportunity to make himself useful to her. All of Anna's monetary commissions were carried out by Ernst Johann von Biron, who in 1722 became a gentleman of the duchess's bed chamber. So it was through Biron that Levy first became involved in Anna's finances.

Lipman apparently attracted the favorable attention of the Russian court. In 1727, when support for Karl Friedrich's claim to the Swedish throne weakened after the death of Catherine I, he lost his influence in Russia and was forced to return to Holstein. Levy, however, remained in St. Petersburg. It is noteworthy that, soon after the duke's departure, on June 26, 1727, to be exact, a decree signed by Alexander Menshikov granted "the Jew Lipman" 6,000 rubles "for producing three Orders of St. Catherine with diamonds." Fabulously expensive rings and "various gold and silver diamond-studded items" were obtained by the young Emperor Peter II and his most august sister Natalya Alexeyevna through Lipman, for which in 1728 he was paid 32,001 rubles. (The ruble was highly valued in those days and by today's standards this is a truly astronomical sum.) Levy was recognized as an authoritative expert in jewels. After the death of Tsarevna Natalya Alexeyevna, it was he who was assigned the task of appraising all of her valuables.

But Levy's greatest success came during the reign of Anna Ioannovna. Whatever her failings, Anna seems to have remembered who helped her in times of need. As the Dane Peder von Haven, who wrote about his travels to Russia, commented, "As soon as the empress ascended to the throne, she gave particularly generous rewards to certain merchants who were given permission to loan money." One of them, doubtless, was Levy Lipman. It would seem that those historians are not entirely correct who presume that he was solely a protégé of Biron and that Anna Ioannovna associated with him only because she was reluctant to go against her favorite. In reality, the empress was torn between the most contradictory feelings. Her innate anti-Semitism muted the gratitude that she felt toward Levy for past services, and intolerance toward infidels was overcome by a burning desire not to be outdone in opulence by the courts of Western Europe. The scales tipped in favor of the "useful" Jew Lipman. "She was generous to the point of extravagance, loves luxury to excess, which is why her court exceeds all others in magnificence," distinguished foreigners said of the empress. And there were none in a better position than Lipman to satisfy the most capricious fancies of this opulence-loving monarch. Even at the very beginning of her reign, on June 30, 1730, "the merchant Lipman…for diamond items obtained from him for the imperial court" was given 45,000 rubles. In 1732, a diamond ring valued at 15,000 rubles was obtained through him, and in 1733 a royal decree stipulated payment to the Jew of approximately 160,000 rubles.

In 1734, an important event occurred in the life of Levy Lipman. The Jew, who was already the *de facto* supplier of the court, was given the official title of Chief Court Commissar (*ober-gof-komissar*), and in 1736 Court Agent (*kamer-agent*). The historian Prince Pyotr Dolgorukov notes that these positions "were created especially for Lipman." In fact it was the other way around. Lipman was created for these positions, which the transformed Russian court so desperately needed to fill.

Anna Ioannovna taught the Russian nobility to live like Europeans. In creating many new ranks for her courtiers she was following the German example. She could not have failed to notice that the courts of Vienna, Hamburg, Frankfurt, and even those of the minor prince electors all had Jews in service. Some had ascended to such heights that they had built themselves magnificent mansions and hosted such lavish parties that even royal personages were not averse to attending them, that they kept an open table, that they drove about in ornate carriages with servants riding the footboards. And these Jews had titles such as Court Factor, Court Commissar, Chief Court Commissar, Court Agent, and some had even been granted noble titles. Of course such a thing could never happen in Russia, since Jews were not even allowed to live there, much less feather their nests so lavishly. But there you have it: Anna Ioannovna reconciled herself to having one court Jew to prevent idle gossip in the West to the effect that Muscovy was still ruled by barbarians. Furthermore, Lipman was someone with a European reputation. His promissory notes were honored from Vienna to Madrid.

And so, like his European brethren, Levy became a Chief Court Commissar and Court Agent and performed duties analogous to theirs. He traded in jewels, was able to send monies to Russian diplomats for urgent needs, arranged funding for the Russian Army abroad, traded in wine and potash, and even oversaw negotiations to hire a foreign theatrical troupe and medical specialists. The sums placed in his hands by the court grew more and more impressive, reaching the tens and even hundreds of thousands of rubles. Suffice it to say that in 1734 alone he was given more than 95,000 rubles.

One could certainly call Levy a full-fledged courtier, and he dressed in livery like everyone else. It is interesting to note that in countries with greater religious tolerance court Jews sometimes preferred to wear their own national dress and did not submit to the dictates of court attire. For example Behrend Lehmann refused a request by August II to shave his beard and wear a dress waistcoat, despite the fact that he was offered 5,000 thalers to do so. And the richest German banker, Samson Wertheimer, also wore a beard and peyos and always dressed "in the Polish manner" observed by Jews in that region. The impression this manner of dress made on Russians is recorded by Andrei Bolotov in his *Notes*. "Their black dress, mottled on the side, their ridiculous skull caps, and the entire image of them was in so many ways strange and unusual that we could not tear our eyes away." Parading before the Russian sovereign with such an appearance would have been considered the height of insolence and was utterly unthinkable. Lipman, understandably, had to adapt to the conditions of Russian court life.

Of course for Lipman's Jewish contemporaries, the sight of him in lavish court dress must have been just as shocking as beards and yarmulkes were for the non-Jewish nobility. In his historical 1936 novel *The Reckless Captain*, writer Leonty Rakovsky, who studied the realia of eighteenth-century court life, paints a vivid picture of Lipman's dress and offers what might have been a typical dialogue between simple innkeepers.

"That fellow is a Jew?"
"Yes, but no ordinary Jew! Look how he's dressed!"
Eliezer screwed up his eyes and shook his head in admiration.

"It has been 15 years since I saw Tsar Peter in Mogilyov, when Jews brought the tsar a live sturgeon weighing one and a half poods. Lipman here is dressed no worse than the tsar's ministers."

"He wears such a fancy *zhupan*?"[2]

Eliezer chortled, "*Zhupan* – ha! That's no *zhupan*, it's a caftan with golden buttons. Truly, if I had even one button from his caftan I would put on a clean shirt every Sabbath!"

"What do you mean, buttons?" Sosya-Basya asked in amazement. "I thought you said he was a Jew?"

"Lipman's a Jew alright, but he wears buttons rather than fasteners like we do. And his cheeks are as smooth as the palm of my hand," added Eliezer, disapprovingly.

Sosya-Basya spat in disappointment.

"He's a scoundrel and not a Jew if that's how it is!"

However, in his depictions of Levy at home, Rakovsky has him wearing a yarmulke, observing the Sabbath and kashrus, and savoring gefilte fish.

Lipman was always able to count on Biron's patronage of his commercial undertakings. Levy was his regular creditor and partner in many large commercial deals, and when Biron became a duke and was placed in charge of Courland, Lipman began to manage the duchy's finances.

In a letter to the historical novelist Ivan Lazhechnikov dated November 3, 1835, the poet Alexander Pushkin reflected insightfully on Biron's position under Anna Ioannovna. "He had the misfortune to be a German. All the horrors of Anna's reign – a reign that reflected the spirit of the times and the prevailing mores – were placed at his doorstep. But in the end he had a great mind and great talents." Lipman, for his part, had the misfortune of being born a Jew, which automatically earned him the animosity of many Russians, despite his intelligence and talents. Anna's favorite Biron may be unfairly remembered by history, but the Court Commissar faired far worse. It is hard to find a more repelling figure in all of Russian historical fiction.

One only need look at how Ivan Lazhechnikov describes Lipman's appearance in the 1835 novel *The House of Ice* to get an idea of the disgust with which he was regarded. "The head that extended out of Lipman's shoulders,

---

2. A pood is an archaic unit of weight equaling just over 36 pounds, so the sturgeon here weighed approximately 54 pounds. A *zhupan* was a colorful over-garment worn in Eastern and Central Europe in the sixteenth-nineteenth centuries.

topped with a ring of red hair, golden rays emanating out from under his black sable hat, with its opened jaws, and watchful eyes that looked ever-ready to snatch up and consume his victim…His eyes caught hold of you like the devil's claws catching hold of a soul." He had a "pale, gangling face, a gaze that radiated a phosphorescent shine," "orangutan ears that wiggled back and forth," and he smiled with "lips that were so big that in hell his multitudinous audience certainly applauded this artful arch-demonic smile." This description certainly deserves no applause, although it is surely the work of a fevered imagination. No portrait of the Court Commissar has survived, so the author had no real evidence of his appearance to draw on and resolved this problem by resorting to tired Judeophobic clichés (the stereotypical depiction of Jews in nineteenth-century Russian literature has been extensively studied by such scholars as Savely Dudakov, Gabriella Safran, and Mikhail Weiskopf).

"A schemer and utter scoundrel" and "traitor of Christ," is what the hero of a story by Vasily Avenarius entitled *Bironovshchina* calls Lipman. "Upon hearing the name of the court banker Lipman, who at the time was a spy, an informer, and a close advisor of Biron, he frowned angrily." And in the fictional chronicle by Valentin Pikul *Word and Deed* (1971), Levy appears as "Count Yid," a crafty rogue, bloodsucker, caring only for his own profit and surrounding himself with disgusting "thieves without family or tribe, craving the silver and gold of Russia." Meanwhile, Biron, although he is delighted with the Jewish financial genius, never forgets the innate mercenariness of his people. "My villainous factor," Pikul has him say to Lipman. "I'm well aware that you know of other sources of income that I have yet to discover. Out with them!"

These fictional descriptions of our hero turn out to be just that, and shatter easily against the hard historical record. It is notable, for example, that the Judeophobic Spanish ambassador to Russia, Duke Diego Francisco of Liria and Jerica (who considered Jews a "filthy and swinish people") in a moment of emotion called Lipman an "honorable Jew." It is also well known that Levy was always ready to lend a helping hand to those in need. At a critical moment and expecting nothing in return, Levy supported the Swiss jeweler Jeremiah Posier (1716-1779) when he was just starting his career. Posier was deep in debt and considering fleeing the country. Lipman not only encouraged him to stay in Russia, but paid his debts and channeled profitable orders his way. Posier later recounted that Levy told him that it was possible to "make a very good honest living" in Russia. Thanks to Lipman the young jeweler became personally known to Anna Ioannovna and his business then took off. In his 1879 historical novel

Love and the Crown, Eugene Karnovich writes, "Distinguished members of the nobility, especially the ladies, invited Posier to come to their homes with his goods and quickly bought them up. These eminent customers often honored his humble abode with their visits."

The fact that Levy Lipman was called "honest" and that he himself spoke of an "honest living" is telling. As much as Marxist ideology may have seen commerce as essentially a mercenary endeavor and equated it with swindling, today, even in Russia, the phrase "honest business" is not taken as an oxymoron. There has always been the concept of a business "code of honor" and "the merchant's word of honor" (as we see in the plays of Alexander Ostrovsky). And it should be said that Lipman always kept his word and was reliable in business. Everyone knew that he was a man you could count on. He knew money and performed his duties impeccably and on time.

The Posier incident reveals another of Levy's qualities: his insight and ability to judge people. After all, he believed in the young Swiss and saw in him the future favorite jeweler of the Russian empress, "the Fabergé of the eighteenth century," as he was later dubbed.

He also reacted quickly when his fellow Jews were afflicted by misfortune. In one instance that took place in 1734, Berk, the young son of a Jew by the name of Kushnel Girshov, from the town of Shklov (in present-day Belarus), was kidnapped by a Lieutenant Bekelman and the soldier Ivanchin. On November 19, a decree was signed by the empress herself demanding that the child be returned to his father and the kidnappers punished. Considering the fact that by law Jews were not allowed to live in the empire, one cannot help but wonder why the empress would suddenly show such concern over the fate of a Jewish child from some shtetl backwater? Of course the concern was not hers, but Lipman's, who saw to it that a copy of the decree reached the proper channels. One can only imagine how much diplomacy and courage it took for Levy to convince the Judeophobic monarch to focus on the plight of his coreligionists.

He, like his European brethren, petitioned the throne on behalf of other Jews, and in this he enjoyed a measure of success. According to a contemporary, the empress granted him permission to keep as many Jews as he wished by his side, although generally speaking they were forbidden from living in St. Petersburg and Moscow. The historian Lev Tikhomirov asserts that it is thanks to Lipman that an entire Jewish colony took root in both capitals. There is evidence that Levy became the center of Jewish life in the same way that in Europe Jewish religious communities formed around court Jews. Lipman maintained close relations – of friendship, not merely commercial ties – with the *otkupshchik*[3] Baruch Leibov (1663-1738). Leibov lived in Moscow, in the German *sloboda* (settlement) "in the home of the goldsmith Ivan Orlet." Along with his son-in-law, Shmerl, who also lived in the *sloboda*, Leibov served as the kosher butcher for Lipman and his servants. This was also a service provided by the Jew Abraham Davydov, who was "blessed by the synagogue in the Polish shtetl of Kopust" for this purpose. David Isakov and Abraham Samoilov were Lipman's stewards, and a man by the name of Faives was Lipman's clerk. They all lived in the home of the "foreigner Boldensha" and made frequent trips to Poland, to the shtetl of Dubrovno, which had a significant Jewish population and was where the family of Leibov's son Meyer lived. This is where, far from prying eyes, the bris (ritual circumcision) of Leibov's newborn grandson, Judah, was performed, as well as that of the ill-fated nobleman and naval officer Alexander Voznitsyn, who was later burned at the stake for converting to Judaism. Faives acted as *mohel* and, as we learn from police records of the Voznitsyn case, was "blessed by rabbis to circumcise Jewish newborns."

But did Lipman really have the sort of influence that would allow him to significantly alleviate the condition of Jews, as Aleksandr Solzhenitsyn suggests? Solzhenitsyn sees Lipman's hand in the fact that two of Anna's decrees were never implemented: the 1739 decree prohibiting Jews from renting lands in what was then called Malorossiya ("Little Russia," present-day Ukraine) and her 1740 decree ordering the expulsion of 600 Jews from there. Evidence suggests that the bungling of the local authorities and the interests of local landowners had more to do with this than any actions by the Court Commissar. Levy's lack of influence can also be seen in Biron's actions in Courland, where he reigned supreme. Jews had lived there for generations and had traditionally worked as craftsmen and in small-scale commerce and leasing. It is indicative that on July 3, 1738, and then again on July 4, 1739, orders were issued demanding that they all, without exception, pay their taxes and leave the duchy by St. John's Day, i.e., by March 8, 1740. Landowners who hid Jews in their homes faced substantial fines. All this took place when Lipman was essentially Courland's finance minister. It is hard, therefore, to believe that Biron did not do anything without "the Yid Lipman's" approval.

If Levy had been all-powerful would he really have allowed discriminatory laws against Jews? Furthermore, he could not possibly have given his blessings to the events of July 15, 1738, when crowds watched as Baruch Leibov was burned

---

3. A tax farmer. See explanation, page 20.

at the stake alongside Alexander Voznitsyn, whom he had supposedly enticed to convert to Judaism. But Lipman did show himself to be a selfless friend in this instance. The 75-year-old Leibov was falsely accused of proselytizing Judaism and sentenced to an agonizing death. He was to be interrogated on the rack in the notorious Secret Chancery. Levy, of course, could not prevent the execution, but he did everything possible and impossible to alleviate the plight of his friend. He was not afraid to draw ire on himself and appealed to Anna Ioannovna, who was infuriated at this "Jewish seducer," to spare the elderly man torture. In this, he succeeded.

Some historians assert that Lipman and Biron were extremely close. But their closeness is far from certain. For one thing, the Jew was not the duke's only source of credit. Biron was in constant need of money and borrowed it from anyone and everyone (even his own valet). There were wealthy people without a drop of Jewish blood who accommodated the empress' favorite with far greater sums than the Court Commissar.

It is unlikely that Lipman himself acted as an informer for the duke, as some assert, or that he covered the palace with a tangle of spy networks working on his behalf. Some say that he warned his patron about a plot being hatched to overthrow him. The playwright Nikolai Borisov in his historical comedy Biron (1899) invents a scene where the favorite responds to such a warning with a horrifying German accent. "Vat utter nonsense you babble ...Oh, Lipman! Who vuld raise a hand against my person?" Yet such a carefree attitude does not seem to fit with the duke's innate suspiciousness and is therefore doubtful. A contemporary memoir recounts how heartrendingly the flabbergasted Biron cried out on the night of November 9, 1740, after 80 guardsmen stormed into his bedchambers to arrest him. It was clear that the regent's dethronement took him completely by surprise.

Another reason to doubt the closeness of Biron and his "trusted henchman" is the fact that after Biron's downfall Lipman was unscathed. Meanwhile, the new regent, Anna Leopoldovna (by marriage, Anna Brunswick-Wolfenbüttel), settled accounts with the rest of the duke's close associates. When foreign newspapers reported that the financier had relinquished his post, on January 13, 1741, *St. Petersburg Vedomosti* set the record straight. "Ober-Commissar Lipman," the newspaper wrote, "continues to conduct commerce and is present at all public occasions of the Imperial Court." True, some sources said that Levy held onto his post under the new regent because he told her where Biron's capital was stashed. But this supposition is obviously absurd, since it is well known that Lipman himself was unable to retrieve the large sum that Biron owed him. The reason behind Levy's "unsinkability" lay elsewhere. Monarchs had a taste for luxury and he knew how to help them achieve it. Suffice it to say that, after a year on the throne, the Brunswick family had acquired diamonds and jewels through the Jew worth approximately 160,000 rubles.

However, everything in Lipman's life fell apart when Peter the Great's daughter Elizabeth ascended to the throne, despite the fact that she has gone down in history as the most fanatical lover of jewels and clothing that ever sat upon the Russian throne. As her contemporary Mikhail Shcherbatov wrote, during her reign "imitation of the most sumptuous peoples grew, and respectability was measured in terms of the magnificence of one's residence and dress." One might have thought that such a highly competent Chief Court Commissar, capable of pleasing the most demanding monarchical tastes, would have been very useful to her. Historians, however, describe her mystical terror of Jews. Although Elizabeth's anti-Semitism was primarily based on religion (once she became empress, she promoted several Jewish converts to Christianity, including the twice-baptized Sergeant of the Guards, Peter Grunstein), there was also a visceral aspect to her prejudice. "There are multitudes of Yids: and I saw them, the dogs," her closest friend Marva Shuvalova wrote to her in 1738 from Nezhin. Evidently, the hatred this "jolly tsaritsa," so wild about fashion and foppishness, felt for these "dogs" outweighed her love of luxury and opulence.

Just how odious Lipman appeared in the eyes of Elizabeth and her associates before she ascended the throne can be seen in the writings of Jacques-Joachim Trotti, Marquis de La Chétardie, with whom she was extremely close. This French aristocrat, who lobbied Elizabeth's interests at the Russian court when Anna was on the throne (for which he later was awarded the Order of St. Andrew), repeated the myth of the all-powerful "court Jew" and spoke of his cunning and ability to "unleash and set in motion all manner of intrigue," concluding that "one could say that Lipman rules the empire."

After the downfall of the Brunswick family, Levy presented a bill for the outstanding balance on everything he had acquired for the former regent, her husband, and lady-in-waiting, Juliana Mengden. The new empress ordered an investigation be conducted to confirm that the money was truly owed to the Jew. Although everyone confirmed the accuracy of Lipman's bill (only Anna Leopoldovna's husband, Anthony Ulrich, disputed 14,000 rubles), there is no evidence that the banker received the requested sum. What we do know is that Elizabeth, having made the famous statement, "I have no desire for profit from the enemies of Jesus Christ," made it clear she would not put up with a "traitor of Christ," especially at the helm of power, and immediately expelled him from the Court. The very positions of Chief Court Commissar and Court Agent, which reminded her of the hated member of an alien creed, were abolished. (It is amusing to note that she showered favors on the diamond jeweler Jeremiah Posier and drew him into her inner circle, where he acquired great influence. Had she only known how much her beloved jeweler owed to the "bloodsucker" Lipman!)

Now Levy was given the humble position of "office worker" and there was very little profit indeed. There has survived a "Catalogue of Paintings and Other Curious Items" that Lipman acquired for the Kunstkammer (Russia's first museum, established by Peter the Great) and assessed at a value of 252 rubles. On April 15, 1742, the librarian of the Imperial Academy of Sciences, Johann Daniel Schumacher, ordered that the master of paintings, Johann-Elias Grimmel, estimate the value of these items and submit a report on the matter. What is striking here is not merely the triviality of the sums that the former financial magnate was now dealing with, but the lack of trust in him as an expert in valuables and *objets d'art*. After all, when Levy had been assessing royal adornments of astronomical value his opinion had never been questioned.

It is also noteworthy that the empress dismissed Lipman's financial partner, the agent Simon, who represented Russia's commercial interests in Vienna. The monarch "did not deign to have a single Yid in her service," despite the fact that Simon "desired no salary whatsoever."

On December 2, 1742, her most gracious Majesty Elizabeth decreed that "under threat of Imperial wrath and grave torture for failure to comply ...from all of Our Empire, including Great Russian and Little Russian cities, towns, and villages, all Yids of both the male and female gender, whatever rank or merit they may have...are to be immediately expelled beyond the border and henceforth are not to be allowed into Our Empire under any pretext."

The last mention of Lipman dates to December 1742, after the decree expelling Jews from the country. According to the journal of a colonel, the Christianized Jew Yakov Markovich, Levy welcomed him and some of his friends to his Moscow home, where they enjoyed a meal together. After that, we lose all trace of Levy Lipman.

However he is not lost to the history of Russia. The anti-Semitic witch hunt that took place in the nineteenth century turned Levy into a predator, a bribe-taker, and a Russophobe, credited with many of the sins and abuses that took place during the reign of Anna Ioannovna. Writers and nationalistic historians endeavored to make Lipman into some kind of power behind the throne but – and this is important – they considered it inconceivable that Russia could be ruled by an unchristened Jew. A puzzling case indeed! The treatment Lipman receives in Lazhechnikov's *The House of Ice* is typical. "He was born a yid, he remained a yid, although he tried to pass himself of as some sort of holy ghost!" Lazhechnikov calls him a convert, but he was wrong. Lipman, like his European counterparts, did not try to hide behind a cross and remained firm in his Jewish faith.

The court Jews of Western Europe helped to liberate their brethren from the medieval ghetto, to emancipate and assimilate them. In Russia, where there was almost no Jewish population, Lipman settled for simply "remaining a yid" and did for the handful of his fellow Jews living in Russia what he could. His fate is interesting in that his remarkable mind and talents – despite infernal obstacles – allowed him to reach an eminent position at the Russian court while remaining true to his people.

His story brings to mind the line spoken by Alexander Pushkin's Covetous Knight: "Cursed Yid! Esteemed Solomon!" These words aptly convey a historical reality: although Jews were often cursed, when they were needed they suddenly became "esteemed." So it was in the life of Levy Lipman. However, the heightened attention paid to this court Jew by both historians and contemporaries, the exceptional importance that they attributed to him, speak only to the fact that Levy Lipman was a striking, major, and memorable figure. He was well known in Europe and it is still possible that new evidence about this extraordinary man, who continues to spark our interest, will be uncovered in European or, perhaps, Russian archives.

GRIGORY POTEMKIN

CATHERINE'S RIGHT-HAND JUDEOPHILE

During her travels through the recently absorbed southern reaches of the empire in 1787, Catherine the Great received a delegation of Jews. The delegation submitted a petition requesting that the insulting word "Yid" (*zhid*) no longer be used in Russia. The empress agreed and directed that henceforth only the word "Jew" (*yevrey*) would be used in official documents. The ease with which Catherine agreed to this request is perfectly understandable. After all, she was committing to no more than a minor linguistic change, not the eradication of ethnic and religious intolerance toward Jews. A precedent for this sort of eighteenth-century political correctness already existed: not long before, the empress had issued a decree prohibiting the use of the demeaning word "slave" (*rab*) in the valediction of letters addressed to the royal person and mandating its replacement with the more enlightened "loyal subject." The poet Vasily Kapnist wrote an "Ode to the Elimination of the Vocation of Slave" in reaction to Catherine's epistolary reform, interpreting it as tantamount to the liberation of the serfs. How did Catherine react? She ordered the presumptuous versifier be told, "You want to destroy slavery in actual fact? Be satisfied with words!" The empress might have said the same to Jews, especially inasmuch as the taboo against the abusive word Yid only applied to official documents. In oral speech, as well as in *"belles lettres,"* there were no prohibitions whatsoever against the term.

As for the attitude toward Jews held by the "Semiramis of the North" herself (as Voltaire famously called Catherine, comparing her to the legendary queen of Assyria), we can clearly see a driving desire to reconcile the irreconcilable: on the one hand the progressive ideas of the Age of Enlightenment and the associated strivings to emancipate this small nation and integrate it into the empire's multi-ethnic patchwork, and, on the other, the age-old, callous hatred toward Jews felt by the majority of the population, a hatred flavored with religious anti-Semitism and xenophobia. A glimpse at the image of the Jew within Russian "folk wisdom" is offered by Ivan Turgenev in his classic, *Fathers and Sons*, which depicts Bazarov's mother, the devout Arina Vlasyevna, sincerely believing that all Jews have a bloody spot on their chests.

Catherine, fortunately, was free of such prejudices and was not, by nature, predisposed toward Judeophobia. Among her associates we find Jews, including some who had not converted: the physician Mendel Lev, the chemist Samuel Shvenon, the banker Levin Wolf, and contractors we know only as Abramovich, and "Zhid David." The monarchy also closed its eyes to the presence of several Jews living illegally in St. Petersburg, in the house of her spiritual advisor, of all places. "They are tolerated in violation of the law; everyone pretends not to know that they're in the capital," the empress confessed.

Catherine's personal feelings about Jews were one thing, matters of state quite another, and she adapted herself to the political demands of the moment. Here is what she recorded in her *Notes* about how the question of permitting Jews to settle in the country was handled in the Senate:

> On the fifth or sixth day after taking the throne she [throughout, Catherine refers to herself in the third person] went to the Senate…It so happened, unfortunately, that the first matter on the agenda for this session…was a draft proposal to permit Jews entry into Russia. Catherine, hindered by the present circumstances from giving her consent to this proposal, which was unanimously recognized as beneficial, was rescued by the senator Prince Odoyevsky, who stood and said to her, "Would not Your Majesty desire first, before deciding, to look at what Empress Elizabeth wrote in her own hand on the margin of a similar proposal?" Catherine ordered that the record be brought to her and found that Elizabeth…had written in the margins: "I have no desire for profit from the enemies of Jesus Christ!"

Repeating that not a week had passed since her ascension to the throne, Catherine continues to write about herself in the third person:

> She was placed on the throne to protect the Orthodox faith; she had to deal with the pious, with the clergy, who had yet to have their estates returned to them and who lacked the necessities of life…; minds, as they always are after such a

Empress Catherine II

Prince Grigory Potemkin

great event, were in a state of the utmost agitation: undertaking such a measure was no way to calm [minds], yet recognizing it as harmful was impossible. Catherine simply addressed the prosecutor general, after he gathered the votes and approached her for her decision, saying to him: "I desire that this matter be postponed until another time."

Summing up the situation, the empress wrote, "Often it is not enough to be enlightened, to have the best intentions and the power to carry them out; even then, often reasonable behavior falls prey to unreasonableness."

Evidently it was fear of this "unreasonableness" that led Catherine to insert the stipulation "except for Yids" in her "Manifesto On Permitting Foreigners to Settle in Russia" (issued at the very beginning of her reign on December 4, 1762). The Moscow historian Dmitry Feldman sees this as a nod toward the old-fashioned political views that predominated in Moscow and especially the memory of the recently deceased and devoutly pious Empress Elizabeth, who was distinguished by a vehement intolerance toward non-Christians.

But once she consolidated her position, the pragmatic Catherine began to make different decisions. Guided by ideas of "social utility" and "profit" (which had earlier been rejected by the Orthodox Elizabeth), she alleviated the plight of Jews. The empress was well aware of their role in commerce and industry and considered them useful to her government. At the same time she was concerned that Jewish commerce might represent too much competition for ethnic-

Russian merchants, "Since," as she confided to Denis Diderot, "these people manage to get everything for themselves." It is interesting in this connection to recall that in his day, Peter the Great, who refused to give Jews the right to trade and settle in Russia, made the exact opposite assertion: "Although they [Jews] are considered skillful swindlers in trade throughout the world, I doubt that they will be able to trick my Russians." Who is right? Probably Catherine, who was well acquainted with the character of the merchant estate in Russia and the ability of Jews to compete with it. Of course it was not a matter of swindles and deceptions by Jews, but rather their particular ingenuity, resourcefulness, and toughness.

Seeing the colonization of the Black Sea region as a critical step in establishing Russia's control of the sea itself, in 1764 the empress used Jews to settled what was being labeled "New Russia" (Novorossiya) and granted them the right to register as merchants and urban commoners (two of the social estates or *sosloviyas* into which the Russian population was divided). Some Jewish financiers were allowed to live in Riga and even in St. Petersburg. During this same period, Jewish merchants were permitted to spend limited amounts of time in "Malorossiya" (literally, Little or Lesser Russia, the term used for present day Ukraine).

Historians have commented on the secretive nature of the actions the empress took on behalf of Jews. Indeed, in her early letters and reports we find no direct mention of Jews, as if the monarch was ashamed to pronounce this embarrassing (for her) word. For example, in a letter to the Governor General of Riga dated April 29, 1764, Catherine demanded that merchants from Novorossiyskaya Province (in present-day Ukraine) be issued passports with no indication of their ethnicity or religious affiliation. The reference was, of course, to Jews, and Catherine wrote in her own hand, "Keep this confidential."

However there was one eighteenth-century Russian statesman who did not beat around the bush when it came to the rights of Jews. The man in question was Catherine's powerful cohort and favorite, His Highness, Field Marshal Prince Grigory Alexandrovich Potemkin of Taurida (1739-1791). A brilliant administrator and military commander, the conqueror of Crimea, and the builder of the Black Sea fleet, Potemkin was a charismatic figure. "A genius, and then a genius, and still a genius," is how one contemporary paints his psychological portrait. "An innate intellect, exceptional memory, a loftiness of soul, cunning without malice, guile without deceit, a fortuitous combination of whimsy, majestic generosity in handing out rewards, exceptional subtlety, a gift for figuring out what he himself doesn't know, and the most magnificent knowledge of people." Potemkin's influence on the empress is hard to overestimate. "Your diligence and hard work," Catherine wrote to him, "would augment my gratitude, if only it was not already so great that it could not be increased."

The years of the dizzying ascent of the empress' virtual co-ruler (1772-1790) overlapped with the first partition of Poland, as a result of which a Jewish population of 100,000 came under the Russian scepter. Largely thanks to the prince, these newly absorbed Jewish subjects benefited from Age of Enlightenment advances.

"Almost uniquely among Russian soldiers and statesmen," the English historian Simon Sebag Montefiore writes, "Potemkin did more than just tolerate Jews: he studied their culture, enjoyed the company of their rabbis, and became their champion." Where might we seek the source of such goodwill on the part of His Most Serene Highness toward "the sons of Israel"? He came from the Smolensk area, where Jews had lived since days of old (this was where the distinguished Shafirov and Veselovsky families originated). We know that Potemkin's ancestors interacted directly with the local Jewish population. One of them, the Smolensk nobleman Nikolai Potemkin, even investigated a complicated case involving the "grievances of Shklov Jews and Russian merchants." No record remains of any contacts specifically between Grigory and local Jews, but it is evident that he interacted with Jews during his young years and the affinity he developed wound up benefitting them.

After the monarch gave him the vast estate of Krichev-Dubrovin in the Mogilyov region of Belarus, which fell partially to Russia after the first partition of Poland, the prince welcomed business people there regardless of race or creed.

Potemkin was distinguished by exceptional religious tolerance: not for nothing was he named "guardian of Tatars and non-Christians" within the Commission for the Codification of Laws. And in the cacophony of languages around him, Yiddish could clearly be heard. Furthermore, His Serene Highness' interests extended beyond the realm of practical matters. He was also captivated by material of a more elevated nature: poetry, philosophy, Greek, and Latin, and especially theology ("I would definitely like to be a bishop or minister," he often told his friends). One contemporary tells of Grigory Alexandrovich's passion for theological debate. "He surrounded himself with learned rabbis, schismatics, and all manner of erudite persons. Among his favorite things to do was wait until everyone started to depart a gathering, then summon them to him and pit them against one another, so to speak, and in so doing refine his own knowledge."

It is entirely possible that Potemkin influenced Catherine's 1772 decision to grant Jews living in the newly acquired territories certain rights of citizenship. An official placard dated August 11, 1772, proclaims, "Jewish communities residing in cities and lands that have been joined to the Russian Empire will retain and preserve those freedoms that they currently enjoy, in keeping with the law and their property." It should be noted, however, that although Jews were given the right to perform religious rites and own property, cautious Catherine did not give them all the same rights given to her other new subjects. Unlike newly absorbed non-Jewish populations, they were not allowed freedom of movement across the rest of Russia.

In 1775, when policies were being designed to attract settlers to Russia's new southern provinces, it was Potemkin who insisted on inserting an unprecedented stipulation in the plan – that it include Jews. He presented an entire program for attracting Jews to southwestern Russia in order to develop trade in conquered lands as quickly as possible. Enticements included the following: taxes would not be levied on them for the first seven years, they would be given the right to trade in spirits, and they would be provided protection against marauders. Jews were permitted to open synagogues and establish cemeteries. To promote more rapid absorption of the territory, Jews were encouraged to bring women from the Jewish communities of Poland to New Russia (and, somewhat later, to Taurida, which comprised the Crimean Peninsula and adjacent portions of present-day Ukraine). For every potential bride that was brought to the territories, His Serene Highness paid five rubles. The historical record informs us that one man assigned to help implement this act was a certain "Jew Shmul Ilyevich." Soon the towns of Yekaterinoslav and Kherson had sizable Jewish populations.

Like Christians, Jews were entitled to affiliate themselves with a particular estate (*soslovie*), depending on the nature of profession they were engaged in and whether or not they owned property. All Jews wound up included among either the merchant or urban commoner estates (the latter – *meshchanstvo* – is also translated as "*petit bourgeoisie*"). They paid taxes and came under the jurisdiction of magistrates and municipal courts. In other words, in essence, the Christian population was encouraged by the imperial government to interact with Jews as their equals. It is illustrative that St. Petersburg's response to a 1783 inquiry on this matter was unequivocal: citizens are taxed and participate in municipal administration with "no distinction made as to faith and law." A senate decree dated May 7, 1786, confirmed that Jews were supposed to enjoy full equality in rights. As historian Richard Pipes points out, the decree "for the first time formally proclaimed that Jews are endowed with all the rights of their estate and that discriminating against them on the basis of religion or ethnicity was illegal."

In order to appreciate just how progressive and unprecedented were the laws Potemkin inspired Catherine to institute for Jews, it is instructive to look at what was taking place in "enlightened" Europe at the time. We see the Judeophobe King Friedrich II of Prussia, who initiated brutal persecution against Jews, and the barbarous anti-Semitism of Maria Theresa, empress of the Holy Roman Empire, who compared Jews to a plague contagion. In fact, the only country in the world that endowed Jews the same rights as the overall population was Tuscany.

In the first volume of his 2001 book, *Two Hundred Years Together*, Aleksandr Solzhenitsyn argues that Jews held a more privileged position than the absolute majority of the Russian people: "From the start, Jews in Russia enjoyed personal freedom that the Russian peasant would not achieve for another 80 years." True, the government treated non-Christians better than their own serfs, but the Jews are hardly to blame for this!

Potemkin surrounded himself with a number of outstanding Jews, both christened and not. Every last one of them is worthy of a separate chapter, however we must limit ourselves to brief profiles.

After converting to Lutheranism and moving with his father to Prussia, Karl Ludwig von Hablitz (1752-1821) became an outstanding botanist. He was granted honorary membership in the Russian Academy of Sciences and the rank of Privy Councillor. He went on to found colleges of forestry in Russia. Hablitz carried out various assignments for Potemkin, some of them secret, and in 1783 he was appointed Vice Governor of Crimea. The prince gave him the job of writing a scholarly work: *A Physical Description of Taurida Province In Terms of Its Location and the Three Kingdoms of Nature*, which was published in 1785 and expanded and republished in 1809. The book also described the peninsula's Jewish residents. For example, here is his description of the so-called "Jewish Fortress" (known today by its Tatar name, Çufut Qale) near Bakhchisarai:

> [It] stood on the very top of a steep stone mountain, and its position clearly shows that it was built...by a people that was ancient, oppressed, and sought

a safe haven for themselves...Now only Yids have been living there for a long time...; and they have chosen this place to stay despite the lack of water, which must be carried up by hinny from the very base of the mountain.

One of Potemkin's trusted associates, Nicholas Stieglitz (who died in 1820, see page 196), was descended from the family of Jacob von Hirsh, the "court banker" at Munich. He also settled in Russia around the end of the eighteenth century. A Kherson merchant, Stieglitz had an office in Odessa and owned a concession for the mining of salt from lakes. Under the prince's patronage, he enjoyed a thriving business in the Crimea. After Potemkin's death he was baptized and became a prominent official in the Ministry of Finance. Stieglitz later was given the title of baron and became a banker for Russian emperors and patrons of the arts.

The Jew Nota Notkin (who lived until 1804, see page 165) was a Mogilyov merchant and Court Councillor. He supplied Potemkin's army with food and forage, risking life and limb in the process. It was said of him that "he served the Fatherland with all possible zeal." Later Notkin presented the authorities with a "Proposal for the Resettlement of Jews in Colonies in the Fertile Black Sea Steppe for the Breeding of Sheep, Farming, Etc..." Under Alexander I he was a member of the Jewish Committee and earned a reputation as "defender of his people." Indeed, he is considered one of the founders of the Jewish community in St. Petersburg.

Potemkin's circle also included quite a few artists, among whom was the "the Jewish disciple" Kifa Itskovich.

But perhaps the greatest influence on Grigory Alexandrovich was exerted by the prominent businessman and learned Hebraist, Joshua Zeitlin (1742-1822). He traveled with the prince, managed his estates, built cities, arranged loans to equip armies, and even headed the mint in Crimea. The pupil of rabbi and Talmudist Arie Leib, Zeitlin was an eager participant in all theological debates, and he maintained piety and wore traditional Jewish clothing. According to eyewitnesses, he often "walked around with Potemkin like his brother and friend." By the will of his lofty patron, in 1791 Joseph became the owner of a lavish estate in Mogilyov Province. An un-christened Jew suddenly became the owner of hundreds of Christian souls – an unprecedented occurrence in Russia! But who could argue with the all-powerful ruler of Taurida?

It could very well be that it was Zeitlin who instilled in Potemkin an interest in Judaism. Suffice it to say that in his personal library the prince kept a valuable scroll of fifty hides containing the Five Books of Moses, most likely copied in the ninth century.

In discussions between the two friends, an idea was generated that was as fantastic as it was audacious: to relocate Jews to Jerusalem, after it had been taken from the Turks. Historians see in this an "attempt to create a link between 'strategic' Jewish interests and Potemkin's visionary impulses." One contemporary commented that Potemkin "began to develop the idea that, once the Ottoman Empire was finally destroyed and Constantinople and the strait were in Russian hands, then Jerusalem would also no longer be under the authority of infidels. And then all Jews should be moved to Palestine…They would be reborn in their native land." It is therefore no exaggeration to state that His Highness the Judeophile was the first (and only) statesman in Russian history to be a fervent supporter of the Zionist idea.

This was more than empty talk. The prince actually tried to bring the idea to life. In 1786, Potemkin created an "Israelite Cavalry Regiment" comprised entirely of Jews, which was ultimately supposed to be sent to a liberated Palestine. This was the first time since the Roman Emperor Titus destroyed the Second Temple of Jerusalem in the year 70 C.E. that an attempt was made to arm Jews!

It has to be admitted that Potemkin's Israelite Regiment did not hold a candle to today's Israeli Army. Surviving accounts of the combat readiness of the Jewish warriors are mocking in tone. For example, the historical novelist Nikolai Engelhart offers ironic descriptions of their lapserdaks (long coats), beards, and peyos, and describes how they had trouble staying in the saddle. The assessment of the "Jewish regiment" left by Prince Charles-Joseph, 7th Prince de Ligne, is in much the same spirit, although he always sympathized with Jews and has even been called one of the first Zionists of the eighteenth century.

The Israeli historian Savely Dudakov suggests that these belittling descriptions are skewed by tendentiousness and bias and points out that quite soon after the events described the Kościuszko Uprising broke out in Poland, in which another Jewish Cavalry Regiment took part under the command of Berek Joselewicz. Five hundred volunteers proved their courage and determination and died heroes' deaths during the storming of Warsaw in November 1794.

The prince organized Jewish pilgrimages to Palestine. We know, for instance, that he arranged for the July 1, 1784, issuance of a passport to one Joseph Sishman, who was traveling to Jerusalem together with a group of Jews.

Russian Jews, for their part, viewed Potemkin as a hero and understood that in him they had a reliable defender and patron. Eyewitness accounts have survived of the enthusiasm with which they received visits by His Highness and we find extravagant odes written in his honor. Indeed, as long as the Prince of Taurida was alive, nothing seemed to threaten their peace and prosperity. But on October 5, 1791, while traveling outside Jassy (the present-day Romanian city of Iași) in the hills of Bessarabia, His Serene Highness breathed his last.

Immediately after Potemkin's death, the government made a marked retreat from the progressive reforms that had been initiated during his lifetime. By December 23, 1791, Catherine the Great signed notorious decrees that remained in force until the February revolution of 1917. Jews were relegated to a "Pale of Settlement" and the most reactionary of anti-Semitic laws was enacted: "Whatever Jews are not explicitly permitted, they are forbidden."

Historians agree that Jews' sudden fall from grace in the eyes of the monarch was prompted by an external event: the French Revolution, whose National Assembly, in the fall of 1791, made Jews equal with other citizens.

Perhaps had Potemkin been alive he might have cooled Catherine's anti-Jewish ardor. But as we all know, history has no subjunctive mood.

One thing is indisputable: Grigory Potemkin symbolizes an entire epoch, one that can be called "Russian Jewry's golden age." The prince's tireless concern for the sons of Israel makes him an emblematic and exceptionally appealing figure, and not only for Jews, for everyone fighting for personal rights and universal human values.

NOTA KHAIMOVICH NOTKIN

THE ADVISOR FROM SHKLOV

"A most noble fellow, even if he is a Jew!" This chauvinistic verdict was handed down about the subject of this chapter by Count Semyon Gavrilovich Zorich (1745-1799), the former favorite of Catherine the Great and owner of lucrative estates earned in that capacity. Coming from the mouth of this inveterate Judeophobe, such a testament to the character of the Jew Nota Khaimovich Notkin (1746-1804) surely bespeaks no favoritism and therefore is as flattering as it is just.

There is only meager information about the first half of Notkin's life. He was born in the town of Shklov in the Mogilyov region of what is now Belarus, which was part of the Polish-Lithuanian Commonwealth before the 1772 partition of Poland (other variants of his name use Nathan as his first name and Shklover as his last). For a long time he was a Mogilyov merchant, and for his fruitful commercial activity the Polish king granted him the rank of Court Councillor. The first documentary mention we find of the "Jew Nota" relates to Vitebsk and dates to 1770.

Later he entered into partnerships with Russian merchants, and in the early 1780s he was engaged in large-scale trade in Moscow. Beginning in 1788, during the Russo-Turkish War, he supplied the army of the "magnificent Prince of Taurida," Grigory Potemkin. Here is what Zorich had to say about how Notkin acquitted himself in this area: "He served the Fatherland with all possible zeal. Being used in the commission of secret assignments, he risked his life more than once and supplied the troops with food and forage and the front and hospitals with the necessary provisions at a time when nobody but he wished to step forward." Potemkin's sudden death led to Notkin's financial ruin, since the treasury refused to reimburse him the money he was owed (approximately

200,000 rubles). Perhaps if this Jew had sought the protection of the cross (as many of his more calculating coreligionists had done), he might have been paid. But Nota Khaimovich chose another path: he remained a Jew, felt all the pain of his people, and acted on their behalf. In essence, he became the forefather of the Russian Jewish intelligentsia.

After Potemkin's demise, Nota returned to his native Shklov. Jews had lived in this town for many centuries, and they constituted more than 47 percent of the population. According to the historian David Fishman, this city was the "metropolis" of Russian Jewry and became the center of rabbinic scholarship as well as the wellspring of scientific knowledge and Haskalah ideas that spread into Russia during the Jewish Enlightenment. The town featured a yeshiva and a large, stone synagogue, and there were stormy debates between the Hasidim and the so-called "wise men of Shklov" about the essence of faith.

However back then it was the aforementioned Count Zorich who presided over Shklov, and Notkin became his financial advisor. Catherine's former favorite lived here like a local tsar with numerous courts and royal outings, balls, and even a theater that staged French operas and Italian ballets. The Count spent lavishly. A notorious cardsharp with a reputation for negligence and poor manners who was accustomed to having his every whim fulfilled, the "despot of Shklov," as he was called, liked to be fawned over and tolerated no recalcitrance. Zorich was particularly extravagant when it came to celebrating graduations from the Shklov Academy of the Nobility, which he had founded. In the historical novel, *The Ninth of Thermidor* (part of a trilogy), author Mark Aldanov describes graduation day:

> Semyon Gavrilovich arranged a particularly lavish graduation celebration in 1792. By then construction was nearing completion on the new three-story building, a crescent-shaped stone structure more than 400 feet long that overlooked the Dnieper from its high right bank. *Nota Notkin, Zorich's Minister of Finance, had obtained a great sum of money for the Count* [emphasis added], and the students were in newly tailored dress uniforms.

We also know that Nota procured a magnificent set of china from Saxony for Zorich that was worth 60,000 rubles.

The fact that Notkin made himself useful to His Excellency the "despot of Shklov" is forgivable. After all, this was the eighteenth century, and rank had to be taken into account. But there is one aspect of this relationship that is hard to understand at first glance. Zorich was cruelly abusive of Shklov's Jewish population. His mistreatment of Jews was truly criminal: the count "left them without payment, nothing but air," as they later complained to the emperor, and even subjected them to corporal punishment, as if they were his serfs. But Nota, rather than refusing to do business with this petty tyrant, sought out his help, connections, and influence. What was going on here? Was this cowardice? Conformism? Reproaches do not appear to be in order, since Notkin's subsequent actions demonstrate that he made use of Zorich's goodwill for tactical ends, seeing an opportunity to draw the attention of higher authorities to the needs of his people.

Semyon Zorich

In fact, on May 24, 1797, Zorich sent Nota to St. Petersburg with a letter to Prosecutor General Prince Alexei Kurakin. In this letter, he asked Kurakin to offer Notkin his patronage and reward him for his efforts. This was a reference to the money owed him for his procurement services during the war. However, Nota Khaimovich also had other things on his mind. He took advantage of the opportunity to submit to the influential courtier a document he had prepared entitled, "Proposal for the Resettlement of Jews into Colonies in the Fertile Black Sea Steppe for the Breeding of Sheep, Farming, Etc.: While There to Establish Cloth, Textile, Spinning, Rope, and Sailcloth Mills Close to Black Sea Ports, Wherein the Skilled among this People Would Be Trained." In speaking about Russian Jewry in this document, Notkin displays impressive erudition and creative thinking. He draws on the legislative experience of many countries of the *Galus*, in particular Austria and Prussia, where manufacturing among Jews was variously encouraged. It is noteworthy that in this proposal he expresses a thought that had yet to be voiced in Russia: the idea of using Jews as manufacturing labor. Arguing for the need to gradually shift Jews away from the sale of alcohol, he advocates that they be brought into agriculture, debunking the myth that Jews are innately unsuited to work the land. In so doing he alludes to Biblical times: "Jews used for [agricultural labor] will grow their nourishment with their own hands…in imitation of their ancient forefathers, and with time they will bring the state significant benefit, and with time necessity will teach them to find their bread through farming." Notkin also insisted on settling Jews primarily in colonies along the Black Sea coast, which promised Russia great advantages due to the fertility of the land there and the proximity to ports for transporting agricultural commodities.

Although the proposal was not met with an immediate response, its author had made a name for himself and was considered a voice of authority in St. Petersburg circles. Emperor Paul himself knew and valued Notkin. In recognition of services to Russia, he gave him a lucrative estate in the Mogilyov region.

Draft of a letter to Notkin asking him to be a member of the Jewish Committee.

Nota Khaimovich brought up his proposal again in 1800. The occasion was Senator Gavrila Derzhavin's visit to Belarus in connection with his work to revise laws concerning Jews. Notkin took the opportunity to acquaint Derzhavin with his ideas. Derzhavin did show an interest in some of them, but (and there is a "but") only those having to do with channeling Jewish labor into activities that would benefit Russia. In other regards, Derzhavin, one of the greatest Russian poets of the eighteenth century, earned himself the questionable distinction of being an advocate of mandatory, restrictive, repressive, and even brutal measures in regard to Jews. We will not spell out Derzhavin's views on this question in detail (they have been quite thoroughly described in the works of historians Yuly Gessen and Mikhail Edelman and are not the subject of this chapter). Let us simply say that the suggestions by some Russian nationalists that this poet and statesman was the victim of a Jewish conspiracy does not merit serious discussion.

However, the irreconcilability of Derzhavin and Notkin's positions was not immediately apparent. At first they developed a friendly rapport. "I need someone like you who possesses qualities like yours and is not blinded by prejudice and ingrained habits and who so ardently desires every good for his nation," Derzhavin wrote to Notkin and invited him to take part in the work of the committee that had just been established by Alexander I in 1802 to draft a "Jewish Statute." Once he became a member of the Jewish Committee, Nota's efforts on behalf of Jewish interests began to take the form of civic duty. Had the culmination of his dreams finally come true? Would he soon be able to petition the Russian monarch himself on behalf of his fellow Jews?

Notkin now moved to St. Petersburg (together with his son Sabbatai). By early 1803, when members from all the Kahals (community councils) had started to arrive in the northern capital, a Jewish community of several dozen people had taken root here. And the soul of this community was "the venerable and respected Nathan Note from Shklov," as he is referred to in the "community book," a record of its members. This small, cohesive group observed Jewish traditions and even maintained its own *reznik* (kosher butcher). It was thanks to Notkin that the Jews were given a portion of the Lutheran graveyard for their use (what later became the Volkovo Cemetery), the first Jewish cemetery in St. Petersburg.

During the time Notkin served on the Jewish Committee, his concern for his fellow Jews became closely intertwined with the activity of another remarkable Jew, the writer Leib (Lev) Nevakhovich (1776-1831); see page 183. In 1803 Nevakhovich published *The Lament of the Daughter of Judah*, which he then issued in Hebrew under the title *Kol Shav'ath Bath Yehudah* and dedicated to Notkin, "the defender of his people." It is noteworthy that this book was published in Notkin's home town of Shklov. It features an ardent call to Christians to be tolerant of Jews. There are lines here that express the mood and feelings of all Russian Jews in the early nineteenth century, feelings that were certainly close to Notkin's own heart:

> The name [Jew] has become something defamatory, disdainful, cursed, a means of frightening children and the feebleminded… Oh, Christians, renowned for meekness and charity, have pity on us, turn your tender hearts our way! Oh, Christians, you seek Judea in the man – no. Better to seek the man in Judea, and you will undoubtedly find him… But heed my words… I swear that a Jew who preserves a pure image of his religion cannot be an evil person, nor a poor citizen.

The book, however, ends with a hint of pessimism: "And so cried out the mournful daughter of Judah, wiped her tears, groaned, and was still unconsoled."

"The Opinion of Senator Derzhavin on Preventing a Grain Shortage in Belorussia by Reining in the Mercenary Designs of Jews and Their Transformation, Et Cetera," which was submitted to the committee and based on obvious ethnic prejudice, did nothing to encourage in its Jewish members notions of a rosy future for Jews in Russia. Notkin was stunned by the barefaced anti-Jewish thrust of Derzhavin's "law-making" after what had seemed a fruitful collaboration. Now it appeared that the information he had shared with Derzhavin about the daily life and customs of Jews had been distorted in order to prove the malevolence of the "Christless," who were depicted as leading a parasitic way of life based on the exploitation of Christians, whom the Jews corrupted with drink and swindled. In order to limit the evil wrought by Jews, Derzhavin proposed that their rights be further restricted. How disheartening this must have been for Notkin, after he had opened his heart to Derzhavin about the true plight of Jews in Russia!

Historian Semyon Reznik writes about Notkin's efforts to persuade Derzhavin:

> Nota Notkin explained to Derzhavin that the vast majority of Jews clustered in the cities and towns of former Polish provinces could find no outlet for their labor. They were prohibited from owning land or entering government service. Most of them were small-scale tradesmen, artisans, innkeepers, and brokers, or filled a variety of roles as intermediaries, but there were too many of them for the region's rather stagnant economy. They lived half-starving, mercilessly competing amongst one another and against Christians working in similar areas. Furthermore, they had no rights and were despised, which was something that local government exploited by demanding bribes from them, corrupting both themselves and the Jews in the process...

In the eyes of the surrounding population, Nota Notkin explained, Jews were considered rich and greedy because they demanded money for their services and knew their worth. Furthermore, too many Jews…were forced to engage in the distillation and sale of alcohol. The income from this industry went to landowners, since the monopoly on alcohol belonged to them and the state. The Jewish distillers had to pay such high lease fees that they could barely make ends meet, but in the eyes of the population all the money was disappearing into their pockets and they were corrupting the people with drink. The absurdity of this calumny is obvious: in the Russian heartland, where there were and are no Jews, people drank no less and lived no better.

Notkin decided to issue a strong response to Derzhavin's Judeophobic "Opinion," and in May 1803 sent the Committee his Memorandum on Reorganizing Jewish Life. The gulf between these two documents is enormous. Notkin countered Derzhavin by proposing that the Jews be given rights equal to those enjoyed by other subjects, as well as permission to settle anywhere they are able to make a living, and that they be relieved of the burden of double taxation and granted the right to buy and lease land. Derzhavin favored forcing Jews to work in agriculture and manufacturing and exiling those who refused to Siberia, "to work the rest of their lives in mining enterprises and without their wives." Notkin favored the voluntary involvement of Jews in these same areas. It would not have been possible to transform all Jews into farmers, as Nota pointed out in his Memorandum. "That would be ridiculous. Not everyone can lead the same sort of life. Jews are engaged in the trades for which others lack skills." He advocated leaving them in peace "to earn their keep through useful labor." What should be done first and foremost, Notkin insisted, was to "gradually create conditions for this people that will prevent abuses on its part and, most important, eliminate the source of abuses: poverty." The prohibition against living in villages, he felt, was counterproductive. Where would 100,000 impoverished Jews go? And if they were resettled in "vacant lands," where would they get the money they needed to establish themselves or buy food? And to whom would they sell their produce? He also spoke of Jews' need for a general education and called for the opening of Jewish schools in every society with instruction in general subjects, including foreign languages. As a true son of the fatherland, he favored making Russian the language of instruction (rather than Hebrew). Furthermore, he proposed that educated Jews with a knowledge of Russian be encouraged to enter government service, even that they be selected to work in ministries, and that discrimination against them be prohibited.

While in St. Petersburg he continued to keep a close watch over the situation and the mood of Jews in the most remote shtetls. Suddenly word reached him that a rumor was circulating among Belarusan Jews that the Jewish Committee represented a danger to them and threatened their very way of life. Notkin immediately used his connections to arrange to have local governors sent a reassuring letter to be circulated to each town and village refuting these rumors as malicious lies. When overzealous local officials developed a plan to expel Jews from Smolensk, Notkin wrote an emotional plea to Minister of Internal Affairs

Count Viktor Kochubey in which he stated, "This expulsion is unpleasant for the Jewish people and only aggravates its dejection and produces in them lamentable conclusions concerning the fate that awaits them…Take pity upon this unfortunate people! Magnanimously fortify their dejected hearts!" The resettlement was immediately canceled.

The historian Yuly Gessen writes:

> Silently and tirelessly, calmly and steadily, he worked for the good of Russian Jews. Through his proposals and memoranda, over the course of long years, Nathan Note placed before the government the grief and tears welling the depths of Jewish life. In acquainting the government with the needs of the Jewish masses, Nathan Note did what he could to write the history of the Statute of 1804. This was the tremendous service he performed.

But it is fair to ask what this Jewish Statute of 1804 meant for the Jews of Russia. True, some of the most odious measures proposed by Derzhavin were rejected by the members of the Jewish Committee (an outcome in which Notkin's counterproposal may very well have played no small role). But the laws that were passed in 1804 were just as cruel as past laws: the Pale of Settlement was made official and the prohibition against leasing and buying land remained in force. Jews continued to be forbidden to live in villages or work in government service. So, during the era that Alexander Pushkin poetically labeled "the beautiful beginning of Alexander days," the situation for Jews remained far from "beautiful." They still faced indignity and a lack of rights.

Perhaps it is fortunate that Nota Khaimovich did not live to see the passage of the Jewish Statute. It is safe to assume that it would have been a tremendous disappointment to him. After all, he fervently believed that a state guided by reason, with the enlightened and reform-minded Tsar Alexander at the helm, could put an end to entrenched animosity toward Jews.

There is a story passed down by the ancestors of our Jewish advocate. As legend has it, Notkin's home was once visited by Alexander I himself. "Stop!" Notkin suddenly exclaimed upon seeing the tsar. When the sovereign asked for an explanation, his host explained that human happiness has a limit, and when it reaches its outer boundary it begins to recede. "My happiness upon your arrival in my home, Your Majesty," Notkin continued, "has reached its apogee. I therefore cried out for it to stop."

Of course Alexander respected and favored Nota Khaimovich as a person (we find a record of imperial decrees expressing his gratitude and giving him a valuable snuffbox, gold and diamonds, etc.), but this is not what was most important to Notkin. For him what mattered more than anything else was the interests of all Jews. He therefore would not have been pleased with the policies of the tsar he so idolized if he had lived to see how Jews would suffer under his scepter. When misfortune afflicted his Jews, the thing to say was not "Stop!" but "Sound the alarm!"

But from the Jewish cemetery in St. Petersburg that Notkin himself established we hear not a word. Here, on a tombstone in the first row are engraved the words: "The high-ranking and distinguished gentleman Nathan Nota of Shklov." From his eternal resting place, Notkin was fortunate enough to never learn just how futile his long and inspired labors proved to be.

ABRAHAM PERETZ

HOT PEPPER

In Russian the word *perets* means pepper, and the homophony between this pungent food and the name of this chapter's subject – Abraham Izraelevich Peretz (1771-1833) – was a source for puns at his expense. For example, one nineteenth-century memoirist reproduced a typical dialogue:

> "Who is this Peretz I've heard about?"
> "Peretz is a rich Jew who holds major government contracts, especially to transport and supply salt to state stores."
> "I suppose that's why they say, where there's salt, there's pepper."

But the linguistic significance of Abraham Izraelevich's name goes even further. In the Russian edition of this book the chapter about him is entitled "*Ostry perets*," which would translate as "hot pepper," but the Russian word *ostry*, which is used to describe spicy food, also suggests a sharp wit and keen intellect, both of which our subject possessed. An 1822 Russian Academy dictionary defined this quality as "the mental ability to quickly understand something, penetrate something...acuity of mind, comprehension." This fits Abraham Peretz – a Russian-Jewish public figure and prominent banker and businessman – to a T.

Indeed, Abraham Peretz began to sharpen his mind from an early age by studying the Torah and Talmud. It was his father, a rabbi in the town of Lubartow in Lublin Province, where Abraham was born, who familiarized him with these texts. Young Abraham was given a traditional Jewish education, first in the home, and later at yeshiva. He was also well-educated in secular knowledge and spoke fluent German and Russian. But the most profound influence of his adolescence was exerted by an outstanding Talmudist and adherent of the ideas of the Haskalah (the Jewish Enlightenment), the chief rabbi of Berlin, Hirschel Levin (1721-1800), also known as Hart Lyon and Hirshel Löbel. Levin happened to be Abraham's uncle. Because the nephew spent so much time in his uncle's home, as a young man he became personally acquainted with many German *maskilim*. Like other adherents of the Haskalah, Peretz opposed the cultural isolation of Jews and saw a European education as key to improving the plight of his tribe.

In Berlin, Peretz developed a close relationship with his enlightened compatriot, Joshua Zeitlin (1742-1821), and this friendship was fated to play a major role in the young man's fate. Born in the city of Shklov, Zeitlin was a learned Hebraist and astute interpreter of the Talmud, but also a major merchant and someone who assisted Prince Potemkin in regard to both his personal estates and government procurement (Zeitlin also nurtured Potemkin's interest in the Talmud). As a result of the Prince's friendship and patronage, Zeitlin had been given the title of Court Councillor and the estate of Ustye in Mogilyov Province, complete with 910 serfs. Jewish patron of the arts that he was, Zeitlin

Abraham Peretz

founded a *bet ha-midrash* (literally, house of study) where Talmudists were able to live and make use of the unique library Zeitlin had assembled. A number of *maskilim* also benefited from the financial support of the "Jewish landowner," including the famous writer and pedagogue Mendel Levin; the expert on Hebrew grammar Naphtali Herz Shulman; and the rabbi, astronomer, and popularizer of science, Rabbi Baruch Schick.

Zeitlin traveled often to Berlin, and there is evidence to suggest that while there he repeatedly visited one of the founders of the Haskalah movement, the philosopher Moses Mendelssohn. It should be mentioned, however, that despite all the similarity of views between German and Russian *maskilim*, there were also serious ideological differences. The first generation of Jewish proponents of the Enlightenment in Russia (the *maskilim* of Shklov, first and foremost) remained under the influence of rabbinic culture, most brilliantly represented at the time by the Vilna Gaon, Elijah ben Solomon Zalman (1720-1797). In essence, many of them combined the ideals of the European Enlightenment and Jewish intellectual traditions.

From the very start, Zeitlin felt a particular liking for Peretz that endured for the remainder of his life. Perhaps there was something about Abraham that reminded Zeitlin of his young self: the abilities of a promising Talmudist combined with the commercial acumen of the businessman. It is therefore not surprising the Joshua decided to bring Abraham into his family by marrying him to his beautiful daughter Sarah, who was nicknamed "Feigele" (little bird) for her diminutive stature. By the age of 16, Peretz was not only a married man, but the "right hand" of his renowned father-in-law, whom he joined in Shklov. However, even the birth of a son, Hirsh, and daughter, Tsirel, did not make Peretz's marriage a happy one. Around the turn of the century, when Abraham left for St. Petersburg, where he would represent his father-in-law's financial interests, his wife did not accompany him. The children remained with her, and only in 1803, after his Bar Mitzvah, was Hirsh allowed to go and live with his father.

After settling in St. Petersburg in the late 1790s, Peretz immediately became a part of the small Jewish community that lived (with the tacit permission of the imperial court) in the capital despite laws prohibiting Jews from residing outside the Pale of Settlement. Abraham's business thrived in "the Palmyra of the North" (as the Russian capital was known). Past connections established through Prince Potemkin did not hurt (the prince himself died in 1791), and neither did his own keen intelligence and resourcefulness. Peretz soon achieved prominence as a wealthy *otkupshchik* (tax farmer) and shipbuilding contractor, and even many years later was long remembered in the capital for his merits and his immense undertakings. In association with Kherson merchant Nicholas Stieglitz, Peretz signed a contract with the government granting him the right to farm Crimean salt. The contract was discussed in the Senate and was personally approved by Paul I, who simultaneously gave Abraham Peretz the title of Commercial Councillor.

Over time, Peretz's ties to the upper echelons of St. Petersburg society strengthened. He was particularly friendly with the emperor's favorite, Count Ivan Kutaysov, as well as with the prominent statesmen Georg von Cancrin and Mikhail Speransky. The latter even lived for a while in Peretz's home on the corner of Nevsky Propect and Bolshaya Morskaya Street (today, the site of the Barrikada movie theater). Apparently Peretz kept an "open house" that welcomed and regaled "the entire city," regardless of rank, family, or tribe.

Some have said that once Peretz moved to St. Petersburg he cut his Jewish roots. The evidence, however, does not support this, since it has been established that Abraham associated closely with eminent representatives of the Haskalah: Mendel Levin and the prominent follower of Moses Mendelssohn, David Friedländer.

One episode is noteworthy. Although in the account by historian Yuly Gessen, Peretz is cast in a negative light, in fact the incident attests to the concern he showed for his coreligionists. At the time, Shklov belonged to the former favorite of Catherine II, Count Semyon Zorich, who was bankrupting and oppressing the local Jews. This population endured insults and even beatings by the petty tyrant Zorich for a long time, and only in 1798, when their fellow Jew Abraham Peretz became friendly with the all-powerful favorite of Emperor Paul, Ivan Kutaysov, did they come forward with accusations against their oppressor. It is hard to agree with Gessen that only "financial dealings were behind the closeness between Peretz and the royal favorite Kutaysov" or that "Peretz enjoyed an acquaintance with influential officials only with a view to his own advantage," without consideration of his own people. By all appearances it was not Peretz but Kutaysov who "used every subterfuge and intrigue to acquire Shklov from Zorich" and exploited complaints against the count in pursuit of his own mercenary objectives. On the other hand, Abraham, who played the role of the *Shtadlan* (an intercessor on behalf of the Jewish community), only wanted to alleviate the plight of his fellow Jews any way he could, and therefore resorted to the help of the self-interested Kutaysov.

There is evidence to suggest that Peretz thought about the fate of his people in historical terms. The memoirs of the writer Fyodor Glinka give an account of conversations with Peretz's son, Grigory, who shared some of his father's innermost thoughts. As Glinka tells it:

> One morning [Grigory Peretz] started waxing poetic about the need for society to liberate the Jews scattered all over Russia and even Europe, to settle them in Crimea or even the East as a separate people; he said that his father, I think, ... had the idea of gathering the Jews together; but for this you'd need to gather together capitalists and the help of scholars and so on. He also went on and on about how Jews would be brought together, in what triumphal processions they would be conducted and so on and so forth. I remember that in response to all this I said, "Yes, evidently you want to bring the end of the world closer? They

say that in Scripture it's written (back then I had almost not looked at Scripture) that when the Yids get their freedom the world will come to an end."

It would indeed appear that Glinka had barely looked at Scripture. But the well-versed student of the Torah Abraham Peretz was certainly familiar with the prophesy that so uplifted his heart: "Then the Lord your God will restore you from captivity, and have compassion on you, and will gather you again from all the peoples where the Lord your God has scattered you... The Lord your God will bring you into the land which your fathers possessed, and you shall possess it..." (Deuteronomy, 30: 3, 5).

It is worth noting that the person who had first introduced the idea of creating a Jewish state to Abraham was that selfsame Joshua Zeitlin, who had in the past discussed it with Grigory Potemkin. The prince had gone so far as to devise a plan: after the Turks were defeated he thought of gathering all the Jews together and settling them in liberated Palestine. These were not empty words – Potemkin had formed an Israelite Cavalry Regiment made up exclusively of Jews to carry out this daring plan. And although this project was left unrealized, it evidently continued to excite the imaginations of enlightened Jews.

But for Peretz, it was not enough to be Jewish: as a true Misnaged, he strongly rejected Hasidism and its leaders, believing that they had achieved their authority only due to popular ignorance and superstition. As the son-in-law of the Talmudist and seeker of knowledge Joshua Zeitlin, and as someone with a secular education, he was bound to feel enmity for a religious movement that did not consider knowledge a worthy pursuit.

In 1802, by which time Alexander I had taken the throne, when a Jewish Committee was convened to consider the drafting of laws affecting Jews, Abraham Peretz was one of the few Jews invited to participate. Other Jewish experts serving on the committee were the prominent businessman Nota Notkin and the writer Lev Nevakhovich. However, while Notkin devised projects for improving the situation of his coreligionists and Nevakhovich spoke out in the press against the spread of anti-Jewish prejudices in Russian society, Peretz's role as a defender of the rights of Jews was less obvious. Strange as it may seem, it is his enemies who best describe his efforts. "Speransky," wrote the Judeophobic Senator and renowned poet Gavrila Derzhavin, "was quite devoted to Yids, through the prominent businessman Peretz, with whom he quite openly socialized and in whose home he lived." Indeed, Speransky was one of the Committee's most vocal proponents of a humane attitude toward Jews. In his opinion, what Jews needed was not punishment and restrictions, but more rights and opportunities. The idea was that, once they had education and access to industry and trade, they would be able to apply their abilities for the good of the fatherland and abandon parasitic and unproductive practices. "As few restrictions as possible, and as much freedom as possible!" is how Speransky envisioned imperial policy toward Jews. And Peretz was rightfully called "Speransky's Jewish helper" in this matter.

Meanwhile, their relationship was and is often misconstrued. For example, quite recently Archpriest Lev Lebedev declared, "A very wealthy Jew, Peretz, paid a large bribe to Speransky, and, after accepting it, this statesman saw that things took a certain turn." The groundlessness of such an assertion was demonstrated in the nineteenth century by the very well informed Baron Modest Korf, who left the following assessment:

> Speransky was truly close with Peretz…, but despite our best efforts, we were unable to find anything reliable either about the origins of these relations or their significance… Most likely our statesman maintained this connection more because he was drawing practical information from Peretz's vast financial knowledge that both as a result of his own upbringing and his sphere of activity he himself lacked. In fact, there would have been nothing shameful for anyone in having a connection with Peretz… who was renowned for his commercial mind.

We also find a possible explanation for the fact that Yuly Gessen underestimates Peretz's role in efforts to emancipate the Jews. The historian points to two dedications prefacing Nevakhovich's book, *Kol Shav'ath Bath Yehudah* (*Lament of the Daughter of Judah*). The first dedication was to Notkin as "the defender of his people," and the second was to Peretz, "councillor of commerce." This evidently led Gessen to assume that Notkin was engaged exclusively in Jewish affairs while Peretz concentrated on finance and trade. But why dedicate a book of this nature to a financial genius? Perhaps the dedication read as it did because Peretz's most prominent feature was his commercial acumen, but obviously what earned him Nevakhovich's tribute in the first place was that he applied his talents and connections to alleviate the plight of his people.

In much the same way that Joshua Zeitlin earned the trust of Prince Potemkin, Peretz, emulating his father-in-law's example, cultivated a friendship with the most prominent reformer of the early nineteenth century, Mikhail

Speransky, who, like Potemkin, was also predisposed to sympathize with Jews. The years that he spent in constant contact with his Jewish friend generated not one, but a slew of ideas. Among them was the financial reform of 1810-1812, the success of which is generally attributed to "guidance by the banker Peretz" (who conceived the overall plan).

During the war against Napoleon in 1812-1814, Peretz invested his entire fortune in organizing the feeding of the Russian army, however the treasury was slow to reimburse him and he was forced to declare bankruptcy. His property was sold for 1.5 million rubles, at a time when the money owed him by the state treasury totaled 4 million.

In 1813 Peretz became a Lutheran. The reason for this dramatic step is generally considered to be his disappointment with the document produced by the Jewish Committee, the 1804 Jewish Statute, which, in the end, represented the triumph not of Speransky's policies, but the timeworn compulsory and limiting measures that other officials had been advocating. This dashed any hope Peretz had for emancipating Russian Jews. But another factor in his decision to convert might well have been the love he felt for the Christian Carolina de Lombor (1790-1853). His first wife Sarah had passed away, and he married de Lombor as soon as he was baptized. The marriage produced four sons and five daughters.

How did his contemporaries interpret Peretz's conversion to Christianity? Here is a bit of evidence left for us by the writer Nikolai Gretsch about our subject's relationship with a Pavel Bezak:

> The wealthy *otkupshchik* Peretz, a Yid, but someone kind and truly noble, knowing Bezak's intelligence, ability, and experience, offered him a position assisting in his office with a salary of 20,000 per annum plus the gift of a house of stone. Bezak decided to accept this position and was able to repair his finances, but ruined his career by becoming known as a "Yid clerk." How unfair the judgments of society can be! What is so wrong and reprehensible here? But it's simply not done and that's all there is to it.

Paradoxically, Bezak was called a "Yid clerk" in 1815, after Peretz donned Christian garb and technically was no longer "Yid."

And how did Jews feel about his conversion? A surviving testament by Hasidim, who never forgave Peretz his opposition to their movement, gives us one perspective: "As far as that snitch Peretz is concerned, may his name be cursed, for his meanness is now common knowledge since he, to the embarrassment and shame of the Misnagdim, has changed religions." It is telling that in the majority of copies of Nevakhovich's book that we have seen, the dedication to Peretz has been somehow cut out, further evidence of Jewish attitudes toward his defection.

Only Joshua Zeitlin maintained his ties with his former son-in-law after his baptism and second marriage. He not only mentioned Abraham in his last will and testament, but granted him a privilege to obtain his Ustye estate. It is clear that the deep spiritual connection between the two men withstood life's trials.

All we know of Peretz's last years was that he was impoverished. In an 1822 letter he wrote in Hebrew to his relative Solomon Zeitlin, Abraham complained, "My affairs are in a terrible state, and there is no one I can turn to but our heavenly father, who gives subsistence to each and everyone of us. I hope that he will not leave me a laughingstock before my enemies." The last mention of him is found in Nevakhovich's 1830 last will and testament, which names Peretz executor of his estate. Abraham Izrailevich Peretz died in St. Petersburg some time after 1833.

A few words should be said about his descendants. His oldest son Grigory (Hirsh, 1790-1855) took part in the Decembrist Revolt. He was educated at Zeitlin's Ustye estate. Beginning in 1803 he lived with his father in St. Petersburg and in 1809 entered government service with the rank of Titular Councillor. He was accepted into a secret organization affiliated with the Union of Welfare in 1820, and, based on his suggestion, the Hebrew word for freedom – *herouth* (or *herut*)– became its password. Despite the fact that Grigory left the society in 1822 (three years before the actual uprising), when the revolt was put down he was tried and exiled for life. Only in the late 1840s did he receive permission to settle in Odessa. Another of Peretz's sons, Alexander (1812-1872), was a mining engineer. He played a prominent role in the industrial development of the Ural region and in 1861-1866 served as head of a corps of mining engineers. The youngest son, Yegor (1833-1899), held a number of high positions within the civil service before becoming a member of the State Council. Part of the liberal bureaucracy and an advocate of reform, he later wrote in his memoirs, which were published only in Soviet times, about the State Council's debates concerning the Jewish question. Abraham's great grandson, Vladimir Nikolayevich Peretz (1870-1935) also became well known as a literary scholar and a member of the Russian Academy of Sciences (beginning in 1914) and the Ukrainian Academy of Sciences (beginning in 1919). His scholarly opus includes works on the

Judaizers and the influence of medieval Jewish literature on Russian literature. Varvara Pavlovna Andrianova-Peretz (1888-1972), Vladimir's pupil and wife, was a marvelous scholar of Old Russian literature who held a doctorate in philology.

Today, we do not run across the name of Abraham Peretz much in historical literature, and it is almost forgotten. But it lives on in the folklore of St. Petersburg and puns about salt and pepper.

LEV NEVAKHOVICH

RUSSIAN LITERATURE'S FIRST JEW

The expression "Russian-speaking writers" began to be bandied about during Gorbachev's *perestroika*. It was coined by ethnically Russian writers of a nationalistic stripe who wanted to distinguish themselves – *Russian* writers and "true patriots" – from non-Russians (i.e., Jews) who wrote in the Russian language. In the eyes of these nationalists, such writers were not true children of the motherland. However much they might make the sign of the cross, write of the anguish they felt over the fate of their country, and sometimes even revile Israel and its culture (as was done, alas, in 2007 by a group of talented Russian Jewish writers at the Jerusalem International Book Fair), they would never be more than "stepchildren" of their native land.

However the first Jewish cultural figure to fit their definition of "Russian-speaking writer" appeared in Russia back in the early nineteenth century. The life and fate of this writer is quite instructive inasmuch as he succeeded – as shocking as this might be to "Russian patriots" – in combining within himself that which they might have thought could not be combined: concern over the fate of Jews and an ardent love of Russia and the Russian people. The man in question is the essayist, dramatist, and philosopher Judah Leib (Löb) ben Noach or, as he was known by his Russified name, Lev Nikolayevich Nevakhovich (1776-1831).

Little is known of Nevakhovich's early years. He was born in 1776 in the medieval Polish town of Letichev (mentioned in thirteenth century chronicles) in the Podolian Voyvodeship (now Ukraine's Khmelnytsky Province). This area had been home to Jews for centuries, and they constituted a fairly significant portion of the population. The town featured a synagogue and two Jewish houses of worship. When Judah Leib was one year old, Letichev was devastated by Haidamak rebels who committed pogroms and beat the town's Jewish residents, many of whom were forced to flee. But, by the will of God, Nevakhovich's parents survived this bloodbath. All that we know about them is that they were devout Jews and that the *pater familias* worked for some time as a banker in Warsaw. It can be presumed that the elder Nevakhovich invested in his son's education and, apparently, instilled in him an avid, all-encompassing love of learning. The facts speak for themselves: even before his bar mitzvah Judah Leib was given a universal, truly encyclopedic education. In addition to Hebrew, German, Polish, and Russian, all of which he spoke fluently, Judah Leib was able to translate from many of the languages of Europe. He had a profound understanding not only of the wisdom of the Torah and Talmud, but was extremely knowledgeable about contemporary Russian and German literature. Driven by an insatiable impulse toward self-education, he was perpetually expanding his intellectual store.

In 1790 our protagonist made his way to the Belarusan city of Shklov, recognized as the world center of the eighteenth-century Jewish Enlightenment, and soon became the teacher of Abraham Peretz (1771-1833), who would later go on to become a major figure in the world of commerce. Nevakhovich and Peretz became comrades-in-arms and life-long friends, a relationship explored below. For now, let us ask ourselves what extraordinary knowledge one would need to possess in order to qualify as the mentor of Peretz, who was extremely knowledgeable. After all, by the time he met Nevakhovich, Peretz had already been given a traditional Jewish education (having graduated a yeshiva), spoke fluent Russian and German, had a solid grounding in the secular sciences, and was an ardent adherent of the Jewish Enlightenment. Clearly, teaching such a "learned scholar" was as much an honor as a responsibility.

Upon arriving in Shklov, Nevakhovich immersed himself in the town's intense intellectuality. Shklov had already become a refuge for the Haskalah's most outstanding representatives. Peretz's father-in-law, Joshua Zeitlin, a prominent Hebraist and interpreter of the Talmud, had founded a *bet ha-midrash* there, a sort of Jewish academy. There, many *maskilim* were provided all of life's basic necessities and were able to give themselves over entirely to their studies. Judah Leib also developed a friendship with a physician and pioneer of the Haskalah in Belarus, Baruch Schick, as well as with the famous writer and teacher Mendel Levin (Satanower) and the expert in Biblical language and its grammar, Naftali Hirtz Schulman, among others.

Nevakhovich too became a fervent follower of the teachings of Moses Mendelssohn. However, unlike Zeitlin and Peretz, who were influenced by the Misnagdim, with their sharp opposition to the Hasidic spiritual movement, Nevakhovich exhibited an admirable broadmindedness and tolerance, focusing attention not only on what divides Jews, but what unites them. Another trait that set Nevakhovich apart even in his youth was his unwavering and genuine interest in the Russian language, which he was able to speak and write flawlessly. This was in sharp contrast with other *maskilim*, who were quite cosmopolitan in their outlook. Even Solzhenitsyn commented on this: "Nevakhovich was a humanist enlightener, but rather than being a cosmopolitan, he was closely bound to Russian cultural life, an exceptional phenomenon among Jews."

In the late 1790s, Judah Leib settled in St. Petersburg, where he lived in the home of his former pupil and friend, Abraham Peretz. The two were immediately integrated into the capital's Jewish community that had been established by another native of Shklov, Nota Notkin. Here, they were able to maintain their spiritual ties with the Haskalah.

In 1798 and 1800, Nevakhovich became involved in translating from Hebrew to Russian materials pertaining to the case of the Belarusan Hasidic leader, Rabbi Schneur Zalman of Liadi, who was twice arrested by Russian authorities, based on unfounded denunciations by the Misnagdim. Not only did Nevakhovich sympathize with the unjustly accused Hasid, but, as the historian Andrei Rogachevsky suggests, he played a vital role in Zalman's release. In order to fully appreciate just how unusual and daring Nevakhovich's role in this episode was, one has merely to contrast it with the treatment of Schneur Zalman by Abraham Peretz, who cruelly insulted the Hasid and forcibly locked him in his (Peretz's) home, bringing back memories of a time when Zalman had been forcibly confined by the Secret Chancery.

A man of the book, Nevakhovich gave himself over completely to his writing, committing to the page his innermost thoughts and spiritual experiences. "Some mysterious force calls me to the pen," he confessed. Judah Leib's debut as a writer came with his "Verses" commemorating the day Emperor Alexander I ascended to the throne on March 12, 1801. He signed them "Your Most Loyal Subject, the Jew Leib Nevakhovich." This ode was written in Biblical Hebrew and accompanied by a Russian prose translation. As the cultural scholar Vladimir Toporov wrote, "this ode is utterly devoid of servility or over-glorification. It is, however, extremely diplomatic…, the author underscores both his Jewishness and the poeticism that he has chosen, a poeticism centered around images of

Jewish Biblical tradition." Here is the sort of panegyric the poet addressed to the emperor:

> The beauty of Joseph shines in the features of His image,
> And the wisdom of Solomon reigns in His soul.
> The peoples are delighted by Him in the depths of their hearts,
> And call out as once before Joseph: This youth,
> In the prime of life, yet in learning already a father!
>
> The peoples living under his Scepter alone foresee that
> Never will there be among them sedition out of lack of
> Tolerance and differences of faith.

The use of classically Slavic attributes of elevated style for this genre of celebratory ode is entirely justified and understandable. But there is something else here that is worthy of attention: the intentional usage by a Jewish author of Old Testament allusions (King Solomon, the Biblical patriarch Joseph). As the philologist Oleg Proskurin has noted, "in all the major languages of Europe...the very mention of Jews seems to attest to a division that has taken place between modern Jews (who bear the 'stamp of damnation') and ancient, Biblical reality."

It is noteworthy that in Nikolai Karamzin's *Letters of a Russian Traveler* (published around the turn of the nineteenth century) such a division and even contrasting juxtaposition is quite evident. He writes:

> I wanted to see their Synagogue. I stepped inside as into a gloomy cave, thinking: God of the Israelites, God of the chosen people! Is this where one must come to bow down to Thee? Lamps shone faintly through the fetid air. Dejection, bitterness, and fear could be seen on the faces of those praying; there was no sign anywhere of tender emotion; no cheeks flowed with tears of grateful love; no eyes were turned toward Heaven in reverential rapture. What I saw were criminals, trembling as they awaited their death sentence, scarcely daring to implore their judge for mercy.

For Nevakhovich, concerned by the lack of rights enjoyed by his fellow Jews, it was important that this "stamp of damnation" be removed. He therefore, through the use of Biblicisms, pointed to the very spiritual succession, the

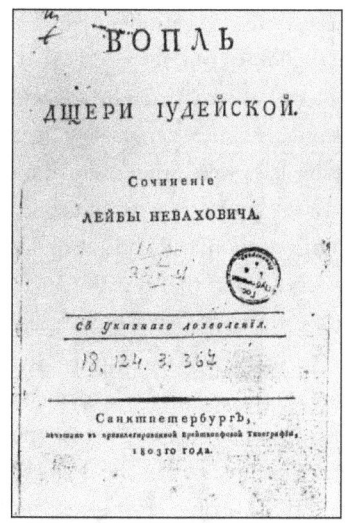 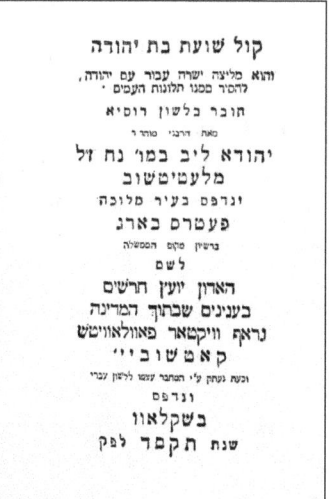

Title pages of Leib Nevakhovich's books Lament of the Daughter of Judah *(in Russian, left, and in Hebrew, right).*

connection between the Jews of his day and the prophets and thinkers of yore. In this regard one line of the poem – "In Thou dwells the heavenly soul of Catherine the Great" – takes on special significance. It was, after all, this empress who mandated that the derogatory word "Yid" (*zhid*) be replaced in government documents with the Biblical word "Jew." When Nevakhovich states that his ode was "Written in Hebrew [by the] Jew Leib Nevakhovich," it is as if he is emphasizing that his work was written by a representative of the people chosen by God, in the language of Holy Scripture. Nevakhovich was not the only proponent of Jewish rights to resort to comparisons between Jewish contemporary reality and that of their ancient forefathers. A striking example of this is Nota Notkin's 1797 memorandum, in which he bases the suitability of Jews to agricultural labor upon Old Testament tradition.

In 1802, the Committee to Improve the Lives of Jews (known simply as the Jewish Committee) was established, with Nevakhovich playing the auxiliary role of consultant to committee members Notkin and Peretz. It was specifically in connection with his work for the Committee that in 1803 Leib published the book *Lament of the Daughter of Judah*, an allegorical depiction of the situation of Jews in Russia in the early nineteenth century, with a dedication to the Minister of Internal Affairs, Viktor Kochubey. In 1804, a revised version of the book was published in Hebrew in Shklov (home to a Biblical Hebrew printing press) under the title *Kol Shav'ath Bath Yehudah,* with dedications to Notkin ("the defender of his people"), and Peretz ("councillor to commerce").

Lament of the Daughter of Judah is the first literary work written by a Jew in the Russian language. It is symbolic that it came out at a time when, raising their voices in defense of their human dignity, Russian Jews were arguing for their people's right to civic freedoms. So it was not just the lament of a daughter, but of all Russian Jews, who had been degraded both economically and morally. For the author of this work it was the moral degradation that was harder to bear than the day-to-day consequences of social ostracism. Nevakhovich laid bare the emotional wounds born by Jews. "To be despised – on top of other troubles!" he writes. "Oh, torment, exceeding any worldly sorrow! Oh, torment, the measure of which no mortal can express! If thunder, wind, storms, and the deafening crash of the ocean could combine with the howl of the despised person to form a single voice: only then would this horrible cry express the magnitude of his suffering."

Possessed of a determined temperament, the author, in a fit of heartfelt indignation, wrathfully unmasks the tired, age-old hatred toward Jews:

> Throughout the ages, people have blamed the Jews...if not for sorcery, then for infidelity or superstition...Before the ages are able to discover the futility of one set of designs against them, new ones have already appeared. Like links in an unbreakable chain, these designs are united in the cause of persecuting this people alone, whose lot is much like that of an unfortunate son, suffering within a family that despises him. His brothers cast his every deed in the worst possible light, and, when his innocence is discovered, ashamed of their past errors, they try to bring down on the sufferer new accusations, as if to prolong his suffering and silence their own pangs of conscience.

The text appeals to the finer sentiments of Christians living side by side with Jews:

> Oh, Christians, renowned for meekness and charity, have pity on us, turn your tender hearts our way! Oh, Christians, you seek Judea in the man – no. Better to seek the man in Judea, and you will undoubtedly find him. But heed my words...I swear that a Jew who preserves a pure image of his religion cannot be an evil person, nor a poor citizen!!!

Writing in the voice of the daughter of Israel, he aims his thoughts and feelings directly at Russians:

> Beloved Russians! It is primarily to you that I address myself, before you I dare to open my mouth, before you, who would condescend and not consider it shameful to engage in conversation with the unfortunate daughter of Israel, despite the fact that I am of another tribe, and law, and that my lot in life is humble…I pour out my heart to you. Finding myself in an abyss of paltriness, I have seen the beneficent son of eternity, the recently-passed eighteenth century, a century of humanity, a century of tolerance, a century of humility, a century without precedent in History, a century that has elevated Russia onto a higher stage of well-being – Russia, which has accepted me as a daughter.

Nevakhovich was insistent in emphasizing that he was a son of the fatherland, that he believed himself to be *a Russian adherent of the law of Moses*. "Love of Tsar and Fatherland, delight in these enlightened times, pleasure and a certain ambition and pride in the fact that I can call Russians my countrymen, along with the commiseration for my fellow tribesmen that consumes my soul – this is how I would describe the spirit that guides my weak pen," he writes in the foreword to his book. The historian Yuly Gessen sees a certain duality in Nevakhovich and points to the fact that he expresses commiseration with his coreligionists while at the same time singing the praises of a people that was often intolerant toward Jews, calling them "a renowned people, a great people." But there is no contradiction here. The affection he feels toward Russians indeed did not come second to his feelings for his own people. If anything, it was stronger. As for the prevalence of anti-Semitic inclinations among Russians, Nevakhovich's goal was to swell the ranks of proponents of Jews – a chimerical thought, but what art is completely devoid of chimera?

The English historian John Klier sees in Nevakhovich's work the direct influence of the ideas of the Haskalah and the eighteenth-century French Enlightenment, as well as the theories of John Locke. He also mentions the "sentimental style" of the narrative. The American scholar Daniel Shiffman discerns here the influence of the father of Russian sentimentalism, Nikolai Karamzin. Indeed, Nevakhovich appeals here not so much to the mind as to sentiment, *to the heart* (he often uses this word) of his "fellow countrymen." The compassionate depictions of Jews in Karamzin's *Letters of a Russian Traveler* were something that the Jewish writer cherished.

The *Statement Concerning Jews* that was released by the Jewish Committee in 1804 was bitterly disappointing to Nevakhovich and dashed his hopes for the emancipation and integration of Jews – even enlightened and virtuous Jews! – into Russian society. The writer drifted away from Jewish topics, but patriotism sounded ever louder in his works. In 1804 he published a philosophical treatise, *Man in Nature: A Correspondence between Two Enlightened Friends*, which is permeated with the ideas of enlightened rationalism. One might think that this was just abstract theorizing, but in the very first letter the author suddenly avows his love for his native land – this despite the fact that the peoples who settled Russia profess a different religion and that among them are those, as he writes, who "do not recognize him as a brother." He professes a belief in the triumph of reason over "prejudice," extolling tolerance and the "fraternal" coexistence of peoples, without wars, plundering, and mutual "callousness."

Worthy of note is an 1806 article Nevakhovich published in the journal *Lyceum*, titled, "Comments Concerning a Review Published in *Allgemeine Literaturzeitung* on 'The Experience of Narratives about Russia' by Yelagin." The author does not so much defend Ivan Yelagin's historical work from the attacks to which it was subjected by foreign critics as muse upon the prestige and authority of Russia. In the very first phrase of his "Comments" he admits, "For a long time now I have wanted to say something in regard to the unfavorable opinion foreigners hold of Russia." He continues in a purely Russophilic spirit: "As unforgivable as it is, on the one hand, that foreigners permit themselves to thoughtlessly condemn Russia and base their judgment on superficial information alone, so too, on the other, is it equally deplorable that Russians hitherto *have permitted* foreigners to think falsely and reprehensibly of them."

He calls Russians "a people famous for quick and extraordinary successes" and makes the following appeal: "The most insulting complaints must at last ignite the fervor of Russians." After condemning certain absurdities concocted by foreign historians writing about Russia, he insistently emphasizes that, "Foreigners, not knowing the Russian language, do not know and cannot know the *spirit* of the Russian people as they exist today...Russians have always had a brave spirit and a language of both depth and breadth."

Here Nevakhovich undergoes a troubling metamorphosis. In 1803, in the *Lament of the Daughter of Judah*, he posed the rhetorical question, "If we renounced our law in order to gain equality of rights, would we make ourselves anymore worthy by doing so?" But in 1806 he abandoned Judaism and converted to Lutheranism (as would his friend Abraham Peretz somewhat later) and married a Christian woman, the German Catherine Michelson. There can be little doubt that Judah Leib, who now went by the name of Lev Nikolayevich, took this step based on purely career-related considerations. Indeed he lost none of his former interest in his fellow Jews. Take, for example, the following bit of evidence: in 1809 we find his name among subscribers to the journal *Me'assef* ("The Gatherer"), which played an important role in the Haskalah cultural movement (it was produced with the involvement of such prominent apologists for the movement as Moses Mendelssohn, Salomon Maimon, and Naftali Wessely [Weisel]).

Lev Nikolayevich's career finally took off. After his christening he was granted hereditary nobility and the rank of Collegiate Registrar, and soon promoted to Provincial Secretary. In 1809 he was given a junior managerial position in a Ministry of Finance revenue office. It turned out that he had a talent for entrepreneurship and, in parallel with his civil service job and in collaboration with the financial genius Peretz, he successfully entered the world of commerce, dealing in military supplies. He gradually developed ties within the bureaucratic world (his close acquaintance with the influential senator, Commissar of the Kingdom of Poland Nikolai Novoliltsev, was particularly useful) and business circles. In 1815 he was promoted to Titular Councillor.

On May 30, 1809, his tragedy, *The Suliots or the Spartiates of the Eighteenth Century: A Historical Tale in Five Acts*, was performed on the stage of the Alexander Theater and was a rousing success. Timed to coincide with the arrival of the king of the Greco-Albanian Republic of Suli, who attended the premiere with Alexander I, the play was all the more topical in that it told of the heroic struggle of the Greek Suliots of lower Albania against their Turkish conquerors. The successful outcome of this struggle for independence was certain to captivate the Russian audience, to say nothing of the tsar himself. In discussing the play, scholars have noted the "exalted patriotism of the 'fearless Greeks,' the exoticism of the staging, the use of choruses in the battle scenes, and the particular attention paid to the feminine heroic nature." The final scenes of the play take on significance specifically for the Russian patriot. The tragedy's heroine, Amseka, the inspiration for victory over the Turks, exclaims, "Descendants of the Lacedaemonians! *Worthy brothers of the valiant Slavs!* [Here is the key idea.] From your own deeds you will learn what a unanimous people can achieve if it truly loves the fatherland – a people that does not want to be defeated is filled with love and trust for its leader and places its trust in God! Let us hurry to the temple to give thanks for the salvation of the Fatherland."

The author dedicated the play to the lady who was well-known to be the tsar's true love, maid of honor Maria Naryshkina, and was shown the monarch's highest favor in being called to the imperial box and given a diamond-studded golden snuffbox. St. Petersburg's best actors took part in the play, including Alexandra Karatygina, Yekaterina Semyonova, Maria Valberkhova, Rykalova, Bobrov, and Sakharov. It is said that when the curtain fell at the end of the premiere, the ruler of Suli and a delegation of Suliots brought Karatygina (who had played the role of Amaseka) valuable gifts. "This drama is among the outstanding works of its kind," gushed the writer Nikolai Gretsch. It continued to be performed for almost two decades.

It seems only natural that Russian patriotism would lead Nevakhovich to become a proto-Slavophile. As early as 1805 we find him defending the poetry of Semyon Bobrov, a follower of the Old Believer and vocal linguistic conservative Alexander Shishkov. In an article entitled "An Opinion on Analyzing the 2nd Canto of 'Taurida'" (*Severnyi vestnik*, 1805, No. 8), he defends the metaphorical complexity of Bobrov's style, arguing that inspiration cannot be subjugated to rules. In 1809 he became close with Alexander Shakhovskoy, the well-known poet, dramatist and future stalwart of the conservative literary society "The Colloquy of Lovers of the Russian Word," in whose home he even lived. Shakhovskoy was engaged in writing a play on an Old Testament theme, *Deborah, Or the Triumph of Faith*, and turned to the Jew Nevakhovich as an expert in scripture and the history of Israel. Shakhovskoy later wrote:

> It is my duty to say that Mr. Nevakhovich, the author of *The Suliots*, was of great assistance to me not only in providing information on Jewish literature, but even (following an outline we devised together) wrote certain scenes of the first and second acts that I proposed…; many thoughts and sayings in the role of the high priest were taken by him from Holy Scripture; almost the entirety of Deborah's political speech was written by him. It is my great pleasure to acknowledge publicly that his gifts, knowledge, and sound mind contributed greatly to the play's success.

The tragedy's plot is based on the Biblical story of the feat performed by the prophetess Deborah, who delivered her people from Canaanite oppression. However, within the context of Russian civic and patriotic poetry of the early nineteenth century, Biblical imagery – specifically that of the Old Testament – took on a special meaning and significance. In the Russian consciousness (especially on the eve of Napoleon's invasion), civic responsibility for the fate of the fatherland was associated with the Old Testament, with the struggle of the ancient Jews to free Israel. Nevakhovich's Jewishness therefore became a positive and meaningful feature within the conceptual framework of Russian patriotism.

It is interesting that those on the other side of the debate between linguistic conservatives and innovators (as represented by the Arzamas Society) that was raging in Russian society at the time exaggerated Nevakhovich's role in composing the tragedy. The writer Dmitry Dashkov penned an acrimonious lampoon entitled "The Buffoon's Wedding" that included the lines:

> Deborah, my tragedy, was very hard to write.
> I had my Jew compose it; my writing's rather trite.
> Since few will read it anyway,
> Why should I labor on my play?

(As an interesting historical side note, Alexander Pushkin, who was a 16-year-old schoolboy at the time, copied these lines into a notebook.)

Nevakhovich's next work was a tragedy, *Oden, King of the Scythians* (1810), a translation from Swedish. It was devoid of literary merit and received a scathing review by Alexander Ismaylov, who called it "the handiwork of the Israelite Nevakhovich." He wrote, "Since the world was created, the theater has not known such a ridiculous play, but this play is a tragedy, and our audiences love a tragedy." The play was short-lived and was only produced twice.

After this debacle, Nevakhovich found new success far from the niceties of literary grandiloquence. In 1813, with the patronage of the all-powerful Novosiltsev, he moved to Warsaw and became the main supplier of food and forage for the Russian army in Poland. He was successful in displacing importunate competitors and in 1816 (again, with help from Novosiltsev) was granted the right to manage the Kingdom of Poland's tobacco monopoly. Expanding on his success, he took control of the sale of spirits and meats in Warsaw and of the collection of revenues on the sale of kosher products there, among other dealings. Beginning in 1821 he served on the Government Finance Commission in Warsaw and was given the Orders of St. Stanislaus and St. Vladimir, both fourth class, as a reward for diligence and zeal. The favor showed him by the powers that be made Lev Nikolayevich one of the richest men in the Kingdom of Poland, the owner of many houses and a luxurious three-story mansion in Warsaw. Although in business circles he earned a reputation as a reliable partner and skilled logistician, small tradespeople and the Polish gentry considered him a plutocrat who was bankrupting their country. It is therefore not surprising that on the very first day of the Polish uprising of November 2, 1830, Nevakhovich's Warsaw home was destroyed by a mob. Fortunately, its owner was unharmed. He had fled a month and a half before this incident, taking money and valuables with him. He would later leave his children a sizable fortune, having appointed his childhood friend Abraham Peretz as the executor of his estate.

But what about his writing? Having achieved success and prosperity in the field of commerce, Lev Nikolayevich seems to have found peace and wrote only infrequently. Gone were the days when he could thrill an audience of readers and theatergoers. The once talented writer had lost his touch. Nevakhovich's later-life efforts deserve no more than a passing mention. In 1817, his translation of T.F. Reinbot's "Sermons on Enlightenment" appeared in the journal *Son of the Fatherland* (Nos. 30-31); in 1823 his Polish-language play *Abu Hassan or the Schemer* appeared briefly on the Warsaw stage. In 1829 Nevakhovich published a translation of the first five books of *Outline of a Philosophical History of Humanity* by the German philosopher and man of letters Johann Gottfied Herder. The translation was subjected to blistering criticism by the journal *The Moscow Telegraph* (1829, No. 17). In 1832, one year after his death, his "historical representation," *The Sword of Foresight, or Nader Tahmasp Qoli Khan*, was performed at the Imperial Theater, but generated little interest.

Nevakhovich is buried in St. Petersburg's Volkovskoye Lutheran Cemetery. The following words are engraved on his tombstone: "There are dwellings, worlds, and space – they all shine with perfect youthfulness, after the passage of millennia; the vicissitudes of time do not deprive them of a radiant light. Here, under your gaze, all is reduced to dust and time threatens the destruction of earthly splendor and earthly happiness. From the works of the deceased."

The cultural historian Vladimir Toporov comments insightfully on Nevakhovich's life:

> He tasted his share of bitterness, experienced failure, ingratitude, disappointment, and the shattering of illusions. Just how he looked back on his "Russian" life from his deathbed we will never know, but in Russia on the cusp of a new century and new millennium, his memory is preserved, or rather has thawed after decades

of being frozen in oblivion and indifference. This memory is appreciative and grateful; it is first and foremost of the man himself and the best of what he did.

NEVAKHOVICH'S MARRIAGE TO Catherine Michelson (1790-1837) produced two sons and a daughter. The older son, Alexander (who died in the 1850s), was a playwright in charge of the repertoire of the Imperial Theater and a translator of vaudeville from the French. In 1829 he staged *Guzman de Alfarache*, a comic farce that enjoyed great success among audiences and, in 1849, *The Poetry of Love*. The younger son, Mikhail (1817-1850), a brilliant writer and caricaturist, was the father of Russian literary caricature and publisher of the popular journals *Yeralash* and *The Magic Lantern*, among others. Two of Lev Nikolayevich's grandchildren (by his daughter, Emilia) were the world famous scientist and Nobel Laureate Ilya Mechnikov (1845-1916) and his brother the famous geographer and sociologist, Lev Mechnikov (1838-1888).

NICHOLAS AND LUDWIG STIEGLITZ

THE BANKER BARONS

It is heartening that the services of the Russian Empire's Barons Stieglitz have now been generally recognized. Their ethnicity, however, is at times treated with embarrassed silence or misrepresented altogether and they are portrayed as Russified Germans. This tendency was pointed out by Dr. Boris Klein who, in an article entitled "Jewish Ethnicity: Facts and Versions," criticized a documentary about the Stieglitzes that was recently shown on Russian television. According to Klein:

> The broadcast repeatedly emphasized that, in terms of ethnicity, the Stieglitzes were Russian Germans. They were distinguished by an innate honesty (a trait we expect in Germans)...The director of the Hermitage Museum, curators of archives, the head of the State Bank, and other distinguished officials took turns developing the documentary's storyline. The general thrust seemed to be that it was high time these patriots were returned to the Russian pantheon.

The historical record tells us that the founder of the dynasty was Lazarus Stieglitz (who died in 1798), a court Jew under Prince Waldeck of Arolsen. Lazarus married a Jewish woman by the name Federica Louisa Marcus. By the standards of the time, the six sons produced by this marriage were given a first-rate education. The oldest, Johann, studied at the renowned University of Göttingen. There is little doubt that Johann, like his brothers, identified with the interests of the German cultural elite. He eventually became a prominent physician and medical advisor in Hanover.

His brother Friedrich set out for northern Slovakia and eventually continued on to Hungary, where we lose track of him. The four remaining brothers –

Nicholas Stieglitz

Ludwig Stieglitz

Emil, Bernard, Nicholas, and Ludwig – entered the sphere of commerce and, sensing that they would be more successful outside of their native land, set out around the turn of the century to seek rank and fortune in distant Russia, which represented great opportunities for financial genius.

Nicholas and Ludwig went on to earn distinction, and while their path was not a bed of roses, in the end Fortune smiled on them and they enjoyed successful careers.

At first Nicholas Stieglitz (1772-1820) lived in southern Russia, where, beginning in 1799 and in collaboration with the well-known Jewish entrepreneur Abraham Peretz, he held major government contracts, supplying Crimean salt to the empire's western provinces.

Nicholas was then granted a government contract to sell liquor. The performance of the duties associated with this contract brought him to the attention of the government. In 1801 he moved to St. Petersburg, where he founded his own trading house.

In 1811, Stieglitz arranged the import of products from the colonies of Western Europe via recently-annexed Finland. He also played an energetic role in the vast undertaking of feeding the Russian Army during the 1812 war against Napoleon. After the war, Emperor Alexander I granted Nicholas nobility in recognition of "great services." The tsar also entrusted the businessman to act as banker in transactions of a "delicate nature." We know, for example, that he used Stieglitz as an intermediary in the 1809 transfer of 13 million rubles of his own money abroad.

Nicholas was also a major patron of the arts. He donated 100,000 rubles to establish Odessa's renowned Richelieu Lyceum, which still exists today. In 1817 he was appointed director of the State Commission to Extinguish Debts. As Minister of Finance Count Georg von Cancrin stated in a report to the tsar, his "zeal and efforts...facilitated our first loans and accelerated the achievement of government goals in one of its most important financial operations." In 1818 he was elevated to the rank of Court Councillor and in 1819 was awarded the Vladimir Cross, fourth class.

After his death in 1820, all of his millions, along with hundreds of thousands of acres and sheep farms that raised a special breed of Spanish sheep, were inherited by his brother Ludwig Stieglitz (1777-1842).

Nicholas had helped his younger brother establish himself, loaning him "seed money" of 100,000 rubles, introducing the relatively inexperienced Ludwig to the St. Petersburg business world and teaching him how to navigate the treacherous seas of Russian commerce. When Ludwig's business floundered, it was Nicholas who put his faith in the lucky star that seemed to shine over the Stieglitz family and again came to his aid, making him another loan.

His faith was not misplaced. Ludwig Stieglitz turned out to be a natural born entrepreneur and the most successful of the Stieglitz brothers. His intelligence, resourcefulness, and foresight ensured his rapid and sustained commercial success. Furthermore, Ludwig was distinguished by a strong work ethic and sense of honesty, two traits that became the hallmarks of his banking house. The bank was established in 1805 under the name "Stieglitz & Co." (by then, its owner was a First Guild merchant). Its offices were located on the English Embankment, in the most prestigious and aristocratic section of St. Petersburg.

In addition to its export operations (of grain and lumber), Ludwig Stieglitz's trading house engaged in the import of goods into Russia that were in particularly short supply. In 1807 he was granted the status of "eternal subject of the Russian state."

Little by little, Ludwig Ivanovich Stieglitz (as he came to be known in Russia) earned the respect of the business world and a reputation that "inspired boundless trust wherever he went." His entry in the *Russian Biographical Dictionary* notes that, "His commercial and manufacturing undertakings enjoyed credit far and wide. A promissory note from Stieglitz, according to his contemporaries, was as good as cash, and his word was more valuable than any promissory note." Stieglitz's popularity was also enhanced by the fact that, unlike foreign banks and Russian moneylenders, he charged a moderate interest rate – 10-12 percent – rather than the traditional 30-40 percent.

Ludwig Stieglitz also made great sacrifices for the sake of the Russian Army during the war against Napoleon, for which Alexander awarded him a bronze medal to be worn on the ribbon of the Anna Cross.

But Stieglitz had even greater ambitions – to serve as personal banker to Alexander I. Holding such a title was a sign of exceptional royal favor, implied enormous trust, and meant arranging all domestic and foreign loans to the Russian government. Ludwig had "friends in high places," such as Minister of Finance Georg von Cancrin and the diplomat Karl Nesselrode, advocating on his behalf. Of course the personal qualities of the candidate himself were his strongest asset, since he had a reputation for consideration and levelheadedness. The staunchness of his character was legendary. There is a story, for example, about how at one point Ludwig Ivanovich found himself suddenly short of urgently needed funds. He turned to a certain influential individual for help but received a refusal. The gentleman in question watched from the window to see how the entrepreneur would behave himself and was struck by his self-possession. Upon stepping outside, Ludwig stopped to pick up a pin that had dropped to the ground and stuck it into the lapel of his waistcoat, behavior that seemed to indicate utter peace of mind. The prospective creditor, intuitively sensing Ludwig's exceptional character, sent a servant after him to give him the necessary sum. It is therefore not surprising that in 1819 "the entire commercial estate pointed to Stieglitz as someone worthy of holding the place of primacy in the St. Petersburg stock exchange."

The prominent Siberian merchant Vasily Basnin, who arrived in the capital in the 1820s, wrote that Stieglitz was always in the thick of people and events. "I spent a long time observing Stieglitz, the well-known wealthy businessman. One could say that he is the soul of the local stock exchange. For three hours without pause he was occupied by the questions and answers of the exchange's brokers, who now total almost one hundred people." The empire's most influential subjects were among the clients of Stieglitz & Co.

On July 22, 1826, in association with the coronation of Nicholas I, Ludwig Stieglitz was elevated to the hereditary rank of Baron, "for services to the government and diligence in the advancement of commerce." Just what services to the government justified endowing an ethnic Jew with such a lofty title in the eyes of the Judeophobic emperor? The fact of the matter was that Stieglitz's reputation for honesty proved to be of exceptional value to the country's finances.

After all, the budget deficit (which annually totaled more than 120 million rubles) and the reform of its financial system compelled Russia to constantly seek funds from abroad, and Ludwig Stieglitz was able to arrange a series of low-interest loans for more than 230 million rubles. Emperors Alexander I and his successor Nicholas I were extremely pleased with these accomplishments. Russia's primary creditors were the major banking houses of London, Paris, and Amsterdam, which at first regarded the royal intermediary with wariness but were soon assured by Stieglitz's impeccable reputation and substantial influence at the upper echelons of Russian imperial power. For anyone preparing to loan money to Russia, the mere mention of his name served as assurance that their money would be in good hands.

Ludwig Stieglitz was involved in a stunningly diverse array of businesses. He owned large sugar-processing and candle plants, the Katerinhoff cotton mill, and merino sheepfolds. He was also one of the first to bring insurance to Russia, another potential source of substantial profits. In 1827 he headed the First Russian Fire Insurance Society, to which he gave the clever name "The Phoenix of St. Petersburg." The idea of an "imperishable" mythic bird rising from the ashes as a symbol of fire insurance certainly shows creative flair.

The renowned Stieglitz stock exchange *artel* (cooperative association) was established in 1833. It resulted out of the merging of two St. Petersburg associations, the Sharapov and Betling *artels*. The *artel* existed under the Stieglitz name into the mid-1920s, outliving both Ludwig Stieglitz and his son Alexander. In 1917 it was renamed the Petrograd Artel and later the Stieglitz Leningrad Artel of Social Labor. The Neva Cotton Mill that he founded, also in 1833, exists to this day (under the name of the Kirov Spinning and Thread Combine).

The first Russian steamship line is also associated with the Stieglitz name. Organized with his active participation, the Society of Stockholders to Establish Continuous Communication between St. Petersburg and Lubeck was granted the privilege of carrying "freight and passengers into and out of the harbors of the Baltic Sea." Another important endeavor for Russia was the creation of the first railroad from St. Petersburg to Moscow. It was through the mediation of the Stieglitz & Co. banking house that in 1841 a foreign loan to the Russian government for 50 million rubles was obtained to build the railroad (which began regular operation in 1851, after Ludwig's death). Also during 1841, Ludwig Stieglitz chaired a committee to build a permanent bridge across St. Petersburg's Neva River.

Among his companies' products that earned gold and silver medals at the All-Russia Exhibitions of 1833 and 1839 were merino wool, cotton, and stearin candles.

"For labors and diligence on behalf of domestic trade and industry" the baron was awarded the Orders of St. Anna second class (1831) and St. Vladimir third class (1836). In 1839 he was entered into the book of noble families of St. Petersburg Province.

His contemporaries remembered Stieglitz as a learned man with an open mind who liked to relax in the company of enlightened people. He intently followed not only Russian, but European literature and was always expanding his collection of books.

Ludwig Ivanovich Stieglitz has also gone down in history as an eminent Russian philanthropist. He provided scholarships to students of the Technological Institute, the Commercial College, and the College of Commercial Seafaring. He also donated 20,000 rubles toward the construction of a three-story stone building with a church at the Commercial College.

His philanthropy went to benefit a vast array of causes. He contributed substantial sums to almshouses and financed a children's hospital. A model home for 150 orphans was established in St. Petersburg exclusively with his funds. However he was not a self-promoter and conducted his charity without fanfare. Stieglitz was inclined to do his good anonymously, without thought of gratitude or rewards. In general, modesty was his dominant character trait.

Ludwig Ivanovich Stieglitz died suddenly on March 6, 1843, of "a nervous stroke." He was 65 years old. On the day of his funeral the St. Petersburg stock exchange closed in mourning. He had indicated his wishes in advance for a simple, low-key funeral. Nevertheless, on his final journey he was accompanied by foreign ambassadors, ministers, and prominent military and civilian officials, as well as members of the Russian merchant estate. A contemporary leaves us the following description:

> The coffin was covered with garlands that loving children had woven out of fresh flowers. There were no baronial coats of arms or crowns. No magnificent carriage followed the coffin, just a modest carriage that the deceased had used in everyday life, covered in black fabric. A large number of those partaking in the procession walked on foot. When the hearse entered Nevsky Prospect it had to stop. This broad avenue up to the intersection with Liteyny Prospect was

completely filled with people. Further on, crowds lined the usually empty streets leading to Volkovo Field.

Ludwig Stieglitz was buried at St. Petersburg's Volkovo Cemetery.

After his death, his 30 million ruble estate went to his son Alexander, who was destined not only to carry on his father's business, but to augment its renown. The services of Baron Alexander Stieglitz to the Russian state are so great that they deserve an entire volume. But throughout his life, this outstanding entrepreneur was always guided by the image of his father, an ethnic Jew who showed him just how a baron should behave.

ALEXEI KOPIEV

THE DISSIDENT JESTER

Although this is not a profession with which Jews are associated, the Russian jester Alexei Danilovich Kopiev (1767-1848) was of Jewish descent. According to the Russian-language *Jewish Encyclopedia*, the progenitor of the Kopievs was "Stepan Ivanovich Kopiev, a Christianized Jew who became a Russian subject with the conquest of Smolensk in 1655." Alexei was not the first Kopiev who was close to the Russian court: Stepan's daughter, Anna (Alexei's great aunt), was married to Peter the Great's vice chancellor, Pyotr Shafirov, to whom the Kopievs were distantly related. Anna's brother (Alexei's grandfather), Samoilo Stepanovich, served as a member of the Collegium of Auditors, while his son, Danilo Samoilovich (the father of our jester), served as first vice governor of Penza Province beginning in 1791 (he died in 1796). The historical record suggests he had a remarkable personality and was "a shrewd person" and "judicious old man." Prince Ivan Dolgorukov refers to his eloquence and perspicacity: "With whomever he spoke he was always very keen-witted," and his "conversation was honeyed."

According to Prince Pyotr Vyazemsky, Alexei resembled his father and "had a rather imposing face; …was very swarthy, with expressive black eyes that were constantly blinking; he spoke with somewhat of an impediment." But if there was a "Kopiev type" it was not limited to physical characteristics. Surely it was from his father that Alexei inherited his insightfulness, his ability to imitate, his brilliant and lively mind, which would later become the calling card of this splendid entertainer and jokester. But Alexei's contemporaries saw no connection between his artistry as a jokester and his Jewish roots. "Is it true that his father was of Jewish descent?" the memoirist Philip Vigel wrote, adding,

"What difference does it make; it is sufficient for me that Daniil Samoilovich Kopiev…belonged to the nation of men who think and act honorably."

Alexei spent his childhood, until his father's death, in Penza, however at the age of eight he was enrolled in the Lifeguards and in 1778 promoted to sergeant in the privileged Izmailovsky Regiment. He entered the regiment, which was garrisoned in St. Petersburg, still wet behind the ears, but with the encouragement of some of the regiment's more experienced and reprobate members, he quickly achieved renown as a first-rate wisecracker. Vigel, his contemporary, had the following to say of the newly fledged sergeant:

> He exhibited neither malice nor a lack of intellect, not a single youthly vice, some of which persist to old age; but on the other hand, there was little to praise him for. All his young contemporaries paraded their impiety and immorality in word more than deed, and this created an impression of jovial but insufferable shamelessness. He tried to outdo them.

Kopiev was especially well known for his mockery of their commander, A.I. Arbenin, a man who was honest and stern, but also extremely kindhearted. Due to his commanding officer's spinelessness and absentmindedness, Alexei was able to get away with it all, which only served to egg him on.

Word of this reckless jokester reached Catherine the Great's favorite, Count Platon Zubov, who drew Kopiev into his circle during the period he was close with the empress (1791-1796) and turned him into something akin to head jester within his rather large and extravagant retinue. As the minion of this all-powerful patron, Kopiev could behave outrageously with impunity, but also enjoyed the benefits of rank, having leapfrogged several grades in the Table of Ranks to become a Lieutenant Colonel in the army. It is not surprising that he soon joined the retinue of Gustav IV Adolf of Sweden, the fiancé of Grand Duchess Alexandra Pavlovna. As Kopiev's old friend Prince Ivan Dolgorukov put it, "He was renowned as an extraordinary mischief-maker. Who did not know him? Who did not remember his countless pranks? Smart, witty, a good writer, simply a wag." Almost no examples of Alexei Kopiev's wit from his days in the service of Zubov have survived. We find only one anecdote about Kopiev, who was known for not feeding his horses well. One day our jokester was riding down Nevsky Prospect in a carriage pulled by a rather emaciated team of horses when he saw Sergei Pushkin (the father of the great poet) walking in the same direction. Kopiev offered to give him a ride. "Thank you kindly," Pushkin replied. "But I cannot: I'm in a hurry!" We also have a clever epigram written by Kopiev about a local beauty:

> Since, Lord, you saw fit to make her,
> Either slake the fire in me,
> Or add to the charms you gave her
> Just an ounce of sympathy.

Eyewitnesses recount that Kopiev was a virtual wellspring of rhymes like these and many that were far racier. Alas, they have not survived.

The talents of Kopiev the satirist found their fullest expression specifically under the protection of Catherine and Zubov, earning him a place among other fine comic playwrights of late eighteenth century Russia. The year 1794 saw the production of two of his comedies in St. Petersburg: *The Converted Misanthrope or the Lebedyan Fair* and *We Don't Even Need What's Ours*. The first is distinguished by lively language, a refreshingly original portrait of daily life, and colorful characters. The protagonist is a landowner by the name of Gur Filatych who is made the subject of ridicule. He is the nephew of another fictional character – Prostakov from Fonvizin's immortal play, *The Minor*, and is just as self-satisfied, limited, and obtuse. Yeremeyevna, the nanny of Fonvizin's eponymous minor, Mitrofanushka, also figures in the plot, but now, having been given her freedom, she is transformed into an unprincipled and pushy matchmaker. The comedy revolves around the idea of the prevalence of "bad will." As evidence, we are given characters such as Gur and Yeremeyevna, along with noblemen with "speaking" names: Prostofilin (Simpleowl), Zateykin (based on the word *zatey*, meaning venture or undertaking), and Nadoyedalov (from the verb *nadoedat'*, to be tiresome), who "tires everyone out with his tiresome existence." They all enjoy the fruits of Catherine's governance, first and foremost the gift of liberty embodied in the 1785 Charter of the Rights, Freedoms, and Privileges of the Russian Nobility. The eminent philologist Pavel Berkov expressed the opinion that every character in this comedy "reflects the intelligent observations of the author, the keen ear of someone with fine knowledge and appreciation of the Russian language, and a penetrating sense of humor that in places turns into sarcasm." After the comedy's premiere, the empress gave Kopiev a diamond-studded snuff box.

The second play, the insightful *We Don't Even Need What's Ours*, is equally interesting. The literary scholar Efim Kurganov points out that in this comedy the author "takes an ironic approach to the long-standing ethical and behavioral norms that he spent a lifetime masterfully undermining and furthermore parodies the positions of his contemporaries, who wound up being the stunned and dumbfounded witnesses of his escapades." Here is a taste of the sort of comic dialogues that were enjoyed at the court of Catherine the Great:

> PRICHUDIN: You're no fool, yet your tomfoolery is endless. You know that in the city they see malicious intent in all your frivolity and caustic abuse in all you pranks, and that many people simply think badly of you for no particular reason.
>
> POVESIN: There's nothing for it, my good man! He who thinks badly, although he seeks the bad, at least thinks. The ones I fear are those capable of thinking neither bad nor good. This sort leaves one no recourse whatsoever!
>
> PRICHUDIN: As usual, you seek consolation in puns.

For Prichudin it is difficult to understand why Povesin (whose name is based on the word for rake or libertine and whose character is a thinly disguised stand-in for the author himself), being a smart man, chooses to excel in the art of acrimonious tomfoolery. For Kopiev, puns and wordplay were his *raison d'être*. According to one eyewitness, "For the sake of a fine word, he might spare his father, but not his mother and sisters, despite the fact that he was very fond of them."

In the memoirs of Varvara Golovina, one of Catherine the Great's maids of honor, Kopiev is described as an "utter parasite, buzzing about the grandees." She obviously had in mind the fact that, during Zubov's reign as Catherine's favorite, our comedian poked fun at anyone, so long as it pleased the powers that be, who rewarded him for this amusement. However, if we look further into the future, to a time when Zubov had fallen from grace and Catherine's son Paul I had assumed the throne, it becomes clear that it was not only unfair but downright absurd to call Kopiev a careerist. Now our jokester – who dared mock the emperor himself, knowing full well how quickly this unbalanced and cantankerous monarch would be to exact revenge – begins to look more like a dissident than a toady. We can only wonder at the depth and subtlety of Kopiev's insight into the psychology of this ruler, who considered the rigorous and conscientious execution of duty to be the highest virtue.

Kopiev's numerous pranks made comic sport of the very thing that the emperor romanticized above all else: blind devotion and loyalty to the tsar. According to one story, Alexei took it into his head to take snuff from Paul's personal snuffbox. At the crack of dawn, the jokester approached the emperor's bed, took his snuffbox, and noisily opened it, making a great show of snorting its contents.

"What are you doing, mischief-maker?" the waking tsar cried out in fury.

"I'm taking some snuff," Kopiev replied. "I've been on duty for eight hours now and sleep was beginning to overcome me. I was hoping that this would refresh me, and I thought that it would be better to violate etiquette than lapse in my official duties."

"You're absolutely right," was Paul's response. "But that snuffbox is too small for two. Take it for yourself."

There is also a story about how Kopiev bet his friends that he would yank the emperor's plait as they dined. Indeed, while sitting at the royal table, he grabbed the monarch's braid and pulled it so hard as to cause pain. When Paul angrily asked for an explanation, everyone present was terrified.

"Your Majesty's plait lay crooked," Kopiev replied calmly. "I permitted myself to straighten it."

"You did well," the tsar replied. "But you might have done so with greater care."

Both of these anecdotes show Kopiev surviving unscathed. One can only assume that this is because the monarch saw his actions as the zealous execution of duty and not as mockery of his royal person.

However, Kopiev had a much sharper and more lethally targeted barb in store for Paul, one to which the emperor could hardly fail to react. The emperor, who had long been captivated by the Prussian military aesthetic, adopted the Prussian dress uniform for his own army, something that was a cause of discontent among his soldiers and officers. Around the time this change was being implemented, our jokester decided to dress himself in a caricature of the Prussian uniform. As the writer Nikolai Gretsch tells it:

> He had a uniform tailored for him with long, broad tails, fixed the sword to the waistband in the rear, and applied a braid [to his wig] that extended down to the knees and fashioned huge ringlets, atop which sat a repulsive three-cornered hat with broad gold galloon, and wore gloves…that extended to the elbows…He assured everyone that this was actually the new uniform.

"Just fine. Very nice!" said Paul once he saw this buffoonish outfit. "To the ranks with him!" That very day Kopiev was dispatched to an army regiment to serve as a soldier. Before his departure he managed to play an exquisite joke on the mean-spirited chief of police, Yefim M. Chulkov (whose last name is based on the Russian word for stocking). The police chief called the comedian to his office and showered him with insults and mockery and finally inquired, "They say you write verse?"

"Yes, sir. There was a time I dabbled in writing."
"Then write me an ode of praise, you hear?"
"Yes, sir, Your Honor!" Kopiev replied and penned the following:

Your father was a stocking;
Your mother was a shoe.
One cannot help from asking,
What kind of bird are you?

But even once he was demoted to soldier, he was no less successful at angering the powers that be, and his irrepressible buffoonery earned him broad renown. Posterity attributes to Kopiev the following epigram, which was surely stinging to Paul, as it mocked one of his pet undertakings – the construction of the brick Mikhailovsky Castle atop the marble foundation of a palace built by Empress Elizabeth.

One ruler built this place
Of marble sure and thick
Another changed its face
And gave it walls of brick.

In the end, even Emperor Paul succumbed to the charms of wit. According to one account, Kopiev wrote him humorous letters and managed to melt the heart of the sovereign, who relented. Paul not only forgave the jester, but restored him to his former rank of Lieutenant Colonel.

A typical episode related by Prince Pyotr Vyazemsky (Kopiev was a frequent visitor to his parents' home) dates from this period. A conversation was underway about a certain man who held a distinguished place in society.

"Evidently you judge people by their rank," Kopiev commented, obviously insulted. "If that is the case, I refuse to return to this house until I hold the rank of general." After making this statement he stormed from the room.

Indeed, Kopiev made a triumphant return to the Vyazemsky household wearing pants with a stripe indicating the rank of general, for his meritorious service had earned him a promotion to Major General. By then, Alexander I was on the throne. It is assumed that Zubov had a hand in this promotion during the short period of his influence over the young tsar.

Kopiev's record also includes service on a commission to deal with Finland, which had recently been absorbed by Russia, and the compilation of a genealogy of the nobility of the Shlisselburg District, but these duties did not change him. In remarks about the 1813 fair in Nizhny

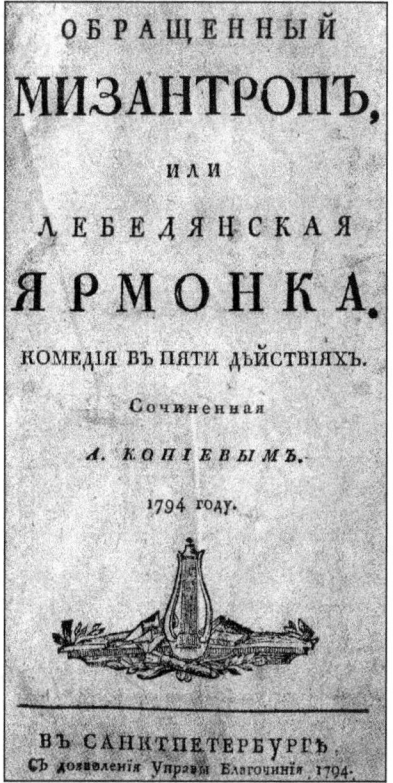

Title page of Kopiev's play The Converted Misanthrope or the Lebedyan Fair.

Novgorod, Prince Ivan Dolgorukov wrote, "I saw the author of *Lebedyan Fair*, the incisive Kopiev. Who does not know him? Always and everywhere he is the same: he jokes, he makes up stories, he laughs from dawn to dusk; …everyone around presses in, listens, and wherever he is there's a crowd."

Whatever apt turn of phrase our jokester came up with, it instantly entered the lexicon of wit. A striking example of this is the story of four young sisters who one day were all awaiting their intendeds and were constantly looking out the window of their Moscow home in anticipation. Walking by, Kopiev commented, "A pancake in every window!" From that time on, the sisters were known as "the Pancake Princesses."

Alexei Kopiev almost never associated with writers and journalists. We do know, however, that he lampooned the avid poet and writer Dmitry Khvostov.

There is also evidence to suggest that the renowned fabulist Ivan Krylov wrote his famous fable "The Liar" after a conversation with Kopiev.

With the passage of time, as Prince Vyazemsky commented about Kopiev, "There were still some attempts at wit, but they lacked the ardor and sparkle that had once been…While the Russian joke remains young, Russian jokesters, like everyone else, can easily age."

Toward the end of his life, the spark of humor disappeared altogether, and the former comedian was consumed by indescribable miserliness and his cynical disregard for the opinions of others only prompted the scorn of those around him. He began to engage in malicious and tedious lawsuits and was constantly buying and selling real estate. According to Philip Vigel, Kopiev also began to exhibit the sort of slovenliness that Russians associate with Plyushkin, the miser of Gogol's novel *Dead Souls:*

> Everything is frayed, everything is stained, everything is soiled, not out of carelessness, but because it has been worn too long. He wore the same green waistcoats for an eternity; people said that for this he buys worn fabric from billiard tables and that you can even see the marks where the balls had once stood.

The loathsome behavior Kopiev exhibited in old age suddenly reminded people that he was a Jew. That same Philip Vigel (who had never had anything bad to say about the Jewishness of Alexei's father) suddenly pointed to "the unabashedly displayed, absolutely Jewish greed for profit, without the slightest twinge of conscience" seen in the former wit in his declining years. One might argue with the memoirist that philanthropy is a trait encountered among Jews much more often than miserliness or acquisitiveness. But what is important here is something else: when Kopiev had been at the height of success and fame, nobody seemed to care about his ethnicity. But as soon as he stumbled, the fact that he was a Jew immediately floated to the surface and was held up as a reproach. Such is life in Russia.

Fortunately, the details of Kopiev's ignominious old age are known to few, while the multitude accounts of his wit are the domain not only of Russian, but of European culture. Many of his witty stories and jokes resonate internationally. They were published repeatedly throughout the nineteenth century in French newspapers and in 1860 Alexandre Dumas included them in his famous *Adventures in Czarist Russia* (although he does not mention Kopiev by name).

The inveterate wit Kopiev became a legend in his lifetime. But today we can take a more thoughtful look at his Jewishness than did his contemporaries. Who knows? Perhaps the time is near when some scholarly investigation will study his jokes, farces, and puns to find traces of a humor that is characteristically Jewish in nature.

GEORG VON CANCRIN

THE ENDURING FINANCE MINISTER

"In the Russian state there are two men who are obligated to serve unto death: I and you," Emperor Nicholas I once said to Count Georg von Cancrin, better known in Russia as Yegor Frantsevich Kankrin (1774-1845). The tsar was not the only one to place such a high value on the work of this statesman. The count's services to the Russian state were, and indeed still are, universally recognized. In his more than 20 years as finance minister, Cancrin made himself utterly indispensible to Russia. He reined in inflation, balanced the budget, strengthened the ruble, and promoted the development of Russian industry.

Born in Hanau in the Hesse region of Germany, he practiced Lutheranism and looked every bit the Prussian. He spoke Russian with a strong German accent and never learned to write well in any language but his native one. He was always thought of as an ethnic German and to this day is included in the authoritative reference, *The Germans of Russia*.

But none of this is enough to elude the unrelenting vigilance of Russian "patriots." The anti-Semitic *pochvennik* Andrei Diky tells us that Cancrin was the son of none other than a "Lithuanian rabbi." Aleksandr Solzhenitsyn makes the same claim in his book *Two Hundred Years Together*, stating merely that Nicholas' finance minister was "the son of a rabbi."

In reality, the father of our finance minister, Franz Ludwig von Cancrin, belonged neither to the Jewish faith nor to Lithuania. He was, however, a very prominent figure in his time. He earned his renown as a scholar and writer, leaving his mark on the fields of technology, architecture, mining, and law, among others. In fact, he was so prolific that his works could fill a small library. At a time when Germany was a patchwork of dozens of principalities (nearly a hundred), Franz Ludwig moved from one to the other, overseeing mining, salt-extraction, and construction operations, his unyielding personality never permitting him to serve the same prince elector or margrave for long. Finally, in 1783, his fame earned him a place of distinction in Russia, along with a sizable income and the elevated rank of Actual State Councillor, as well as the important post of Director of Salt Factories. He later became a member of the Collegium of Mines.

Suspicions that Minister Cancrin was a Jew are not without foundation, however it was his grandfather rather than his father who was the rabbi. One well-informed contemporary, Philip Vigel, writes, "Learning was heritable property in his [Cancrin's] family. His grandfather, the Rabbi Cancrinus, who took the name of Ludwig not through holy christening but in the reform manner, was quite well-known, if not to the whole world, at least within the world of German scholarship." The belief that the Cancrins were of Jewish descent is expressed as well by Alexander Ribopierre in his *Notes* and by Benjamin Disraeli in his novel *Coningsby*. The contemporary historian Vladimir Novikov adds that the progenitor of the line, the Jew Cancrinus, also resided in Hesse and adopted a Christian name and faith during the first third of the eighteenth century.

This explains why Georg von Cancrin (and his father, for that matter) was completely unfamiliar with the Jewish religion and Yiddish culture. He seemed barely aware of his ties to the people of Israel. Does that mean, however, that there was nothing characteristically Jewish in his way of thinking? For the time being we will merely point to the remark by Philip Vigel that "despite the fact that he liked to pass himself off as a German..., the vibrancy of another [Jewish] ancestry was manifested not in actions, not in his deeds, but in his words. He had an exceptionally sharp wit."

Georg himself began to manifest the family trait of an "exceptionally sharp wit" during adolescence. The influence of Franz Cancrin, who honed his son's perceptive mind by developing an interest in the technical disciplines and jurisprudence, is unquestionable. Georg was a gifted and eager pupil, always quick to grasp the essence of whatever was under discussion. After receiving a classical education in Hanau (even in his later years he retained a good bit of Latin), Cancrin was first admitted to the University of Hesse, but, not quite satisfied with the level of instruction there, transferred to Marburg University. He graduated in 1794 after a brilliant university career. It was during his student years that Georg first tried his hand at writing, producing *Dagobert, A Novel about the Current War for Liberation*. Suffice it to say that this work is quite conventional and has the expected ventures into the realm of romantic love.

One of the work's more noteworthy aspects is its characterization of Emanuel Kant's philosophy, of which the author states that, although it does not reveal the truth, it is a brilliant breakthrough in this direction and therefore excites a sense of sympathy. Even back then Cancrin showed himself to be a true statist, emphasizing in the novel that the efforts of any government must be aimed first and foremost at promoting prosperity and greatness.

After graduating from university, Georg did not succeed in finding employment in his native Germany. So in 1798, at his father's urging, he set out for Russia. However, due to the obstinate natures of both Cancrins, father and son soon quarreled and Georg found himself with no means of support. Taking up residence in St. Petersburg, he was awarded the not insignificant rank of Court Councillor, but without position or salary. Lacking knowledge of Russian and connections, he was ready to take on any work that came his way and tried tutoring, brokering, and keeping the accounts of a wealthy *otkupshchik* (tax farmer of liquor revenue). For a while, he was secretary to the Jewish entrepreneur Abraham Peretz. Georg lived in near-destitution for three years, a time when he developed the habits of thrift and moderation that would later set him apart from the other men at the upper echelons of imperial power. The extent of his frugality (if not stinginess) would be fully manifested once he wore the mantle of power. After he became minister, he prohibited the use of expensive sealing wax, replacing it with less costly flour paste and causing several sealing wax factories to go bankrupt. Cancrin was not, however, callous, a trait that frequently went hand in hand with miserliness. On the contrary, he was always ready to help the poor and needy, having suffered at the hands of poverty himself.

In 1800, fortune finally smiled on Georg when a plan he had drafted for improving sheep breeding in Russia made a favorable impression on Count Heinrich (Andrei Ivanovich) Osterman, Russia's vice chancellor. Osterman's patronage gained him a job at the salt factories, working as an assistant to his own father, and in 1803, a transfer to the Ministry of Internal Affairs, to work in the Department of State Property. Knowledge, administrative ability, and business acumen combined with an appealing unaffectedness to earn him the respect of colleagues and rapid promotion through the ranks. Within six years he had risen to State Councillor. This rapid rise is all the more noteworthy in that Cancrin never resorted to toadyism or servility. His unwavering self-respect can be seen in a story passed down about an encounter he had with the well-known timeserver Count Alexei Arakcheyev. The Count summoned

Cancrin and addressed him using the familiar second-person pronoun *ty* as he went over a number of issues concerning the management of forests on his estates. Cancrin heard him out in silence and then turned and left the room without saying a word. Arakcheyev then demanded that the Minister of Internal Affairs officially assign Cancrin to work with him. In the end, Arakcheyev appears to have drawn a lesson from the incident and suddenly invited Cancrin to dine with him, henceforth addressing him with all due courtesy and respect.

Georg von Cancrin

His work inspecting and organizing the timber and salt industries took Georg to many of the empire's provinces, including some of its more remote reaches. He became well acquainted with the bountiful resources of his adopted country and developed a true affection for its people and their language. Contemporaries attest to the fact that Cancrin wove Russian proverbs into his conversation, which, due to his imperfect mastery of Russian grammar, at times created a rather humorous effect.

In 1809 Cancrin produced *Passages Regarding the Military Art from the Perspective of Military Philosophy*, which was printed in two editions. In this work he expressed the thought that in wartime the state must take advantage of its geography: the vastness of its territory, the great length of communication lines, the severity of its climate, etc. This work provoked avid interest in military circles, where a debate was raging about whether war with Napoleon, should it occur, would be aggressive or defensive. *Passages* also attracted the attention of Russian War Minister Mikhail Barclay de Tolly, the military theoretician General Karl Ludwig von Phull, and Emperor Alexander I himself, who was informed that Cancrin was a "knowledgeable and capable man, but with a bad character."

Cancrin was promptly put to work developing plans for the impending war, where issues of supply would be crucial. In 1811 he was appointed assistant to the Purveyor-General for all forces, with the rank of Actual State

Councillor. When war did break out, he was elevated to Quartermaster General. It should be noted that, under Cancrin's management, the Russian army was kept continuously supplied by the Jewish entrepreneurs Nicholas and Ludwig Stieglitz, as well as Abraham Peretz (the latter was subsequently ruined by the government's failure to reimburse him). It is a credit to Cancrin's energy and organizational talents that the Russian army was well supplied over the entire course of military operations. In this regard, the war of 1812-1815 differed from later conflicts, such as the Crimean War, during which embezzlement and abuses by officials often left soldiers without bread and proper footwear. Furthermore, expenditures under Cancrin were stunningly modest: 157.5 million rubles for three years of war (while the first year of the Crimean campaign alone cost Russia 300 million rubles). A decisive role was played here by the irreproachable honesty of the Quartermaster General himself. After all, given his unchecked authority over army funds, he would have been able to make millions in bribes. Instead, Cancrin was scrupulous in checking accounts and wound up paying only a fraction of them, demonstrating that many of the charges were fraudulent.

Cancrin's talents were highly valued by Mikhail Kutuzov, who took his advice and often supported his proposals. The Field Marshal particularly appreciated Cancrin's ability to keep units supplied under what seemed to be impossible situations. For example, in May of 1813, during the days of heaviest fighting at Bautzen in Saxony, when 200,000 allied troops were concentrated along a narrow front line, Alexander I, deploring the exceptional difficulty of the situation, personally appealed to Cancrin for help. His confidence was not misplaced. The Quartermaster General succeeded in delivering supplies exactly where they were needed.

It was Kutuzov who saved Cancrin when he was facing imminent dismissal. The Quartermaster had provoked the ire of Grand Duke Constantine by interceding on behalf of the residents of a German town who had suffered at the hands of unruly allied troops. The incident was resolved through the intervention of the Field Marshal, who told the Grand Duke, "If you remove people who are critically needed by me, the sorts you cannot get for a million, then I myself will be unable to remain in my post." For services to Russia during the war of 1812-1815, Georg Cancrin was awarded the Order of St. Anna, first class.

When the war ended, for a while Cancrin was left without a position, although he remained a member of the Military Council. In 1816 he married

Yekaterina Muravyova, the cousin of the future Decembrist Sergei Muravyov-Apostol, after meeting her at a ball at Barclay de Tolly's headquarters. The marriage was a happy one and Yekaterina became muse and faithful helpmate to her indefatigable spouse. They had four sons and two daughters.

It is noteworthy that in 1818 this foreigner in Russian service presented the emperor with a paper titled *A Study of the Origins and Abolition of Serfdom or the Dependence of Farmers Primarily in Russia*, in which he proposed a plan to emancipate Russian peasants by gradually buying their freedom using loans from a special bank. Under this plan, the peasants would have taken over final ownership of their lands by 1850. Unfortunately, the government did not give this proposal the attention it deserved. "If his plan had been adopted," one historian wrote, "our governmental and economic life would have developed more normally and the emancipation of the peasants would not have caused so much upheaval in the economic life of Russia as the reforms of 1861 inevitably did."

Cancrin also made contributions to the literature of economics and finance, enriching these fields and gaining European renown. He published two monographs: *Military Economy in Times of War and Peace* (1820-1823) and *World Wealth, National Wealth, and State Economy* (1821). This second work is of particular interest. In essence, the author spells out his own program for managing the country's finances. In it he writes:

> It is necessary to avoid extremes and elude four great apocalyptic beasts: a decrease in the value of money, paper money, excessive government debt, and the artificial accumulation of commercial capital, as well as to bring expenditures into strict correspondence with natural income, striving to increase the latter *by encouraging the people to work hard through order and good governance, only in the extreme case resorting to moderate debt* so that it can be repaid at the first opportunity.

Cancrin subjected the actions of his predecessor as finance minister, Dmitry A. Guryev, to scathing criticism (Guryev is known to history less for any economic achievements than for a special variety of kasha he invented).

When Cancrin replaced Guryev in 1823, he immediately set about putting his own economic theories into practice with remarkable energy and thoroughness. In the history of the Russian Empire, no finance minister remained in that post longer than Cancrin, who held it for 21 years.

What was the state of the imperial economy when Cancrin came on the job? It would not be an exaggeration to describe it as catastrophic. By 1821 the overall government debt had reached 408 million rubles, and since then expenditures had gone up while revenue had gone down. At times, the deficit had reached one-seventh of total revenues. The manufacturing sector was stagnant. Depressed grain prices were leading to bankruptcies in the agricultural sector. Domestic commerce was languishing. Foreign trade had fallen from 130 million to 92 million rubles per annum. To make matters worse, there had been a significant outflow of metal monies abroad and the value of the assignation (paper) ruble had fallen in value to 25 kopeks. The country therefore lacked a stable currency, with both paper currency and coins constantly fluctuating in value. But the biggest problem was that there was simply no money in the treasury.

First of all, Cancrin focused his efforts on fighting the budget deficit and on creating new monetary reserves. With unwavering firmness, putting in 15-hour days, he fought off all attempts to raid the treasury. He exposed bribetakers, dealt mercilessly with anyone caught embezzling public funds, and was always able to prove that a given matter could be handled with less money than was being requested. As a result, he cut the military budget by 20 million rubles and the Ministry of Finance budget by 24 million rubles. In his first years on the job he cut expenditures by one-seventh and accumulated 160 million rubles of state capital.

In his drive to build monetary reserves, Cancrin at times was compelled to resort to economic measures he disapproved of in principle. For example, in 1827 he restored the *otkup* system, which employed tax farmers to manage and collect revenues from the sale of alcohol through taverns, lamenting that "It is distressing to manage finances when they are based on revenues from drunkenness." However this measure increased revenues from 79 million to 110 million rubles. He raised customs duties, as a result of which the influx of revenues to the treasury from this source increased from 31 million rubles to 81 million. In addition to generating income, protectionism of this sort helped to prop up a frail domestic industrial sector, although (as Cancrin himself understood), as time went on, the absence of foreign competition could harm the empire's economy.

Cancrin also paid close attention to the mining industry, increasing revenues there from eight to 19 million rubles and increasing gold extraction from less than half a ton to more than 18 tons. He also wrote *Instructions on the Management of Mining Facility Forests in the Ural Range Applying the Rules of*

Forestry and Sound Economy, which would become the best forestry textbook of his day. These instructions dealt with many issues, for example the harvesting of bark from young oak trees for use as a tanning agent. He also oversaw an effort to plant trees to stop the expansion of the Alyoshkovsky (Oleshky) Sands in Ukraine, the largest expanse of sand in Europe.

Georg Cancrin deserves recognition for the advances in Russian education that he promoted. "Russia utterly lacks the class of people possessing middle-level theoretical knowledge that it needs for the most diverse fields of endeavor," he wrote to Alexander von Humboldt, the renowned naturalist. In an effort to repair this deficiency, Cancrin founded the St. Petersburg Practical Technological Institute and expanded the Forestry Institute (the latter institute was nicknamed "Cancrinopolis" by his contemporaries). He was also a driving force behind the establishment of the Mining Institute and Gorygoretsky Agricultural Institute. He was a patron of numerous institutions of learning: art schools under the Academy of Arts, one of which featured the first galvanoplastics departments in Europe; Moscow's Gymnasium No. 3; schools of commercial shipping in St. Petersburg and Kherson; and navigation classes in Arkhangelsk and Kem. The special classes that he established for girls represented a great innovation at the time.

Despite his characteristic thrift, the minister was never parsimonious toward the needs of education. "Yes, I'm a miser when it comes to everything that isn't needed," he liked to say. Cancrin arranged to have young Russians study abroad, kept an eye on the latest foreign innovations in manufacturing, and organized competitions among manufacturers. In short, he marshaled every possible resource to advance Russian industry. He established a *Journal of Mining* and *Commerce Gazette* and was the initiating force behind the publication of the *Agriculture Gazette*, which was edited by the former director of the famous lyceum at Tsarskoe Selo, Yegor Engelhardt, an expert in the field. To broaden the reach of this publication Cancrin allocated a governmental subsidy to keep the annual subscription price below one ruble. He also made sure that the newspaper's correspondents included a number of peasants who reported their practical experiences in agriculture. The paper published a piece by Cancrin himself about dividing Russia into climactic zones that attracted the attention of European scholars.

Cancrin managed to convince Nicholas I to invite Alexander von Humboldt to Russia. Significant sums were allocated toward the German naturalist's travels through the Urals, the metal- and mineral-rich Rudny Altai belt, and along the

Caspian Sea coast. Fresh horses awaited him at every post station and a military convoy was provided where safety was a concern. The expedition resulted in Humboldt's monograph *Central Asia*, which represents a major contribution to nineteenth-century science. In 1829, Humboldt wrote to Cancrin of his travels across Russia, "I owe it to you that this year, due to the huge number of ideas I collected over a vast space, became the most important of my life." The year also proved to be one of the most important in Cancrin's life, as this is when the emperor gave him the title of Count. Humboldt wrote in congratulation, "This outward luster will remind posterity of the commemorative time when Russian finance flourished under your guidance." In 1832, Russia's highest honor was bestowed on the count: he was made a knight of the Order of St. Andrew the First-Called "for management of the Ministry of Finance, excellent prudent thoughtfulness and unwavering fervor in the improvement of this important part of governmental administration, and for many useful designs, their painstaking execution and vigilant oversight..." In 1834 he was given diamonds to adorn this order.

In 1838 Cancrin read a series of lectures on the science of finance to the heir to the throne, the future Alexander II, which were published in 1880 under the title *A Brief Overview of Russian Finance by Count Ye. F. Cancrin*.

Cancrin's most significant contribution to Russian history was the monetary reform he undertook in 1839-1843. In June 1839 a decree was circulated proclaiming, "The silver coin will henceforth be considered the main currency. Assignations[1] will henceforth be considered subsidiary symbols of value and their rate of exchange against the silver coin will be set at one silver ruble to 3 rubles 50 kopeks in assignations." Cancrin felt it would be wise to establish a special office to issue notes of deposit in exchange for currency that could be traded in for silver money on demand. It is to his credit that this deposit fund earned the trust of the population and rapidly grew. When it reached 100 million rubles it was moved with great fanfare to the Peter and Paul Fortress in the presence of top government officials and members of the nobility and merchant estate. This event marked Russia's rejection of paper currency and its adoption of monometalism, the basing of the currency on a single metal. Finally, in 1843, a manifesto was issued ordering the destruction of all assignations, which could be exchanged for notes of credit: 596 million paper rubles were exchanged for notes of credit totaling 170 million silver rubles.

---

1. Paper rubles.

The authoritarian Nicholas I was not known for prizing initiative in his ministers and demanded strict adherence to all his orders. He made an exception, however, in the case of his brilliant and independent-minded Minister of Finance. The emperor was even willing to listen to any objections he raised, realizing that statesmen like Cancrin are hard to find. Nicholas forgave the count his unkempt greatcoat, his habit of wearing his trousers tucked inside his boots, and the woolen scarf he kept tied around his neck, although he held others to strict rules of military dress. At one point the emperor made a comment to Cancrin about his attire, to which the count replied, "Your Majesty would certainly not wish me to catch cold and be confined to my bed. Who would work in my place?" The emperor not only resigned himself to Cancrin's manner of dress, but even allowed him to puff away at his pipe, which was stuffed with cheap tobacco, while making his reports, although in general Nicholas did not tolerate smoking.

Cancrin took no pleasure in high society and avoided official receptions, balls, and celebrations. On the other hand, he was an ardent lover of poetry, music (he played the violin), and architecture, penning an original work entitled *Elements of the Beautiful in Architecture* (1836). Despite leading a rather cloistered life, he often invited writers into his home and loved to converse with Alexander Pushkin, Pyotr Vyazemsky, and Vladimir Benediktov, among others. The count wrote theater reviews, as well as short stories, which were published in 1844 in a collection entitled *Fantasies of a Blind Man*. He also kept a journal.

A man of enviable wit, he sprinkled his speech with striking images, metaphors, comparisons, and juxtapositions. His very original way of putting things generated a number of anecdotes, including one in which he complains to the emperor about the large number of flaws in an order that he took part in drafting. "Why did you not raise any objections while it was under discussion?" the emperor asked. "Your Majesty," replied Cancrin, "the text was read so quickly, it was like snipe hunting: paragraphs flew by left and right, like snipes. Some I noticed and shot down in flight, while others flew right by." Another time Cancrin was asked why he never attended funerals. He replied that "There is only one funeral a person is required to attend: his own." Once, when a fellow was talking with pride of an honorable deed he had done, Cancrin broke in with the comment, "He might as well be praising himself for not being born a woman." When it was suggested that he should write his autobiography he replied, "I am too truthful to enjoy a sense of my own truthfulness."

In 1844, a severe illness compelled Cancrin to step down from his post, but even then he was not idle. He continued to work on his main opus, *The Economics of Human Society and the Financial Science of One Former Minister of Finance*. He died in Pavlovsk on September 9, 1845. Not long before he passed away he made the following entry in his journal.

> Over the course of my life, through days of sorrow and joy, I strove to achieve a single goal: to do good for people, to help them succeed, to borrow useful ideas, and to spread knowledge and civilization. Those who know me can say whether or not I achieved anything and to what extent.

But let us return to those who are primarily concerned with the chemical makeup of the blood of this outstanding figure rather than his actual services to Russia. The Russian-born American sociologist Pitirim Sorokin explicitly refers to Cancrin as a Jew in his book *Russia and the United States* (1944). One nationalistic writer refers to him as "the Jew-Count Cancrin." In fact, Georg Cancrin, with only one Jewish grandparent, did not see himself as belonging to an outcast people. Furthermore, he felt no particular sympathy toward Jews. In his book *Tsar Nicholas I and the Jews*, the American historian Michael Stanislawski counts Cancrin among the traditionalist pragmatists who, while disagreeing with some of the tsar's repressive measures, generally shared his chauvinistic views.

Whether he was aware of his Jewishness or not, he exhibited many characteristics associated with Jews. As the historian Rostislav Sementkovsky noted:

> Cancrin really did combine many typical traits of the Jewish tribe. He had a lively temperament, an exceptionally sharp wit, he loved science and literature, but at the same time had an excellent grasp of the demands of real life and was exceptionally practical and prudent, while enjoying poetry and art and loving beauty in all its manifestations, although he himself was far from always making an aesthetically pleasing impression with his brusque, awkward manners, primarily due to the slovenliness of his attire.

Therefore, when Cancrin is falsely labeled "the son of a rabbi," we should not be in any hurry to argue. If "patriots" think they have done harm to the Jewish cause by "exposing" a man like Cancrin to be a Jew, they are sorely mistaken. In so doing, they have revealed another example of the inestimable contributions Jews have made to Russian history and culture.

LEON MANDELSTAM

THE LEARNED JEW

Leon Iosifovich Mandelstam (1819-1889) was the first Jew to graduate from a Russian university and to publish a collection of poetry in Russian. He translated the works of Alexander Pushkin into Hebrew, and the renowned twentieth-century poet Osip Mandelstam was his great nephew. But these impressive facts only begin to tell his story.

In his youth, Mandelstam did something that was utterly unprecedented for a Jew: he left his father's home and set out for Moscow to study at the university. On the road to Moscow he met a cantor who, upon learning of the purpose of his journey asked, "Why go there? You could be the first among your own people, but you are leaving everything behind to be the last among Christian scholars." Mandelstam parried: "It is written in the Talmud that it is better to be the tail among lions than the head among foxes!"

The cantor was certainly not the only Jew to feel baffled by the actions of this young man. Most distressed of all was his own family, who perceived the step he was taking as a step away from their Jewish world. "Your father gave you clothing, and you are going to adopt different dress," his brother appealed. "Your mother played with your curls, and you are going to cut them off. You will be speaking a language that we do not understand, and you will write in a hand that we do not know…"

This is not to say that Leon came from the most orthodox of families. He was born in the town of Zhagory in Vilna Province, located near the border with Courland (a territory that comprised parts of modern day Lithuania and Latvia). Zhagory (present day Žagarė) was an important commercial center with a population of 3,000, half of whom were of Jewish descent. The ideas of the Haskalah, the Jewish Enlightenment, and Moses Mendelssohn, its founder,

Leon Mandelstam

which found lively and striking expression in the German Hebrew-language periodical *Ha-Me'assef*, fell on fertile ground here. The population of Zhagory, which was eager to take part in this Enlightenment, were quite carried away by this periodical.

Leon's father, Joseph (Iosif) Mandelstam, who was born circa 1780, was an erudite and energetic man. An eminent merchant, his business took him far and wide through Russia, Poland, and Germany. He was knowledgeable in the Talmud and Jewish literature and was no stranger to Haskalah ideals. Joseph saw to it that Leon was given not only a traditional Jewish education, but a general one as well, including foreign languages and European literature. Leon himself later wrote,

> Day and night I studied the Talmud, and by the age of 12 I had earned myself the epithet of *iluy* [prodigy] and symptoms of tuberculosis. Thanks to my father and older brothers, I read a great deal by the followers of Mendelssohn and, later, the philosophy of Maimonides and Spinoza.

Along with Hebrew he mastered German and French and even tried his hand at writing in these languages in the spirit of the romanticism, which was popular at the time.

At the age of 16 he began to immerse himself in Russian and mastered it so well that, after a few years, he was able to compose not only prose, but poetry in Russian. He demonstrated such an envious mastery of versification that he was able to contend with the intricate rhythms of the Russian sonnet. His poetic experimentation resulted in a book-length manuscript that he took with him wherever he went.

Mandelstam's self-education was interrupted for a time by his early marriage. Leon's 17-year-old bride (the choice of his father, who insisted on an early marriage) belonged to an entirely different world. In the home of Leon's father-in-law, in the shtetl of Kedainiai in Kovno Province, where young Mandelstam moved after the wedding, militant orthodoxy reigned supreme. His "extracurricular" activities – reading anything other than the Talmud – were viewed as blasphemous. Leon was not able to stay in this house for long. Soon he was again under his paternal roof and shortly thereafter divorced his wife.

Leon was consumed by an impulse to defend and enlighten his people, the great majority of whom, alas, lived in total alienation from contemporary European culture. This sense of messianic purpose overcame him very early. At the age of 20 he committed his innermost feelings to paper.

> Here I now stand – a wild, strong, free son of nature, full of love for my country and the language of my native land, but miserable for the misery of my coreligionist brethren. Their close-mindedness, which undermines their abilities, enrages me, but I am bound to them by ties of blood and a sense of their misfortunes. My life's goal is to exonerate them before society and help them to be worthy of this exoneration.

A thirst for the most diverse knowledge provoked in him the desire for a systematic education, which would only be possible far from hearth and home, in the capital. One is reminded of *The Lottery Ticket*, a story by Sholom Aleichem in which a young Jewish man leaves the shtetl and goes to study in the big city. The story has a tragic ending: in order to get ahead in life, the educated Jew renounces the faith of his ancestors, for which his family curses him and considers him dead. But this was not the case here. Leon not only did not betray his faith, but centered all his aspirations around the Jews, making his concern for his coreligionists the meaning of his life. Here is the "Parting Thought" he dedicates to his native Zhagory the night before his departure:

> Paternal hearth, sleep, for your friend,
> Your genius watches over you;
> For you alone, you can depend,
> He left to join the fray and hue,
> For you he travels hills and narrows,
> For you he faces fortune's arrows,
> No other purpose drives him forward
> You are his glory, his reward.

Mandelstam managed to evade "fortune's arrows," indeed Russian *Fortuna* clearly favored him. He moved to Vilna in order to take an examination at the provincial *gymnasium* to demonstrate he had had an equivalent education. His first attempt did not succeed, which was not a calamity, since his second bore fruit. The superintendent of the Vilna school district wrote about him to the Rector of Moscow University:

> On Mandelstam's second attempt, the council of the Vilna Gymnasium, although it does not recognize in him knowledge corresponding to a full course of *gymnasium* study, finds his knowledge sufficient for entry into the university… Based on this finding and bearing in mind the natural ability of the aforementioned Mandelstam, who constitutes an exceptional phenomenon among his coreligionists, his love for scholarship and extraordinary gift for languages and literature…, I have decided to send him to Moscow University as an auditor.

By order of the Minister of Education, Count Sergei Uvarov, Mandelstam was admitted to attend university lectures "without further examinations."

Rather strange, is it not? The Jew fell somewhat short on the examination, and yet the superintendent gave him a diploma and, on top of that, wrote him a letter of recommendation. His Excellency the Minister immediately enrolled him as a student. Somehow this preferential treatment is hard to reconcile with the Jewish quota system we usually associate with tsarist Russia.

Mandelstam would ultimately live to witness such restrictive (not to say Judeophobic) measures. But then, in the thirties and forties of the nineteenth century, Jews were hardly clamoring to enter universities; they kept to their shtetls, fully walled off from Russian life, language, and culture. For this reason, the government's educational policy toward them was quite different from what it would later be. Blaming Jewish separatism on the Talmud and rabbinical "fanaticism," the authorities proclaimed their main objective to be the moral and religious transformation of the Jewish nation – basically making the empire's Jewish population more like its Christian one. For this it would be necessary to create a network of schools and public colleges in which, together with Judaism (and a modernized Judaism at that, since the goal was to eliminate the Talmud from the curriculum, although study of the Bible in its German translation and with Mendelssohn's commentaries was highly recommended), general subjects would be taught, including mathematics, physics, rhetoric, geography, foreign languages (Russian first and foremost), Russian history, and literature.

The Minister of Education, Count Uvarov, began to bring this reform to life. It was during his tenure that the semi-official division of Jews into "useful" and "useless" began to emerge. The *maskilim* were included among the "useful": the government of Nicholas I was counting on them. Minister Uvarov, unable to find a "Russian Mendelssohn," recruited the German Jew Max Lilienthal to become involved in Jewish education in Russia and corresponded with a number of Western European Jews in order to "import" teachers for Jewish schools. One can only imagine that it must have been music to his ears to hear that, within the borders of the Russian Empire, in Vilna, there was a Jew seeking to enroll in Moscow University. This is why Mandelstam's enrollment in Moscow University (he later transferred in St. Petersburg University) was worthy of a ministerial decree. Furthermore, Uvarov kept close track of Leon's academic progress.

Being, by nature, a rather complex person, Leon combined a propensity for scholarship with poetic dreaminess. Soon after his arrival in Moscow he made his debut as a writer, publishing – under the patronage of an unknown sponsor – *The Verse of L.I. Mandelstam* (1840). If for no other reason, this book is of interest because it is the first collection of Russian poetry published by a Jew.

A letter survives from Mandelstam to a certain Alexander Vasilyevich (possibly the mysterious sponsor?), in which Leon reveals the book's creative impulse, its goal and purpose. He writes of the imperfections of his work and asks critics to point out to him "errors of expression, meter, and word," among other things. But the inspiration of this work is exceptionally significant. Mandelstam writes, "I look at my verse as a translation from Hebrew, a conceptual and literary translation...; the gloomy, martyred specter of a disembodied spirit, like Judaism, weaves its way through my writing...You will find [here] that fervent passion, those anguished sighs, that are characteristic of "the world's unfortunate outcasts."

The creators of today's Russian-language *Short Jewish Encyclopedia* took these words literally and concluded that the verse was actually translated from Hebrew. In fact Mandelstam, who was completely fluent in Russian, had something else in mind: he was referring to that special Jewish spirit that imbues the collection's poems (indeed, the author calls them "the fruits of my soul"). In so doing he underscores that his book does not so much belong to Russian literature as to Russian-language *Jewish* culture. In this he could not have failed to see himself as an heir to the Jewish writer Lev Nevakhovich, the author of *Lament of the Daughter of Judah*, which was written in Russian in defense of his fellow Jews. Summarizing his own work, Mandelstam wrote, "This composition, as a rarity on the part of the Russian Jew, can serve as a pretext for various conversations about my nation, and, if possible, lend my coreligionists a few words of defense and comfort!" He angrily condemned those Russian novelists and satirists who strove to "debase the Jew in society's eyes." Suffice it to recall the caricatures of Jews in the works of Nikolai Gnedich, Faddey Bulgarin, Ivan Lazhechnikov, and even Nikolai Gogol, to understand that Mandelstam had every basis for making such accusations.

But let us turn to the book itself. In a foreword "To the Readers" it is emphasized that "the author was born of Russian Jews and did not have the good fortune to be given a Russian upbringing." It is also explained that the poems were taken from the author's manuscript (and that they represent only a small portion of his work) and that in their sequence "can be seen some sort of connection that, perhaps, will be entirely familiar to his relatives and closest friends." It is obvious that the thread that connects these texts is the author himself. So it was Mandelstam's pen that for the first time in Russian culture turned a Jew into the lyrical protagonist of a book and elevated him into the realm of the aesthetic. The titles of his works ("To the Motherland," "To the Singer," "Reality," "Dream, "Yearning," etc.) lend them a confessionary tone.

> Have not I had all a heart could command,
> Love of family and friends in my father's abode?
> What is it that lures me to venture the road,
> And pulls me away to an alien land?
> For flowers of childhood, so to my heart near,
> In alien regions hot tears I'll be shedding.
> Will they keep from wilting till homeward I'm heading,
> The roses I love in the place I hold dear?

The emotions of a protagonist torn from his Jewish environment are natural and deeply felt, inasmuch as they have been experienced in the author's own life. The poems suggestive of his time in Moscow are also emphatically biographical.

> Oh, center of Russia! My city of dreams!
> Will you take to your breast a poor outcast like me?
> A true child of our land, could I ere to you be?

Your son stands in awe of your beauty's bright gleam,
His heart aches, it races, as hit by a blow,
He thinks of his home and the tears start to flow.

At times the author startles his readers with unexpected images that were clearly ahead of their time. In his programmatic poem "The Poet," in the midst of developing the traditional theme of the creator and the ignorance of the mob, he suddenly exclaims:

The lily of Eden's no good for exchange!
The fragrance of color, the crowd can't conceive,
The sigh of the poet, its ear can't perceive,
And to heaven's son, the earthly is strange!

In the words "the fragrance of color," the entire unique artistic world of the poet is captured. Such a metaphor comes straight from the realm of the twentieth century's Symbolists.

In general, what sets Mandelstam's poems apart are a diversity of meters and, as a rule, rich, precise rhymes, which reveal him to be a skilled versifier. And although his experiments can on occasion feel forced or stray toward the poetic cliché, for a young author writing in a second language, the results are astonishing.

The book was published when Leon was a student. It is interesting that Uvarov kept constant watch over Mandelstam. Consider the following: in 1843 he invited Mandelstam to take part in the work of the Rabbinical Commission. One cannot help but smile imagining the scene: a student, still wet behind the ears, sits at the same table with recognized religious leaders (among whom was the renowned Menachem Mendel Schneersohn) and contributes to decisions about the most important issues facing educated Russian Jewry!

In 1844, after a brilliant student career, Leon graduated from St. Petersburg University and defended a dissertation entitled "The Biblical State." He was given the degree Candidate of Philosophy (the approximate equivalent of a Ph.D.) in literature. With Uvarov's patronage, he set out to continue his research abroad by studying cuneiform tablets. He not only mastered the mysterious writings of the ancient Sumerians, but several European languages as well (including English, in which he penned lively feuilletons). In 1846, when he returned home to St. Petersburg, he intended to publish a Hebrew-language journal for Jewish intellectuals, modeled after *Ha-Me'assef*. The journal, however, never got off the ground, possibly because the St. Petersburg Jewish community was only in its infancy and did not have sufficient funds to support such an endeavor. Another probable factor was that Mandelstam, after returning to the capital, was appointed by Uvarov to the position of "Learned Jew" within the Ministry of Education, a position that left him little time for anything else. After all, he was charged with putting Uvarov's plans for Jewish educational reform into practice and oversaw approximately 150 newly established public colleges. He was rarely in one place for long, with inspections taking him to the school districts of Vilna one week, and Kiev and Derpt the next.

This job turned out to demand not only the talent of an organizer and administrator, but also to draw on Mandelstam's literary gifts. The minister assigned him to compile a series of catechisms and teaching guides for Hebrew, German, and Russian. A passionate propagandist of Russian language and culture, in 1847 Mandelstam published *An Experimental Guide to Practical Russian Language Exercises for Jews*, which (for the first time in history) included line-by-line translations into Hebrew of fragments from Pushkin's novel in verse *The Bronze Horseman* and his tragedy *Boris Godunov*.

Mandelstam also penned a five-volume work *Taken from Maimonides* (1848), written in Hebrew and German. The medieval Hebraist's text, however, was modified and adapted to the conditions of Russian life. Primarily, these adjustments had to do with how relations between Jews and non-Jews were treated. The derogatory word *goyim*, which appears in Maimonides' original text, is replaced with the more neutral *akum*, and it is emphasized that Jews live under the authority and protection of Christians (i.e., Russians) and are obligated not only to respect those of other faiths, but to love them like brothers. In the name of the Torah, he calls upon Jews to rigorously obey the laws of Russia and the will of its most august monarch.

Among the publications the Learned Jew produced we find the Hebrew-language textbook *Chinuch Ne'arim* ("Educating Boys," 1849), and essays on civic duty, *Shnei Perakim* ("Two Chapters," 1852).

Of truly inestimable value were the two-volume *Hebrew-Russian Dictionary* (1859) and *Russian-Hebrew Dictionary* (1860) that Mandelstam compiled, both of which played such an important role in the emancipation of Russian Jewry. Generations of Russian Jews learned Russian thanks to these tomes.

To understand what sorts of ideas Mandelstam introduced to Russian Jews, one must consider his *Textbook of the Jewish Faith*, which was issued in 1870. Here is his commentary to the words of the prophet Moses:

> "Love your neighbor as yourself": Who is our neighbor? Our neighbor is any person, no matter of what people or faith, everyone in need of our help and whom we are able to help…Our Love of neighbor must be extended…even to our enemies.

This precept, especially concerning enemies, is traditionally associated less with Judaism than with Christianity. What we have here are universal values that bring both religions closer together. It is noteworthy that he pronounces the main occupation of Jews to be not the distribution of goods and trade, but the much less popular farming and handicraft (here he very fittingly cites Psalm 128, "You will eat the fruit of your labor, blessings and prosperity will be yours"). He thus called upon Jews to partake in productive activities, an appeal that was fully consonant with the programs of the Russian government, whose policies he, as a government official, steadfastly worked to realize. He paid special attention to the relationship between Jews and their native land: "We must love our Fatherland, we must strive to apply our efforts and resources to promote its prosperity."

Mandelstam's textbooks, which the Ministry of Education made a mandatory part of the curriculum, were rejected by those Jewish conservatives who did not wish to stray beyond the boundaries of traditional education. They disseminated ridiculous rumors to the effect that the new schools would incline pupils to switch religions and that the Learned Jew, having published one textbook after another was lining his pockets with the blood money of his coreligionists. They based their faulty interpretation on the unfortunate fact that the textbooks were excessively expensive and were printed with funds from the so-called "Box Tax" – a mandatory tax on Jews. "There were no purchasers for these books," one contemporary reported. "They were forced on the *melameds* [teachers]. But since the cost (approximately 20 rubles) was sometimes higher than the *melamed's* income for an entire semester, the entire community had to take it upon itself in the form of an additional tax."

While some accused Mandelstam of greedily profiting from his publications, the reminiscences of his contemporaries attest to Leon's extraordinary authorial pride and his sense of the importance of his labor, with no thought of personal financial gain. One witness wrote,

> When Mandelstam took on the publication of some book, he did not ask how many copies could be sold over the course of some number of years, but simply ordered that five, ten, or twenty thousand copies be printed. If the books then languished on bookstore shelves without buyers, he felt no personal remorse, just a sense of scorn for his contemporaries, too few of whom were capable of appreciating something good; and when it came time to publish the next book, he would do the exact same thing. Surely he would not start penny-pinching like some shopkeeper just because these ignoramuses were not able to know a good thing when they saw it?

In 1857 Mandelstam left his post at the Ministry. Historians assumed that this was a result of his lively, independent character coming into conflict with the autocratic manners of some education bureaucrats. But even after he stepped down as the official "Learned Jew," Leon continued to serve in this position *de facto*, a source of legitimate pride for him. His biographer, S.M. Ginzburg, writes:

> Owing to his exceptional standing as the first Jew to finish university with a Candidate's degree, owing to himself alone, to his abilities, energy, assiduousness, combining in himself tremendous Jewish erudition with vast and diverse scholarship in the area of philology and historical knowledge, and having mastered most of the languages of Europe, Mandelstam could not have failed to have a sense of his superiority over the generation of *maskilim* of the thirties and forties, who were not able to participate in the mainstream of European education and, even in the area of their own Jewish knowledge, could not introduce the necessary systemization and discipline...Everything he did he did on a grand scale and at a great pace.

After retiring, Leon Mandelstam took up residence abroad, but did not abandon his educational efforts. He published, primarily in German, major works on studying the Bible and Talmud. He also wrote for a number of German, English, and Russian periodicals. In Berlin in 1862 he published *For the Benefit of Russian Jews*, his Russian translation of the Pentateuch (in 1872 a second edition was published that included a translation of the Book of

Psalms). Here too he was a pioneer, since this was the first translation of the books of the Old Testament into Russian by a Jew. Due to a prohibition on the use of Russian rather than Church Slavonic for scripture, the translation was not sold in Russia. Leon paid for a large number of copies to be printed, which was financially ruinous. Only in 1869 did a decree signed by Alexander II allow the books to be sold within the empire.

Leon was tireless in defending the interests of his fellow Jews and weighed in on the issues of the day. One of his articles – "In Defense of Jews" – was prompted by the polemic surrounding Odessa school superintendent Nikolai Pirogov's article on the Odessa Torah Talmud, which held up an aspect of Jewish education as a model to be emulated by Christian educators. Another, an apologia titled, "A Few Words about Jews in General and Russian Jews in Particular," was published in the popular newspaper *The Russian Invalid* (1859, No. 58).

Mandelstam did not give up his literary endeavors. In 1864 (again in Berlin and again at his own expense) he published a drama in verse entitled *The Jewish Family*. The censors, however, did not permit the play to be published in Russia due to the "tendentiousness and reprehensibility of the content of this work." This, despite the story's spirit of civic loyalty: it concludes with a chorus of "God Save the Tsar!" and repeatedly glorifies a world order "where all the tribes of the Fatherland will stand like a wall around the Tsar!" But the censor did, in his own way, have a point: Mandelstam was not truly objective, and was not capable of being objective, when he sang the praises of the majesty and strength of spirit of his people. Here are some of the words he puts into the mouth of one character from the drama, Rabbi Joseph:

> ...Our books
> Of ages past I need but open,
> And I live, not just again,
> Not just my youth, but lives of thousands
> Of others I have never known;
> Of all the martyrs of our faith,
> Of all the greatest of our wise men,
> Heroes, rulers just and good,
> Sent us by our Lord and maker
> Across three thousand years in time
> And from earth's one end and to the other!

> And therefore it just cannot happen,
> That a people such as ours
> Could perish, disappear, and vanish,
> As long as people walk the earth…

The author valorizes the martyrs of the Jewish faith. For example, Joseph tells his pupils the story of a Jewish child who refuses to bow down to the pagan god Zeus and is brutally executed with the words "Our God is the only God, O Israel!" on his lips.

Here, being a Jew signifies an unbroken continuous connection with the deeds of the renowned forefathers of the chosen people. Against this backdrop, the plight of the family of the Jew Baruch – an honest tailor, yet also a humiliated and persecuted outcast – appears particularly bitter and painfully unjust.

> Not wishing harm, without intention,
> The Jew bequeaths his family
> A sense of shame; my deprivation
> Afflicts my children's destiny;
> Just like a beggar, day in, day out,
> I must beseech work from the grandees;
> They shove me, they humiliate me,
> I am the butt of ridicule;
> They truly think I have no feelings;
> No man am I, I am a Jew.

Mandelstam sarcastically mocks the prevailing anti-Semitic bias of the time. He offers the following words spoken by a hapless Judeophobe, who blames the Jews for Russian drunkenness:

> To best ensure sobriety
> And guard against all rabblerousing,
> In every market in our land
> Let all partake – except the Jews!

The book was not published in St. Petersburg until 1872 and only in a heavily abridged version.

The last work that Mandelstam published was a collection of poetry written in German, *Voices in the Desert: Selected Jewish Songs* (London, 1880), which, like the verse he published in 1840, belongs first and foremost to Jewish culture. Confession and an immediacy of feeling are given an expressive artistic form that is entirely free of grandiloquence and importunate deliberativeness.

As he approached old age, life for Leon, bankrupt by decades of self-publishing, was not easy. He subsisted by writing for several Russian and foreign publications on a wide variety of topics – whatever paid: the working of the post office, the tax on alcoholic beverages, governmental borrowing, the railroad. The vast library that he had lovingly collected over the course of a lifetime was inventoried and, with the consent of his creditors, remained in the hands of its compiler, although, technically, he was no longer its owner. Vitality of spirit, however, did not leave our Learned Jew. In his hours of leisure he worked energetically on a comparative dictionary of Hebrew roots that had entered European languages, including Russian. Even in his declining years, in the words of an eyewitness, Leon exhibited a rare compassion for the misfortunes of others and a heightened sense of pride. "His hospitality, cordiality, and courtesy toward everyone who approached him," writes his biographer, "were reminiscent of the wellborn nobleman of yore and matched his outward appearance, which he maintained with great dignity, even when, alone and forgotten, he lived out his final years in uncomplaining poverty."

The vicissitudes of fate that buffeted Mandelstam in life pursued him beyond the grave. As it turned out, he, a man who had devoted his entire life to Judaism, was at first buried in a Russian Orthodox cemetery. On August 31, 1889, Leon died suddenly on a boat that was crossing the Neva River in St. Petersburg. Since no identifying documents were found on the body, it was sent to a mortuary in the Vyborg district and was then buried in the Uspensky cemetery. Only after he was finally missed and the caretaker of the building where he lived identified his keys and clothing, were Mandelstam's mortal remains disinterred and, on September 6, transferred to the Preobrazhenskoye Jewish cemetery.

The great twentieth-century poet Osip Emilyevich Mandelstam (1891-1938) was Leon's great nephew. Osip's grandfather was our Learned Jew's brother, Benjamin Mandelstam (who died in 1886). Benjamin was also born in Zhagory, but while his learned brother was busy educating himself and studying languages, Benjamin was engaged in commerce. Later, however, he too took up writing and penned several works in Hebrew. He was an exquisite stylist and his writing is distinguished by striking imagery and rich and colorful language. In his book *Hazon La-Mo'ed* ("The Time Has Not Yet Come," 1876), which takes the form of letters and memoirs, he presents a faithful picture of the daily life of Russian Jews in the 1830s-1850s. An advocate of Jewish religious reform, he proposed in this work radical measures that would be needed to create a "hand of authority" to lead the "deaf and the blind along life's path." In a short story entitled "Paris" (1878), written under the influence of fresh impressions of a trip he took there, he focuses on the plight of Jews in France. To his pen also belongs a collection of parables and aphorisms, *Mishlei Binyamin* ("The Parables of Benjamin," 1884-1885). Like his brother, he became an ardent proponent of Jewish participation in Russian and European culture.

And what genetic memories were passed down to the descendant of the Mandelstam brothers, the poet Osip Mandelstam? It would seem that the strongest childhood impression his literary ancestors left on the poet took the form of a book shelf:

> I will always remember the chaos of the lower shelf: the books did not stand spine to spine, but lay like ruins – brown-red *Pentateuchs* with torn covers, a Russian history of the Jews written in the awkward and timid language of a Russian-speaking Talmudist. This was Judaic chaos toppled into dust...

It is surely symbolic that the brilliant Russian poet, who wrote for a Russian-speaking audience, is now revered and read in modern-day Israel. In 2007 Jerusalem's Philobiblon publishing house released *The Times of the Year in Life and Poetry*, which contains 20 poems by Mandelstam translated into four languages, including Hebrew. "Judaic chaos" thus takes on new meaning and significance in apparent confirmation of the old adage: history is cyclical.

JOSEPH, HORACE AND DAVID GINZBURG

THE BIBLIOPHILE BARONS

The history of the renowned Jewish dynasty of the Barons Ginzburg – Joseph (also known as Evzel or Osip, 1812-1878), Horace (Goratsy, 1833-1909), and David (1857-1910) – suddenly became a topic of fresh interest during the waning years of the USSR: 1989-1991. A commotion erupted surrounding the collection of medieval Jewish manuscripts that had been painstakingly assembled by the three generations of barons and that was stored in the manuscript department of the Russian State Library (at the time still the Lenin Library). The unimaginable happened: a group of Hasidim burst into the library demanding their legitimate right to access these sacred texts. To protest the prohibition against using them, they barricaded themselves in the office of one of the library's directors. The protesters insisted that every religious Jew has the right to study any of the library's Jewish manuscripts.

Meanwhile, Russian nationalists (known as *pochvenniks*, from *pochva*, the Russian word for soil) were equally interested in the Ginzburg collection. They called for the Jewish manuscripts to be kept out of reach of "suspicious persons" (in other words, Jews), but they did believe that these historical documents needed to be studied and for a particular purpose. It seemed to these nationalists that a "patriotic" historian might be able to glean from them just how the Jews were planning to subjugate Mother Russia. Passions reached truly Shakespearian heights.

WHAT DID RUSSIAN "PATRIOTS" WANT WITH JEWISH MANUSCRIPTS?

In the March 1991 issue of the right-wing publication *Nash Sovremennik* ("Our Contemporary") there appeared an irate letter by a certain M. Mikhailov. It ran under the catchy heading, "We are not protecting what is ours..." What was Mikhailov so upset about? Was he worried that Russian Orthodox churches were being destroyed by "non-Russians" or the unprincipled scheming of Russophobes? Nothing of the sort. He was writing about medieval Jewish manuscripts, books, and personal papers from the collection of the Hebraist scholar David Ginzburg (1857-1910) that were held by the Lenin State Library. Believe it or not, the author of this letter was alerting Russian patriots that "as the result of an act stemming from the new political agenda, such as a presidential decree, a unique collection could be on its way to our Middle Eastern 'friends'" – in other words, to Israel. (Note Mr. Mikhailov's quotation marks around the word "friends.")

In scrupulous detail, the agitated Mikhailov recounted the story of the longstanding behind-the-scenes struggle for the Ginzburg legacy that was still going on at the highest echelons of power. His account featured a mysterious query from the Jewish Agency submitted to Anatoly Lunacharsky, the People's Commissar for Education in the 1920s, that resulted in a resolution by the Commissar; a 1987 meeting between the vice president of the Soviet Academy of Sciences, Yevgeny Velikhov, and the rabbinical scholar Adin Steinsaltz; and even a special letter from the president of Israel, Chaim Herzog, to Mikhail Gorbachev, which was supposedly delivered personally by Armand Hammer. And, despite the fact that all this was taking place behind the backs of patriots and the Russian people in general, Mikhailov knew beyond a shadow of a doubt that the Ginzburg collection was "one of the key" issues during a meeting between the chairman of the World Jewish Congress, Edward Bronfman, and President Gorbachev.

As evidence of how well informed he was, the patriot introduced an official query labeled Soviet Ministry of Foreign Affairs No. 1112/УБВСА and dated November 6, 1990:

> The Israeli side has shown an interest in the collection of Baron D.G. Ginzburg housed in the Lenin State Library of the USSR. According to the Israelis and based on publications in our possession, the collection was left by him to the Jewish Public Library of Jerusalem (now the Jewish National and University Library). I am requesting information on what we can reply to the substance of this request by Israel, including the actual condition of the Ginzburg collection, its legal status, and the possibility of working with the Israeli side in regard to this collection.

The substance of this request clearly held little interest for Mikhailov, who suddenly turned his attention to Israeli rabbis frequenting the Lenin Library, something that really got under his skin. He goes on to elegiacally bemoan the machinations of "operators such as Armand Hammer" and repeatedly brings up the Soviets' post-revolutionary sale of cultural treasures, forgetting to mention the fact that it was perfectly legal for the first wave emigration to take their own property out of the country. And this is a relevant point. On the eve of the revolution, Baron David Ginzburg's widow sold the collection to a Zionist organization, specifically to Hilel S. Zlatopolsky, for the soon to be opened Jerusalem Jewish National Library. The books were already en route when the October Revolution broke out and they were "expropriated" by the Bolsheviks. A significant portion of the collection was brought to Moscow and placed in the Rumyantsev Museum (now the Russian State Library). The Zionists demanded the return of their lawfully acquired library, but the Bolsheviks asked such an astronomical sum for its return that negotiations ground to a halt and the barons' collection never left Russia.

One might well ask why a nationalistic journal would care about some Jewish and Talmudic manuscripts. What interest could they possibly hold for nationalists who had plenty of their own problems to contend with? Quite a bit, it turned out. Mikhailov lets his readers in on a secret:

> Within the Ginzburg collection is presented (albeit in veiled form) ...world Jewry's idea of "colonizing Russia" with the goal of dismembering and destroying it. The manuscripts collected by D.G. Ginzburg from throughout Russia discuss the practical measures for implementing this idea. And in this, David Ginzburg was true to the memory of his father, who put no small effort into mobilizing the Jews of Europe to enslave Russia.

Well, that explains it. The destruction of Russia is admittedly serious business. However hard Ginzburg (known, among other things, as a world-famous scholar and chairman of the Society for the Promotion of Enlightenment among the Jews of Russia) may have tried to hide his activities, Mikhailov was on to him: he was the head of a secret Judeo-Masonic conspiracy, an enemy of Russia.

Even Alexei Suvorin's ultra-rightwing, prerevolutionary journal, *Novoye Vremya* ("New Times"), had never gone that far! On the contrary, in 1910 it reported on the benefit David Ginzburg's patriotic and educational activities were bringing to Russia. This seems a good time to recall such "interpreters" of Jewish history as former Duma member Nikolai Markov, known as Markov the Second, who ended his "patriotic" career as a consultant to the German Gestapo; or Grigory Bostunich, who rose to the ranks of Standartenführer in the Nazi SS. Was Mikhailov vying for a place among them in the annals of history?

Actually, Mikhailov was not only concerned about international Jewish conspiracies; there was also money at stake. "For just one [Ginzburg manuscript], a Canadian rabbi offered...his entire library several years ago, a collection valued at a million dollars" (for effect, the price of the collection was given in petit font). So, if the manuscripts were to be sold, at least the "patriots" should drive a hard bargain!

Just what made the Ginzburg collection so unique and significant? What did it contain? The *Nash Sovremennik* article provides little to illuminate the reader on this count, only a few quantitative characteristics: it is the "second in the world (after the British Museum's) in terms of the size and value of a collection of medieval Jewish manuscripts, consisting of approximately 2,000 books" and "two-thirds are obscure Judaica, texts and fragments of texts." It is amusing that there is a much more detailed account of these manuscripts in a Jewish encyclopedia published in Russian in the early twentieth century:

> Within the manuscript section [of the Ginzburg library] of particular importance are: *machzors* [prayer books] in Spanish, Italian, Occitan, Afrikaans; Diwans by major poets of the Spanish era; valuable manuscripts of Yemeni works on various branches of science; a portion of an ancient copy of the Talmud salvaged from a fire during the *autos da fé*; a Yerushalmi with commentary by Solomon Sirillo on its kabbalistic and philosophical content, which, incidentally, belonged to Isaac Abrabanel; an ancient biblical manuscript with a *targum* and an Arabic translation, and much more.

Mikhailov makes no secret of the fact that these materials had yet to be made accessible to scholars. It is illustrative that in an authoritative reference published under the aegis of the Lenin Library (*Personal Archival Collections*) there is just one mention of the Ginzburg papers, and it is in a description of a different archive. Surely this state of affairs contradicts everything represented by this marvelous Jewish scholar and educator, who, as Mikhailov recognizes "made it his goal to open a new center of kabbalistic and Talmudic scholarship for world Jewry"?

To give some idea of the ancient Jewish publications from this collection, there are more than 200 of them that by some miracle survived destruction by medieval censors and *autos da fé* (including extremely rare items with pages that were charred by the bonfires of the Inquisition). There are treasures of the incunabula period of Jewish book publishing: Joseph Albo's religious and philosophical treatise, *Sefer ha-Ikkarim* ("Book of Principles") printed by the Soncino family in 1485; Bahya ben Joseph ibn Pakuda's commentaries to the Torah, *Chovot ha-Lavavot* ("Duties of the Heart"), which was released in Naples by the Joseph Gunzenhauser printing house in 1490; an edition of the famous *Canon* by Avicenna dated 1491; a rhymed treatise on ethics by Kalonymus ben Kalonymus (1489); an edition of Moses Maimonides' *Moreh Nevukhim* ("The Guide for the Perplexed") printed on parchment in 1475.

Also represented in the collection is the work of such centers of Jewish bookmaking and culture in the fifteenth-seventeenth centuries as the printers Daniel Bomberg, Marco Antonio Giustiniani, Matteo Zanetti (Venice), Gershon Soncino (Pesaro), Samuel Latif (Mantua), B. Gershon, Samuel and David Nahmias (Constantinople), Judah Gedaliah (Salonica), Johannes Crato (Wittenberg), Rafael Talmi (Bologna), Isaac ben Aaron (Krakow), Gershon Cohen (Prague), and L. Marcus (Amsterdam), among others.

In total, David Ginzburg's collection contained 9,000 printed items. The baron's books were stamped with a Star of David with the monogram of the owner and labeled with two book plates, one artistic and one heraldic. The artistic one featured the aphorism, "Everything passes, everything is forgotten." The heraldic one shows the baron's coat of arms with a shield emblazoned with a beehive, a symbol of diligence, and decorated with another aphorism, a quote from the Song of Songs in Hebrew, "You are all beautiful, my beloved, and there is no blemish in you." (Song of Songs, 4:71).

A large portion of the publications is represented by Bibles, Talmuds, and rabbinical commentaries on them, as well as essays on religious law, philosophy, and mysticism. Among the secular books in the collection are works on history, geography, linguistics, and medicine, as well as references, dictionaries, and textbooks on Hebrew and other Semitic languages. There are also Yiddish periodicals dating back to 1861 from Odessa, St. Petersburg, and other cities. The collection is unique both in terms of its chronological range (from the first fountainheads of Jewish book publishing to the early twentieth century) and geography (it includes books published not only in the major centers of Europe and Asia, but also from North Africa and America). Over the course of his life, David Ginzburg painstakingly collected books that were then extensively used in his own research, which produced comparative studies of the medieval period and writings on Jewish history, the cultures of Russia and Arabia, and the religious singing of ancient peoples.

Back then, one could only guess what amazing finds lay hidden from society in this scholarly collection. But that is just the point. Mikhailov had no intention of making these manuscripts accessible. On the contrary, he was protecting the true-Russian masses from "concluding an inequitable agreement with Israel on publishing the collection's materials."

Who was responsible for curating David Ginzburg's collection? This was a legitimate question. Who in the USSR was assigned the task of preserving and studying this monument to Jewish culture? The amazing inside knowledge possessed by Mr. Mikhailov (if indeed this was his real name) gives him away. Clearly, this was someone working in the manuscript department of the Lenin Library.

Alas, something had been rotten in the manuscript department of the *Leninka*, as this library with its rich scholarly and cultural traditions was affectionately known. I worked in the library for ten years and had first-hand knowledge of this department. The head of the Manuscript Department was a professor who in 1989, during one of the library staff meetings, was publicly exposed as a rabid anti-Semite, something that was reflected in the young "researchers" he hired. I remember that when he arrived in the department we started to see bearded men in black paramilitary shirts wearing pins depicting St. George the Victorious – the uniform of the ultra-nationalist organization *Pamyat* – and maliciously hooting whenever they passed a "non-Russian" in the hallways of this renowned institution. One of them took part in a television show where he represented one of the wings of *Pamyat*. In the reading room of this department they hung a poster showing the Star of David made of skulls and bones with the word "Danger" underneath. When news of this leaked out and they were forced to offer an explanation to the library administration, they claimed that they were expressing their solidarity with the struggling people of Palestine. Very clever.

But perhaps their most pernicious influence was felt in the cultural events traditionally held in the library, which were transformed into festivals of anti-Semitism. Groups of organized young men accompanied by sinister looking women infiltrated these meetings and arranged themselves at either end of the meeting room. If, heaven forbid, an invited speaker said anything positive about a Jew, the hissing and clatter began. Then, right on cue, someone (always an older person with a chest full of medals) would get up and start to rant about the damned Masons and the impending supremacy of Zion. The old man would be loudly supported by a specially assembled cast of extras.

This was the sort of putrid atmosphere of anti-Semitic hysteria in which these relics of the Jewish people were languishing. They had been put in the charge of black-shirted fanatics and were being guarded by Mikhailov and other self-educated experts in Judeo-Masonic conspiracies. So rest assured – these folks were doing a fine job of preserving and "studying" them. And when they were done, they would have sold the collection for as much as they could get. And if selling it did not work out, what was to prevent some hot head, inflamed with hatred for the Ginzburgs, those "enemies of Russia," from taking out his anger on their collection?

During the period of stagnation – the Brezhnev years – soulless bureaucrats placed a taboo on the whole subject of Judaism. Today, thankfully, this is something that can be openly discussed. But it was a bitter pill to have to swallow that the unpublished materials contained in this priceless collection had become an object of political manipulations and the malicious falsifications of pseudo-patriots.

I WROTE ABOUT ALL OF THIS in an article published in the *Jerusalem Post* (June 25, 1991) under the title, "*Pamyat* Controls a Jewish Legacy." Israeli society, which had already taken a great interest in the Ginzburg collection, was thus kept informed about who was controlling these treasures of the Jewish people. It also became fully aware of what kind of a fight the anti-Semites would put up. However this did not frighten the Israelis. They were ready to go up against the likes of Mikhailov if necessary.

It is hard to say who deserves the greatest debt of gratitude – the Israelis, who demonstrated persistence and diplomatic tact, or that same head of the manuscripts department, who suddenly was transformed into a progressive (believe it or not) – but during the summer of 1992 a historic decision was made that suited both sides. The collection itself would remain in what was by then the Russian State Library (RSL) and its inviolability would be assured within this rich depository; the Israelis (in the person of the Jerusalem's Jewish National and University Library) were granted the opportunity to microfilm all of the manuscripts and create their own computer catalogue. As a result, the Jews and Hebraists of the world were given access to copies of unique manuscripts of the eleventh-eighteenth centuries: Bibles, Talmuds, literature in the field of rabbinical studies, halakha, kabbalah, medicine, astronomy, and philosophy, including a number of texts that had been considered lost to history. Now anyone can study these texts on their computer screens, no matter where on the planet they may live. At last there is no need to worry about Jewish manuscripts being under the sole control of black-shirted toughs. The Israelis, however, have not given up their attempts to take possession not only of copies, but of the physical collection itself, in accordance with the dying wish of David Ginzburg. Significantly, during February 2010 negotiations in Moscow between Israeli Prime Minister Benjamin Netanyahu, Russian President Dmitry Medvedev, and Russian Prime Minister Vladimir Putin, the subject of the collection was again raised by the Israeli side.

A large-scale project was undertaken at the RSL to describe and catalogue the entire Ginzburg collection. The first step in this direction was taken in 2003, when the RSL Eastern Literature Center, in collaboration with the Israelis, published a *Catalogue of the Hebrew Incunabules from the Collection of the RSL*, which contains all the collection's earliest books. Next in line are catalogues of paleotypes and other valuable publications from the collection. The books from the Ginzburg library have been displayed at numerous exhibitions conducted under the aegis of the RSL.

Today, the Ginzburg collection is recognized as an exceptionally valuable cultural legacy not only in Israel, but in Russia. It is included in a Russian registry of books considered to be monuments of culture and history and is categorized as a "collection of federal significance." This is deeply symbolic; the barons' tireless efforts are now celebrated as a service not only to their ethnic brethren, but to the entire Russian motherland, for the good of which they labored selflessly for almost an entire century. The remarkable story of this glorious dynasty deserves to be widely known.

BECOMING SELF-MADE

Baron Joseph Gavrilovich Ginzburg (1812-1878) bequeathed that his heirs maintain the faith of their ancestors, but also their Russian citizenship. This renowned banker, gold mine owner, and patron of the arts and culture dedicated his own life to fighting for the rights and emancipation of Jews and, at the same time, to serving tsar and country. For him, combining the two was not only a sensible approach, but the only one possible, since he firmly believed that the prosperity and well-being of Russia were in the fundamental interest of Russian

Jews. He saw the future of his people not in Pale of Settlement isolationism, but strove with all his might to integrate Jews into Russian society and for them to enter the empire's multi-ethnic family on an equal footing, while maintaining their ethnic identity and Jewish religion.

Having worked his way up from the bottom, this Vitebsk Jew was the first person in Russia to found a modern-day bank. He also became a distinguished baron, multi-millionaire, and major landowner. Everything that Joseph Ginzburg achieved in his life was the product of his own abilities, intuition, and business acumen. This gifted Jew was the ultimate self-made man. But it should be kept in mind that to a certain extent these were inherited qualities that crystallized in him after being passed down for generations.

The genealogy of the Ginzburgs (Gintsburgs, also spelled Günzburg and Guenzburg) can be traced back to the mid-fifteenth century. The name comes from the city of Günzburg in Bavaria's Swabia region. The founder of the dynasty was the Rabbi Yechiel of Porto. Fleeing the persecution that Jews were subject to in Germany, his grandson, Rabbi Simeon Ben-Avraam Günzburg (1506-1586), moved to the Polish-Lithuanian Commonwealth and is mentioned in Polish chronicles as a wise man, a mathematician and an astronomer. He left behind six sons.

Joseph Ginzburg

In the seventeenth-eighteenth centuries, their descendants were among the most prominent rabbis in the German duchies and Poland. Joseph's grandfather, Naftali-Gerts (who died in 1797), was the first in the line to break the family tradition and enter commerce.

His son and Joseph Ginzburg's father, born Gavriil-Yakov Ginzburg in Vilna (c. 1793-1853), followed in his father's footsteps, engaging in philanthropy and aiding the poor (his funds built a hospital for the indigent in Sevastopol). He is purported to have loved reading and collected books written in a number of languages. The extreme success of Gavriil-Yakov's commercial activities is attested to by the fact that Emperor Nicholas I made him a hereditary honorable citizen. But this occurred only toward the end of his life, in 1848, by which time he had permanently settled in Sevastopol. In his youth, his commercial concerns required Gavriil-Yakov to move from place to place. During Russia's war against Napoleon he found himself in Vitebsk, where Joseph was born in 1812.

The father gave his son not only a traditional Jewish education, but also a broad general one, and taught him several languages, of which Russian was one in which he gained native fluency. The rudiments of the science of business was also passed down from father to son, and Joseph quickly came out from behind the former's shadow, becoming the cashier and, essentially, manager for a prosperous *otkupshchik*.

As was customary for Jews, Joseph married early, at the age of 16. His bride was the beauty Rasya Dynina (1814-1892), the daughter of David Ziskindovich Dynin, who owned a postal station in the city of Orsha in Vitebsk Province (at the time it was the main postal link between Warsaw, Kiev, St. Petersburg, and Moscow). Dynin was a well-respected, educated, and tactful man. There is a family legend that every time the Emperor Alexander I passed through Orsha, he made it a point to visit the Dynin household, where he took great pleasure in the Jewish cuisine. Joseph Gavrilovich had a happy marriage. Rasya Davidovna, reputed to be a kind and God-fearing woman, bore him four sons – Alexander, Horace, Uri, and Soloman – and one daughter, Matilda.

Ginzburg had barely reached the age of 20 when he became a First Guild merchant. Enterprising and energetic, he mastered the most important skills needed to manage his employer's "tax farm" (taverns) and soon accumulated the necessary funds to buy his own license in 1840, after which he himself became a prominent *otkupshchik*. It should be noted that in those days the distilling of alcohol was the prerogative of the state, and only its sale was handled by private individuals. Licensed *otkupshchiks* had to put timely payments to the government ahead of their own financial needs. For this reason, licenses were given to those who were considered reliable, prosperous, and whose reputations guaranteed the irreproachable fulfillment of their contract with the state treasury. That a license would be granted to a Jew, and such a young one at that, was exceptional to say the least. But the Ginzburgs were accustomed to being the exception.

Joseph established good relationships both with the financial institutions of Podolia and Kiev Provinces, in which he tirelessly ran his business, and with those of St. Petersburg, to which he frequently traveled. Gradually, he developed ties in the capital's highest circles, especially its financial circles, where he was well-liked and earned a high level of trust. He grew particularly close with Minister of Finance Fyodor P. Vronchenko, by whose initiative "for services to the Russian government" he, like his father before him, was named a hereditary honorable citizen. During the Crimean War of 1853-1856 he ran his Sevastopol liquor trade under a state of siege. In the words of a contemporary, he was one of the last to leave the city and departed "almost at the same time as the garrison commandant." This and other brave deeds were recognized by the emperor with two gold medals "For Zeal" to be worn on the same ribbons as the Orders of St. Vladimir and St. Andrew. Many more such signs of distinction lay ahead.

Joseph Ginzburg had a keen sense of politics, a gift that would later bring him great success in the realm of finance. Recognizing earlier than others that the current tax farming system was fated to come to an end and that Russia would inevitability need to be capitalized, he perspicaciously bet on the liberals, who at the time were in disfavor, and developed commercial and financial connections with Prince Alexander of Hesse, the brother-in-law of the future Tsar Alexander II. When the latter ascended to the Russian throne, his reforms were largely influenced by his wife, Maria of Hesse, and her brother's favorite, Joseph Ginzburg, immediately found himself admitted to a circle that was engaged in creating "the infrastructure for a new economy."

When the tax farming system was replaced by a governmental monopoly on alcohol sales, many *otkupshchiki* were ruined. Not Ginzburg. He saw that the reform had created the need for a private banking system in Russia. He first established the Private Commercial Bank of Kiev, followed by the Accounting Bank of Odessa and the St. Petersburg Accounting and Loan Bank. Finally, in 1859, Joseph, together with his son Horace, founded the I.E. Ginzburg Banking House, the largest in Russia, with a branch in Paris (managed by his other son, Solomon). Soon the Ginzburg bank squeezed the renowned bank of Baron Alexander Stieglitz out of the financial market. The Ginzburg banking house worked in close association with the leading banks of Western Europe (Warburg in Hamburg, Mendelssohn and Blechröder in Berlin, De Haber in Frankfurt am Main, and Hoskier and Camondo in Paris, among others). It became the main credit bridge across which foreign money was invested in the Russian economy. The family's role in developing Russian credit and investment banks also cannot be overstated.

The Ginzburg banking house was always characterized by exceptional reliability, in stark contrast with other commercial enterprises, which were often guided by the famous principle, "there is no profit in honesty." This is why, at a time when private banks were vanishing like bursting soap bubbles, leaving their investors destitute, Ginzburg's bank kept growing and expanding. His banking house financed gold mining in the Urals and Baikal region and owned a corporation that ran steamship lines along the Sheksna River, among other enterprises. Joseph became fantastically rich. He had large estates in Bessarabia and Kiev, Podolia, and Taurida Provinces.

The Ginzburg family spent a good deal of time in Paris, where in 1870 Joseph built his own hotel on Rue de Tilsit. They were extremely outgoing and their hospitality soon turned their home into a gathering place for the Russian community of scholars, writers, and artists who found themselves living in France. One habitué of the household was Ivan Turgenev, the renowned author of *Fathers and Sons*. The painter Alexei P. Bogolyubov and the poet Nikolai M. Minsky were also frequent visitors. An Arts Club was founded so that prominent figures in Russian culture could get together, and Joseph Ginzburg was unanimously elected its chairman.

Ginzburg took a particular interest in his children's education and sought out the best scholars and teachers. Among them was a French language instructor named M. Mapu, the famous musician and music historian Jules Massenet, the classical philologist L. L'Abbe, the historian Heinrich Grets and the professor of Hebrew, Salomon Munch, among others.[1]

The fate of his coreligionists was something that was always on Joseph Ginzburg's mind, particularly at the height of his own financial success, when he had the greatest opportunities to come to the aid of those in need. He relentlessly and methodically bombarded the powers that be with petitions to alleviate the plight of Jews. He fully deserved to be considered a *shtadlan*, an authoritative representative of the Jewish community able to intercede with the government on its behalf, but he was his own sort of *shtadlan*. In playing this role he followed his heart, and did not always ask for what his unwitting constituents might have wanted him to seek. Indeed, many of the measures he proposed were far from universally supported by the Jewish population in the Pale of Settlement, which had completely cut itself off from modern Russian life and had no desire for innovation. According to the historian Heinrich Sliozberg:

> The light of day barely penetrated the dark underground of the Jewish ghetto of the cities and shtetls. Everything seemed to be fossilized in the spiritual life of the Jews…A mystical mindset distracted spiritual Jewish dreamers from gloomy reality…[They retreated into the realm] of inner contemplation – mystical

---

1. The sources of this information are in Russian. It is likely that the French spelling of Mapu, Grets, and Munch are different.

contemplation in the case of the Hasidim, contemplation that was purely spiritual and mental, scholastic and dry, in the case of the Misnagdim.

This sort of insularity was the polar opposite of what Joseph Ginzburg had in mind. His objective was the full-fledged participation of Jews in the life of Russia. The ideas of the Haskalah were close to his heart. The founder of this movement was the remarkable German thinker and public figure Moses Mendelssohn, who fought for the full assimilation of Jews and their integration into European scholarship and culture. The first Russian *maskilim* appeared around the dawn of the nineteenth century (Joshua Zeitlin, Abraham Peretz, and Lev Nevakhovich). In Ginzburg's day, it was specifically the *maskilim* that Nicholas I's Minister of Education, Count Sergei Uvarov, was counting on in his quest for a Russian Mendelssohn. Surrounding himself with eminent representatives of the Haskalah (Isaac Bar Levinsohn, Max Lilienthal, Leon Mandelstam), Uvarov, often with their guidance, attempted to transform the spiritual life of Russian Jewry. Jewish colleges were founded to train rabbis where they were given a solid grounding in general knowledge, in addition to a traditional Jewish education. A network of schools that provided a standard education was opened. There is evidence to suggest that by 1855 there were more than 100 such institutions in Russia and no fewer than 3,500 students enrolled in them. A great deal of attention was devoted to the study of languages and, significantly, the Russian language (more hours were allotted to the study of Russian than Hebrew). There can be little doubt that the graduates of such colleges went on to fill the ranks of the Russian-Jewish intelligentsia.

Ginzburg can rightly be considered one of the most ardent *maskilim*. A voracious reader, he laid the foundation for the collection of books and manuscripts that researchers would later call the Baron Ginzburg Collection. Joseph Ginzburg involved such eminent scholars in the development of his library (which started in earnest in 1840, first in Kamenets-Podolsk and later in Paris) as the orientalist Adolf Neubauer and the scholar of Jewish antiquity Senior Sachs. In 1856, the latter was put in charge of the entire book collection. Under Sachs, this repository acquired a large number of medieval manuscripts and rare editions, including manuscripts from the collections of such prominent Hebraists as Seligman Baer, Elykim Karmoli, and Nahman Nathan Coronel, to name a few.

Joseph did more than sympathize with the project to modernize Jewish education. In 1863 he founded the Society to Promote Education among the

Jews of Russia and supported it almost entirely with his own funds. The main tenet of the society's charter reads, "The Society promotes the furtherance of knowledge of the Russian language among Jews and publishes and assists others in the publication of useful writings, translations, and periodicals, both in Russian and in Jewish languages, with the goal of spreading enlightenment among Jews and providing stipends to encourage young people to dedicate themselves to scholarship." The Society was actively engaged in publishing. It released a *Collection of Articles on Jewish History and Literature* (St. Petersburg, 1866-1867) and collections of didactic maxims from the time of the Tannaim to the followers of Moses Mendelssohn entitled, *The Talmudist Worldview, A Collection of Religious and Moral Teachings through Excerpts from the Primary Works of Rabbinical Literature* (Volumes 1-3, St. Petersburg, 1874-1876), as well as an edition of the Torah in a new translation, *The Pentateuch of Moses in the Hebrew Text with a Word-for-Word Russian Translation for Jews* (Vilnius, 1875), along with other books that received wide recognition.

The Society subsidized Jewish periodicals, both those produced in Russian – *Den'* ("Day," 1869-1876), *Yevreyskaya biblioteka* ("Jewish Library," 1871-1880) – and in Hebrew – *Ha-Tsefirah* ("The Dawn"), *Ha-Melits* ("The Mediator") – as well as the creation of Russian-language textbooks for Jews and translations of *siddurim* and *machzorim* into Russian. It also provided financial support to Jewish scholars researching Jewish history and to authors of books of popular science written in Hebrew that promoted the "positive sciences and knowledge of the natural world." Furthermore, it distributed books in Hebrew and teaching aids and helped to establish Jewish public and school libraries. One of the Society's larger budget items funded scholarships to secondary and post-secondary students, including a stipend for Jewish medical students. Ginzburg thus played an integral role in producing the first generation of Jewish graduates of the Russian Empire's medical academies.

Ginzburg did not limit his activities to cultural philanthropy. He also devoted himself to causes that today would fall under the category of "human rights." For example he lobbied the government to grant Jewish artisans the right to live outside the Pale of Settlement. He did not share the scorn with which most Jews regarded craftsmen. With his encouragement, Jews overcame traditional prejudices toward manufacturing. Another area of endeavor Ginzburg strove to encourage was Jewish agriculture, a topic on which he submitted a memorandum to the government in 1862. He also worked with the Ministry of State Property to create a special fund to recognize the best Jewish farms.

Thanks to the tireless intercession of Joseph Ginzburg and the energetic assistance of his son Horace, the following categories of Jews were granted the right to live outside the Pale of Settlement: First Guild merchants (1859); so-called "Nicholas soldiers" or "Cantonists" who had served in the military after being conscripted as children (1867); and those engaged in the "liberal" professions, such as midwives, pharmacists, and dentists, among others (1869).

Ginzburg took a particular interest in the reform of military conscription that was undertaken in the 1870s. Most Jews, given that they did not speak Russian and were meticulous in their observance of rituals and tradition, especially dietary ones, felt that conscription was a terrible hardship for the Jewish people. Joseph, on the other hand, believed that with the rights Jews were being granted came obligations, including the obligation to serve in the military, and if Jews were exempted from certain duties to the state, they could not dream of ever achieving equality in civil rights. Indeed, the military guidelines issued in 1874 made no distinction between Jews and Russians. This is another advancement that can be credited to the selfless persistence of Joseph Ginzburg.

Joseph Ginzburg managed to achieve something that might have seemed impossible – permission from the emperor to build St. Petersburg's Grand Choral Synagogue. For many years he was recognized as the leader of the capital's Jewish community. In 1874 the title of baron was added to his numerous other regalia. This title was granted to Ginzburg by the Grand Duke of Hesse-Darmstadt. The Ginzburgs were now entered into the book of the nobility with honorary titles kept by the Senate's Department of Heraldry.

In January 1878 Joseph Gavrilovich Ginzburg departed this life surrounded by his large family. Death found him on the banks of the Seine where, terminally ill, he sought refuge in his final days from the cold and dank of the St. Petersburg winter. He was laid to rest in the family vault in Paris.

He had been granted the productive and fulfilling life of the creator. Along with the banks, factories, and corporations he created, along with the beneficial changes to the situation of Russian Jews that were brought about as a result of his efforts, Joseph Ginzburg made himself. He was truly a self-made man, a fascinating and exceptionally magnetic personality that left its mark on Russian history.

Horace Ginzburg   *Anna (Rosenberg) Ginzburg*

THE BEAUTY OF ISRAEL

A historical anecdote has been passed down over time: One day Baron Horace Ginzburg (1833-1909) was riding in a carriage with Emperor Nicholas II. A passing *muzhik*, unable to contain his amazement, exclaims, "Well, how do you like that? A yid is riding with the tsar!" The peasant is grabbed and about to be dragged off to prison for insulting the baron when Ginzburg requests that the simple fellow not be punished and even gives him some gold. "For what?" he is asked. For not letting him forget that he is a Jew.

This imposing gentleman, who spoke better French than Russian, was tall and well-built, with an aristocratic bearing and a captivating smile that made him difficult to dislike, and he truly appreciated being reminded of his origins. He was deeply religious and was convinced that Judaism was the precursor of all culture. Whatever the subject of discussion might be, the baron invariably wound up commenting that the solution to any problem related to the well-being of mankind can be found in the writings of Judaism. One of his favorite phrases was, "In the Talmud it is said that…" This conviction was expressed in every conversation he had.

His thorough grounding in the Talmud and ancient Hebrew was acquired in childhood. He was taught by the renowned Hebrew scholar, Mordecai Suchostaver, first in Zvenigorodka in Kiev Province, where he was born and spent his early years, and later in St. Petersburg and Paris, between which the Ginzburg family later divided its time. Like Joseph's other children, Horace was given an excellent education at home, this matter having been entrusted to the best pedagogues and experts. To Horace, his father's authority was beyond question. His guiding principle was "This is how my father did things or felt he needed to do things." This is not surprising, since from an early age he served as his father's right-hand man. At the age of 20 he married his cousin, Anna Rosenberg (1838-1878), also with his father in mind. Horace's chosen helpmate enjoyed tremendous respect within the Ginzburg family and exerted a great deal of influence on her father-in-law.

The rights won by Russian Jews during the 1850s-1870s were unquestionably a product not only of Joseph Ginzburg's efforts, but also of Horace's energy and skill. The son, who was always by his father's side, also made major contributions to his father's successes in banking and finance. Indeed, Horace Ginzburg was fated to surpass his father in many ways and earn himself not just a European reputation, but an international one – and not first and foremost in the sphere of business (although here he not only consolidated but advanced his father's work, becoming the founder of new corporations, large gold-mining partnerships, the owner of sugar factories, and a sponsor of the construction of Russian railroads, to name just some of his achievements). However, it was his activities in the area of philanthropy and human rights that earned him the greatest renown.

Even during Joseph's lifetime, Horace became a prominent philanthropist and patron of the arts in his own right. His exceptional position in Russia was attested to by the fact that in 1868 he was appointed consul general for Hesse-Darmstadt in St. Petersburg, becoming the first non-Christianized Jewish diplomat to the court in St. Petersburg. In 1871, when the Grand Duchy of Hesse became part of a united Germany, Horace (and just three years later his father Joseph) was granted hereditary Hessian nobility, and the title of baron into the bargain.

The scope of Horace Ginzburg's philanthropy was seemingly limitless. There was an impression that no major undertaking in St. Petersburg was deprived of his generous financial contributions and efforts, whether or not they directly benefited his coreligionists. One could point, for example, to the model technical college named in honor of Tsarevich Nicholas, or the special surgical infirmary he set up as part of the Stock Exchange Hospital, where countless people in need were given urgent care by the finest doctors. He was directly involved in the establishment of the St. Petersburg Archeological Institute, which was granted the designation "Imperial," and the "Bestuzhev Courses," which subsisted on private funds and was one of the few institutions of higher learning for women in Russia. He donated appropriations for the Institute of Experimental Medicine founded by Prince Alexander Petrovich of Oldenburg (modeled on France's renowned Pasteur Institute), organized a Society for Affordable Apartments in St. Petersburg, participated in the work of the Society to Improve the Living Conditions of Poor Children, and served as a trustee of the Nicholas II School of Commerce. The causes to which he made significant charitable contributions are too numerous to mention. What is important to note is that a strict condition of his participation in these projects was that they equally benefit all people, without regard to ethnicity or religion. "He did not differentiate between people," one of his contemporaries commented, "since the teachers of the law to which he was ever-faithful did not distinguish between Jew and Greek."

Horace Ginzburg was at the very center of the intellectual life of his time. As his father had done in Paris, Horace opened the doors of his St. Petersburg home to the finest exemplars of the progressive Russian intelligentsia. Close ties of friendship existed between Ginzburg and Mikhail Stasyulevich, a former history professor and founder of the liberal magazine, *Vestnik Evropy* ("Herald of Europe"), as well as with the men of letters who contributed to this publication: Konstantin Arsenyev, chairman of the St. Petersburg Bar; Vladimir Spasovich, outstanding criminologist and professor of criminal law; Alexander Pypin, literary historian; Konstantin Kavelin, professor at the Military Law Academy; and Vladimir Stasov, the outstanding art historian and patron of the arts (who later became an ardent admirer of Jewish talents). The Ginzburg household was also frequented by the writers Ivan Turgenev, Ivan Goncharov, Mikhail Saltykov-Shchedrin, and Pyotr Boborykin; the illustrious jurist Anatoly Koni; one of the founders of modern Russian medicine, Sergei Botkin; and the remarkable philosopher Vladimir Solovyov. Solovyov was a particularly close and trusted friend. It would appear possible that it was Ginzburg who influenced Solovyov to study Judaism through primary sources and develop a profound knowledge of the Talmud. The philosopher's biographers attest that the last words he pronounced on his deathbed were those of the *Shema Yisrael*. Unfortunately, Ginzburg's correspondence with Solovyov, as well as with other prominent cultural figures, which was kept in the baron's archive and are of paramount scholarly importance, were destroyed in a fire, which goes to show that manuscripts do, after all, burn.[2]

---

2. "Manuscripts don't burn" is an often-quoted line from Mikhail Bulgakov's novel *Master and Margarita*.

Horace Ginzburg also developed a rapport with the artist Ivan Kramskoy, who painted a portrait of the Ginzburg family, as well as with the court painter Mihály von Zichy, who produced masterful hunting scenes that were celebrated for their refinement. Horace collected contemporary Russian paintings and his St. Petersburg home held a collection of nineteenth-century portraits. It was he who saw to it that an unknown tailor's apprentice from Vilnius by the name of Mark Antokolsky received an academy education and acquired world renown as a sculptor. And the baron did not forsake Antokolsky when he became terminally ill, arranging for the sculptor to spend his last months amidst the wonders of Switzerland. Ginzburg created a special Academy of Arts fund to endow a prize that would recognize Jewish artists.

Not surprisingly, the world of music was another realm in which Ginzburg had close friends of prominence, including the first director of the St. Petersburg Conservatory, the pianist and composer Anton Rubinstein, the famous cellist Karl Davydov, and the Hungarian violinist and renowned teacher Leopold Auer. Among the young musicians who received financial support from Ginzburg in the form of stipends were Auer's students Jascha Heifetz and Misha Elman.

But Horace Ginzburg's most productive philanthropic and educational work was through the Society to Promote Education among the Jews of Russia, which he took over as chairman after his father's death. For example, in 1880 he established a foundation to help Jewish women achieve a higher education. The society also left an impressive publishing legacy, including *Russian-Jewish Archive* (1882) and *A History of the Jews* by Henrich Graetz (1883). A special Jewish Historical Ethnographic Commission (later the Jewish Historical Ethnographic Society) was set up to research the history of Jews in Russia. It was this commission that published the classic three-volume reference *Lists and Inscriptions* (often cited by its Russian name, *Regesty i Nadpisi*, 1899-1913), an invaluable resource for every student of Jewish history. An ethnographic expedition was organized that resulted in a unique collection of objects of Jewish material culture. This collection later formed the basis around which a Jewish museum was built (later shut down by the Soviets).

The society also made a major contribution in the area of Jewish elementary education. A *Compilation for Jewish Elementary Schools* was published in 1896 and a *Reference Book on Issues of Jewish Education* followed in 1901. Subsidies were given both to Jewish schoolchildren attending general education schools and to Jewish elementary schools. The society also supported efforts to open new schools, with the stipulation that religious subjects and Hebrew be taught.

With the opening of offices in Moscow (1894), Riga (1898), and Kiev (1903), the society's reach was greatly expanded. Toward the end of the baron's life it had 30 offices and 7,000 members and had funded a total of nine libraries. In 1907, with the society's patronage, a two-year teacher college was established in Grodno to expand the ranks of qualified Jewish educators.

Whenever misfortune struck the Jewish community, Horace Ginzburg was there to lend a helping hand. In 1878, Ginzburg reacted with lightning speed as soon as news arrived from the Transcaucasian city of Kutaisi that a group of Mountain Jews had been falsely accused of the ritual murder of a Christian boy. The baron not only hired the best lawyer to defend them, but managed to inspire a professor at St. Petersburg University's School of Eastern Studies, the outstanding orientalist and semitologist Daniel Chwolson, to write a scholarly work on the history of blood libel, discrediting such accusations. The professor's book, *Do Jews Use Christian Blood?*, was published at Ginzburg's expense. The first investigation of this issue in Russia, it was translated into several European languages and had a broad impact. As a result, the Kutaisi Jews were acquitted. Indeed, the very idea that Jews engaged in ritual killings was stripped of credibility.

The ascent of Alexander III, who steered a radically different course when it came to Jews, dashed all hope of positive change. Historians have written about the pathological anti-Semitism of this Russian emperor, characterizing his attitude toward Jews as "the apotheosis of malice, ignorance, and narrow-minded, un-Christian vindictiveness." The acrimony this monarch felt toward the Jewish tribe can be traced back to the Russo-Turkish War of 1877-1878. During this conflict, the Russian army, under the command of (then Tsarevich) Alexander, suffered devastating defeat. The cause, in his eyes, was the administrative inefficiency of Jewish suppliers. His lack of personal exposure to Jews, combined with his feelings of resentment, causing him to feel animosity toward all Jews. Fuel was only added to the fire when the 1878 Congress of Berlin, which handed Russia a humiliating settlement, guaranteed the Jews of Balkan states equal rights, something that had been lobbied for by French and English Jewish leaders (the Alliance Israélite). This brought a temporary liberalization in attitudes towards Jews in Russia as well. One of the forces behind this liberalization, Count Mikhail Loris-Melikov, whom Alexander II had put in charge of spearheading reforms, even pursued the possibility of abolishing the Pale of Settlement.

The future Alexander III did not care for any of this and saw signs of a powerful and united Jewish cabal all around him. Furthermore, once he became emperor, his Jewish (or rather anti-Jewish) legislation was guided not by any rational state interests, but by emotions, prejudice, and preconceptions. It is illustrative that when he was presented with a petition complaining about flagrant discrimination against Russian Jews, he wrote in the margins, "They forget the terrible words of their ancestors. 'His blood be on us and on our children!'! This explains why they have been ruined and cursed by the Heavens!" In other words, to him any legal questions about the rights of citizens were essentially trumped by the notion of a legendary sin and the collective responsibility of the Jewish people before Christianity. It would appear that among all Russian monarchs the one closest to him in views was Peter the Great's militantly Judeophobic daughter, Empress Elizabeth, who famously proclaimed, "I have no desire for profit from the enemies of Jesus Christ!"

The tsar's inclinations were shared by the new Interior Minister, Nikolai Ignatiev, who in May 1882 issued the so-called "Temporary Regulations," draconian laws that, alas, remained in effect until the 1917 revolution. They were based on the perverse idea that Jews themselves were to blame for the new restrictions, since they were guilty of corrupting the Russian people with drink, mercilessly exploiting the peasantry, and of escaping the Pale of Settlement in order to join in revolutionary sedition. The government (which itself had impoverished the peasantry through its ruinous economic policies) felt a need to defend the Russian people, the peasantry first and foremost, from Jewish "bloodsuckers." Under the May Laws (as they came to be called) Jews were to be expelled from villages and forced to settle in cities and shtetls, they were to lose the right to engage in the sale of alcohol, and their access to higher education was to be sharply curtailed. One cannot help but think of Sholom Aleichem's Tevye the Milkman, who was forced to sell his house and cow and leave the village where he grew up. He was just the sort of hard worker that Ignatiev's law hit the hardest. It pulled the rug out from under hundreds of thousands of families who had made a living out of the production and sale of alcoholic beverages. Finally, it certainly revolutionized those who wanted to attend university but found themselves hostages to the quota system. What was an educated, Russophone Jew to do? Many who had already received a top notch *gymnasium* education were shut out of institutions of higher learning. Economic conditions were already bad enough in the Pale of Settlement; more than a million people were destitute, lacking even the means to celebrate

Passover. Ignatiev's laws condemned the Jewish population to poverty and emigration. One and a quarter million left for Argentina, Palestine, and the United States.

Gone were the auspicious days of the Tsar-Liberator, Alexander II, a time when Horace, together with his father, had won rights for their long-suffering people one step at a time. Jewish pogroms, something unheard of under Alexander II, swept the country, perpetrated by urban rabble with the tacit approval of the authorities. Now that the reactionaries were in power there could be no talk of emancipating the Jews. Every effort had to be directed toward preserving what had already been achieved and preventing newly gained rights from slipping away. And what was Horace Ginzburg's role in all this? Later, the jurist Maxim Vinaver wrote very aptly on this subject.

> He alone did not stray from the path he had chosen and continued the fight. The fight…this word seems so incompatible with his kind, soft…face, with his massive but childishly gentle, kind figure. What could he fight with? His sword was his kind, heartfelt smile, and the only armor he had against cruel blows was an endlessly loving heart that was incontrovertibly devoted to his people. He asked and cajoled, walked out, but then returned. More than once critical words from the mouths of his contemporaries condemning his seemingly futile efforts reached his ears. But those who judged him did not understand that it is easier to put up a clamorous fight and even to be heroically struck down in open combat than – day in, day out – to knock on doors, walk away, and come back again and again…To persist all your life, to persist with dignity, with head held high, is something that can only be done by a soul that feels compassion even for the haughty and unfeeling against whose heart of stone all his pleas have been smashed. This is the sort of man he was: he sincerely forgave his enemies, even the enemies of his people.

Every request, petition, and memorandum submitted to the government concerning the rights of Jews always had to get past Horace's strict censorship. An innate sense of tact gave the baron a keen ear for the most appropriate phrasing. He relentlessly crossed out such words as "highly," "extremely," "unquestionably." As a result, any document that benefitted from his pen took on a calm, businesslike, and balanced character and thereby gained in effectiveness. His unique style was respectful, but insistent.

Baron Ginzburg paid close attention to the everyday lives of ordinary Jews and was always ready to come to their defense, standing up for their interests in the Governing Senate. In so doing he relied heavily on the support of a man who was known by his contemporaries as the "righteous judge" – the head of the Senate's First Department, Viktor Artsimovich. A testament to the memory of this highly placed friend to the Jews has been preserved for posterity in a bust by Mark Antokolsky that stood in the baron's study.

In 1882 Horace actively participated in the work of the High Commission to Review Laws Pertaining to Jews, which had been convened by the tsar and was chaired by the former minister of justice, Count Konstantin Pahlen. Pahlen had a reputation as a man who was fair and incorruptible. His Commission took a serious look at the lives of Russian Jews. A number of reports were drafted and published, including on the economic situation of Jews in the Pale of Settlement, the history of laws pertaining to Jews, and the demographics of Russian Jews. The baron saw to it that the facts the Commission was working with were accurate and provided evidence disputing the common belief that Jews evade military conscription. Ginzburg demonstrated that the official figures suggesting that Jews are not proportionally represented in the army could be explained by the fact that they were not being properly registered when enlisted, as well as by the special rules that had been put in place relating to their recruitment. In fact, in percentage terms, the number of Jewish recruits was actually proportionally higher than for other nationalities. His efforts were not in vain. The majority of High Commission members had the courage to recognize that the limitations currently in place would do nothing to resolve the Jewish question and that continuing to follow the current course was unjust, unnecessary, and would only cause harm (including economic harm) not only to Jews, but to the greater population. The Commission proposed gradually expanding the rights of Jews. In short, Pahlen and his staff did not "justify the trust" that the openly chauvinistic and anti-Semitic Alexander III had placed in them.

Unfortunately, in 1887 the Commission was unexpectedly dissolved. The fate of Russia's Jews was then handed over to a Government Council put together by the Interior Minister and chaired by the inveterate reactionary Vyacheslav von Plehve, who at the time was Assistant Minister. A brutish anti-Semite and careerist who was eager to please his Judeophobic tsar, Plehve set out not only to keep the draconian May Laws, but to make them even tougher, taking them to extremes of cruelty and misanthropy. This nineteenth century Haman sought to expel from the Russian countryside even those Jews who were living there legally and felt that, until such a wholesale expulsion was achieved, any Jew who traveled where he was not allowed should be deprived of the right to return to hearth and home. Jewish artisans, who had been earlier given the right to live outside the Pale of Settlement, were to immediately return there. Rental of real estate outside of cities was prohibited. Any violation of these "rules" were to be punished with a prison term.

These "legislative proposals" had to be submitted to the Government Council for approval. Given the circumstances, one might have thought that any struggle for the rights of Jews would have been paralyzed. Baron Ginzburg, however, redoubled his effort. He went into battle calmly and patiently, attempting to demonstrate to the government just how injurious the Plehve initiatives would be. He convinced Finance Minister Ivan Vyshnegradsky that this medieval intolerance toward Jews was monstrous and barbarous. In a report Vyshnegradsky submitted to the tsar, he convincingly argued the benefit Jews brought to the economic life of the country. The minister also pointed out to the autocrat the harmful impact that Plehve's projects would have on imperial finances. In the end, the baron's efforts were successful. Plehve's proposals were not put before the Government Council and faded into oblivion. Ginzburg thus managed to avert terrible misfortune. Even if this was the only service he performed for his people, it would be enough to earn him their eternal gratitude and an important place in Russian history.

The interests of the Jewish people were Baron Ginzburg's primary concern, and Jews throughout Russia turned to him for help and felt unflagging respect and gratitude toward him. "Show me a single shtetl," the Rabbi Vladimir Temkin once said, "that, in a moment of tribulation, has not turned to the baron for help, for protection. Can you find a single Jew who, in a moment of desperation, in a minute of bitter suffering, did not call out to the baron?"

Ginzburg's importance as the organizer and head of the St. Petersburg Jewish community is inestimable. He was behind construction of the capital's synagogue on Ofitserskaya Street, which was opened in 1892 and is still functioning. This great work of architecture, built along the Neva River in the Moorish style, is one of the cities most stunning historical buildings. The baron became chairman of the synagogue's board of directors, and under his leadership a public assistance office was opened to aid the poor. Earlier, Horace's wife Anna had founded a Jewish orphanage on St. Petersburg's Vasilievsky Island.

The causes for which the baron petitioned the government and the Jewish undertakings that he financed are too numerous to list. Ginzburg came to the generous assistance of victims of fires, famines, pogroms, and other misfortunes. But he was also an unflagging Russian patriot, something even his enemies recognized. He loved Russia just as it was, but held high hopes for its future. His patriotism came coupled with a profound loyalty to tsar and government. The regime's failings were perfectly clear to him, but he never opposed the existing order and followed the Talmudic precept that the laws of the state must be rigorously obeyed. It pained him deeply to see so many Jews join the revolutionary movement.

The Russian government recognized Ginzburg's services and in 1889 he was elevated to the rank of Actual State Councillor, the civilian equivalent of the rank of general, and decorated with the highest orders. Most importantly, the baron was seen by the government as the leader of all Russian Jewry.

Horace Ginzburg believed that Jews could thrive in Russia and did not approve of Zionism or emigration to Palestine, Argentina, and the United States, which was then rampant. But he respected the personal choice of his coreligionists and understood that without his participation (including material assistance) it would be impossible for Russian Jews to resettle, so in 1893 he took over leadership of the central committee of the Jewish Colonization Association. Soon there were 507 emigration committees working under his patronage. Later, a farming colony in Argentina came to bear his name.

Baron Horace Ginzburg departed this world in 1909, at the age of 76. Speaking at his funeral, Heinrich Sliozberg delivered a moving tribute:

> Horace Osipovich was the beauty of Israel. It was not his wealth or nobility that made him so, nor was it the fact that he was influential and that his influence was always used to benefit others, nor was it that he always generously shared with those dear to him the riches that fate bestowed upon him...There was no human suffering that he did not feel and that he did not strive to alleviate, regardless of who was suffering – his own people or "others," and for him there really were no "others." But it was not just this that made him the beauty of the Jews. And it was not the fact that, loving beauty, he encouraged art in all its manifestations, and that being enlightened, he enlightened others and sowed enlightenment with his generous hand right and left, and not just in a narrow furrow, confident that however the seeds fell on the grateful soil of the Jewry it would bear rich fruit. He was the beauty of the Jews in that he was the living exemplar of the Jew, imbued

with the spirit of Judaism, with the Jewish ideal, and everything that he did, and everything that he was, manifested his Judaism. Everything he did, he did not, as some would say, "despite being a Jew," but specifically "because he was a Jew." The precepts of the Jewish creed and Jewish morality were always his guide, and never for a minute did he forget that, in the words of our teachers, "the world is sustained by three things: justice, truth, and peace."

Horace Ginzburg bequeathed that he be buried in Paris, by his father's side. His body departed St. Petersburg for Paris amidst great ceremony. Delegations came from many cities for the occasion. The body was accompanied on its journey by specially appointed envoys.

But before long the name Horace Ginzburg began to be forgotten. This is understandable. He was too traditional a Jewish leader, faithfully petitioning the powers that be on behalf of his people. The tsarist government had no desire to alleviate the situation of Jews, seeing in this "alien" nation a scapegoat and a force behind the revolutionary movement. "Let the Union of the Russian People be my tower of strength, serving in every way and every deed an example of legality and order!" was the rallying cry of the emperor of the Black Hundreds, Nicholas II, who had no intention of protecting Jews from pogroms and persecution. Under such circumstances asking was not enough; it was necessary to demand, to cry out, and even to resort to arms. Later came the October Revolution, with its slogans of internationalism and proletarian solidarity, which left no place for Jewish ethnic identity. It is not surprising, therefore, that the name of a renowned Jewish *shtadlan* entered official obscurity. Not a single edition of the Soviet encyclopedia or biographical dictionary mentions his name.

Today, however, this remarkable defender of human rights lives on in the memories of grateful Jews throughout the world: in Israel, Russia, and Argentina. In the United States a special Baron Ginzburg Foundation has been established that recognizes the best works of Jewish history and literature.

Horace Osipovich Ginzburg was a typical Jew, a benefactor and philanthropist about whom even Nicholas II, not known for his love of Jews, said, "Here is a man about whom nobody has a mean word to say."

His is an example worthy of imitation.

THE JEWISH ANTIQUARIAN

I would like to show how poetry gushes like a living spring from the depths of metrics; I would like to show why stilted recitation grates our ear while a skillful reading opens before us new, distant horizons; I would like to show how the works of our great poets should be interpreted and how their natural rhythm must be found in order for them to be truly appreciated; I would like to show how when our inner eye is informed by a correct understanding of meter it is suddenly capable of seeing everything that is happening in their soul at the moment of inspiration; I would like to show how, if we cast off the alien yoke, we can, without cunning philosophizing or arcane theory, write beautiful verse and with full awareness of its internal structure.

This is a brief fragment from the book by Baron David Ginzburg (primarily known to his Western contemporaries as de Günzburg, 1857-1910), *On Russian Verse: Experiencing the Rhythmic Structure of Lermontov's Poetry*. We include this fragment to give the reader an opportunity to hear the voice of an outstanding scholar and educator (unfortunately this book has not been translated into English). *On Russian Verse* is marked by an ardent love of Russian poetry, and one is struck by the amazingly pure but also lively and emotional language of the author. He was nourished not only by the classics, but by the conversations that so often took place in the Ginzburg household among the masters of the Russian word that surrounded David when

David Ginzburg

he was a young boy. The examples from other languages that he offers in his book make clear how knowledgeable and comfortable he was with French, German, English, Italian, Polish, Ancient Greek, Latin, Hebrew, and even Arabic versification, and reveal an impressive philological erudition.

At an early age, as was to be expected in the Ginzburg family, David was already a polyglot. In addition to providing his son with a traditional Jewish upbringing, Horace saw that he learned the major European and classical languages. For his home education, the elder Ginzburg made sure that David had the best mentors, top experts in their fields. One of them, the brilliant scholar of medieval Jewish literature and philosophy, Senior Sachs (1816-1892), proved extremely influential on David. The curator of the Ginzburg library, Sachs was also the compiler of a catalogue of ancient Jewish manuscripts and it was he would instill in David a consuming and enduring interest in rare books and manuscripts. This translated into a passion that David spent a lifetime pursuing. Another mentor was Hirsch Rabinovich (1832-1889), the compiler of a compendium on the natural sciences that was popular among Jews in his day. He was also a gifted journalist and sharp-witted polemicist, something that rubbed off on his pupil. Another major force in David's intellectual development was one of the top humanists of the nineteenth century, the orientalist Adolf Neubauer (1831-1907), who went on to become a professor in the Department of Rabbinic Literature at Oxford University. Neubauer, along with the beauty of ancient Hebrew and Karaite literature, introduced David to the charms of Arabic literature and language.

It became clear early in David's life that he did not have the Ginzburg talent for business and finance, but the makings of a scholar were evident. He was drawn to the cradle of civilization, the Middle East of antiquity, and became absorbed in a quest to comprehend its history and culture. On his own initiative, in Paris David began to attend lectures by the eminent Arabist, historian of Islam, and expert in ancient poetry, Stanislas Guyard (1846-1884). The young baron was inspired by Guyard's theory about a system of versification based on a language's natural rhythm. He would go on to develop this theory in his own scholarly works.

At St. Petersburg University he audited lectures on the history of Middle Eastern cultures and the literature of medieval Arabia and Persia by professor Victor Rosen (1849-1908), the founder of a school of Arabic studies in Russia. Rosen was a broadly learned man with a particular interest in cultural history, an interest he instilled in the young Ginzburg.

The knowledge David acquired through his home education and subsequent self-education prepared him, at the age of 20, to pass examinations at St. Petersburg University and earn a Candidate of Sciences degree (the approximate equivalent of a Ph.D.), despite the fact that he was never enrolled as a student there. He did not stop at that. His thirst for knowledge led him to the oldest university in Europe, the University of Greifswald, founded in the fifteenth century. Here he studied under the famous professor Wilhelm Ahlwardt (1828-1909), an expert in ancient Arabic poetry and oriental languages. Among the things Ginzburg studied there was the Coptic language, making him the only scholar of this language in Russia.

By Ginzburg standards, David married rather late in life, at age 26, choosing his cousin Matilda Yuryevna Ginzburg, who was seven years his junior, as his bride. The ceremony, which took place in Paris, was a traditional *chuppah*. The union resulted in five children: Anna, Joseph-Evzel, Mark, Sofia, and Eugene. All (except for Mark, who died in childhood) lived through the revolution and emigrated, Anna and Joseph-Evzel to France, Sofia to Palestine, and Eugene to Argentina.

The baron proved a highly productive scholar and writer. Among the many works he published was the first edition (in 1886) of *The Topaz* (*Sefer ha-Anak* or *Sefer ha-Tarshish*), a collection of poetry by the renowned medieval Jewish poet, philosopher, and linguist, Moses Ibn Ezra, and an Arabic translation of this work with commentaries (1887). In 1896 a collection he compiled, *The Diwan of Ibn Quzman*, the eleventh-century Muslim poet from Cordoba, was published.

But perhaps his most impressive achievement was a project he undertook in collaboration with the prominent critic Vladimir Stasov, *L'Ornement Hébreu* (1905). This sumptuously produced album, which features examples of ornamentation from Syrian, Yemeni, and African Jewish manuscripts, represented two decades of work with manuscripts from the Imperial Public Library. Stasov's enthusiastic participation in the project is noteworthy and should be instructive to today's Russian "patriots." Here is what the researcher Alexander Kantsedikas had to say on the subject.

> For Stasov, the search for the national identity of Jewish art was closely associated with the main objective of his overall cultural work: the study and introduction into contemporary artistic practice of the distinctive foundations of Russian art. This might seem paradoxical, since today expressions of Russian national feeling are often accompanied by manifestations of anti-Semitism.

David Ginzburg's bibliography is extremely impressive. He appeared in the most authoritative scholarly journals and anthologies of his day, publishing on a wide variety of topics – everything from an essay on the history of the kabbalah in the journal *Issues of Philosophy and Psychology* to an expansive study of the first Jewish school in Siberia for *The Journal of the* [Russian] *Ministry of Education*. His articles were eagerly published by such Jewish periodicals as *Revue des Études Juives, Ha-Meliz, Ha-Yom, Ha-Kedem, Voskhod*, among others, and were sought out by the editors of commemorative anthologies in honor of eminent scholars, including professors Victor Rosen, Daniel Chwolson, Abraham Garkavi, Leopold Tsunts, and Morits Steinschneider. He also completed a fundamental and truly titanic work: a catalogue describing the manuscripts held by the Russian Foreign Ministry's Office of Oriental Languages.

It should be noted that not everything David Ginzburg produced was published in his lifetime. The book on Lermontov cited above came out only in 1915. His *Haggadah* (a collection of Biblical prayers, blessings, and commentaries associated with the exodus from Egypt recited during the Passover meal) was not published until 1962.

Ex libris of David Ginzburg

The unique library collected by three generations of Ginzburgs was passed down to David in his father's lifetime and in the 1880s was brought together in the young baron's house located at No. 4 Pervaya Liniya in St. Petersburg. Some of the books had been kept in Kamenets-Podolsk (where the collection first began) and others were brought from Paris (where, beginning in the 1850s, its most valuable components were kept). The centerpiece of the library was the Jewish manuscripts and books, the number of which expanded greatly under David Ginzburg's stewardship. The Jewish portion of the library was expanded through acquisitions from the leading booksellers of the day, including those outside Russia (Fischl Hirsch, Eliezer Azhkenazi, Ephraim Deinard, among others), and as a result of the purchase of entire collections (for example, approximately 100 extremely rare Jewish publications from the collection of Iosif M. Vyazinsky). One fascinating contribution to the Ginzburg collection was the entire personal library of the philosopher Vladimir Solovyov, including his theological writings.

It would be difficult to compile a list of all the scholarly societies in which David Ginzburg took part. He was a lifelong member of the Russian Imperial Archeological Society and the Paris Société Asiatique and was on the Scholars

Committee of the Russian Ministry of Education. These memberships were far from sinecures; they came with a great deal of hard work. He himself was the driving force behind the creation of the Society for Oriental Studies in St. Petersburg and the Société des Études Juives in Paris. He was intimately involved in the emergence of the Society for Jewish Scholarly Publications. One of the largest projects undertaken by this society was the publication of Russia's first Jewish encyclopedia compiled by Friedrich Arnold Brockhaus and Ilya Abramovich Efron between 1908 and 1913, "a collection of knowledge about Jewry and its culture, past and present." This is still the most complete and wide-ranging (in terms of the volume of text and quality of illustration) Russian-language encyclopedia on this subject; it contains more than 21,000 articles.

"The idea of publishing [the encyclopedia] met with his ardent and energetic sympathy," writes David Ginzburg's Russian biographer, Herman Henkel (German Genkel). "He was the first to support the idea and the encyclopedia owes its existence largely to his assistance." Working in close collaboration with Dr. Lev Katsnelson, Ginzburg became the encyclopedia's editor-in-chief. He also contributed entries on Arabic and Gaonic literature. The articles of this universal compendium, written by the top scholars of the day, has not gone out of date even today (especially when it comes to questions of history, biography, and issues of biblical interpretation).

David Ginzburg was behind the opening of the first secular Jewish institution of higher education in Russia, St. Petersburg's Courses in Eastern Studies. This name was imposed on the baron by officials at the Ministry of Education. It had been Ginzburg's intention to call the college the Institute of Jewish Knowledge. As the historian Mikhail Beyzer remarked, "The Judeophobic Russian government could not allow such an 'unseemly' word as 'Jewish' to appear above the entrance of an institution of higher learning and covered up this embarrassment with an 'Eastern' fig leaf."

The course of study included analysis of the Tanakh and the Talmud, Jewish and world history, philosophy, languages, literature, and art of the Middle East, as well as psychology and pedagogy. Baron Ginzburg himself served as rector. He recruited the best historians, orientalists, linguists, and experts in Jewish literature to join the faculty, which included Lev Katsnelson, Semyon Dubnov, Heinrich Sliozberg, Mark Vishnitser, Isaac Markon, and Abraham Zarzovsky.

Ginzburg lectured on Talmudic, rabbinical, and Arabic literature, Semitic linguistics, and medieval philosophy. According to Dubnow, the baron often invited students to his library, where they took turns reading out loud from the rare volumes that had been laid out on the tables (he would help them decipher difficult passages). He saw the objective of the Courses in Eastern Studies as "creating a learned element among the Jews that would be able to successfully meet the spiritual and scholarly needs of Russian Jewry, serve its interests as public rabbis or teachers, and generally help to uphold the covenants of the past."

As a public figure the baron was a worthy heir to his remarkable father. David became a member of the Society to Promote Education among the Jews of Russia and the Society for the Promotion of Agriculture among the Jews of Russia when Horace was still alive. After his father's death he replaced him as the chairman of the St. Petersburg Jewish community and of the Central Committee of the Jewish Colonization Association. He also founded the St. Petersburg Society to Assist Impoverished Jews and a kosher dining hall for students and served as a trustee of a Jewish orphanage in St. Petersburg, a Minsk farm, and an agricultural school for Jewish colonists in Novaya Poltava.

David Ginzburg was a close friend of the famous archeologist and vice president of the Academy of Arts, Count Ivan Tolstoy, who served as Minister of Education from October 1905 to April 1906. It should be noted that this liberal dignitary proposed eliminating quotas for Jews in institutions of higher learning. In 1907 Tolstoy and Ginzburg, along with the philosopher Ernest Radlov; Yuri Milyutin, one of the leaders of the Union of October 17 political party; Esper Ukhtomsky, editor of the newspaper *Peterburgskie Vedomosti* [St. Petersburg Gazette]; and Pyotr Izvolsky, Ober-Procurator of the Governing Synod of the Russian Orthodox Church, formed the Society for Equality and Fraternity. The members of the society (or rather *kruzhok*, meaning circle), despite diverse political convictions, shared a common mission of restoring "peace, truth, and justice," and "introducing their spirit into the University, the State Council, and the State Duma, and instilling this spirit through secondary and elementary school instruction." The goal was to achieve equality for all the peoples of Russia, with special emphasis on the idea that its participants would have to "fight anti-Semitism through word and deed."

The baron, like his father and grandfather before him, looked out for Jewish interests, and was always prepared to intercede on behalf of his fellow Jews. And he was in a position to do so. A prominent official in the Ministry of Foreign Affairs, he held the rank of State Councillor and was well received within the highest government circles.

He was also a patron of Jewish talent. It was he who saw a major poet in the 15-year-old Samuil Marshak, and he recommended the youth to the influential Vladimir Stasov (later the gifted young man found himself under the wing of Maxim Gorky).

Untimely death (at the age of 53) prevented the baron from realizing his full potential. He outlived his father, a legendary figure, by only two years. For this reason David Ginzburg was fated to go down in the annals of the advancement of Jewish rights as a successor to Horace Ginzburg rather than someone with great achievements in this area in his own right.

Clearly, in his views on the future of Russian Jewry, he was not fully in accord with his father. While Ginzburg senior believed that Jews could thrive in the Russia of the future, the son was an adherent of Russian Jewish resettlement to Palestine. It was for this reason that this Jewish antiquarian bequeathed his collection, lovingly assembled by three generations, to the Jewish Public Library in Jerusalem.

Would Joseph and Horace Ginzburg have approved? Hardly! Wholeheartedly devoted to their native land, they would surely be glad to know that the legacy of the three barons remains, at least for the time being, in Russia.

Brief Chronology of Jewish-Russian History

586 B.C.E.　　The Babylonians conquer the Kingdom of Judah and force some of the Jewish population into slavery in Babylon. In 538 B.C.E. Cyrus the Great of Persia conquers Babylon and allows the Jews to return home, but part of the community decides to remain in Babylon. Other conquests during the Second Temple Period result in the spread of Jews throughout the Greco-Roman world, especially to Alexandria.

70 C.E.　　Jewish revolts against Roman rule result in the destruction of the Second Temple in Jerusalem, the center of Jewish life. In the years that followed, the Jewish diaspora spread throughout the Roman Empire, all along the shores of the Mediterranean and in Mesopotamia.

600s　　Jews from the Middle East and Mediterranean areas migrate into the Caucasus.

700s　　The upper class of Khazaria, a Turkic kingdom located in what is today southern Russia, converts to Judaism.

800s　　Jews in southern Europe begin migrating into the regions of the Paris basin, Champagne, and the Rhine. Many of the European Jews are merchants, some of whom are involved in long distance trade with India, China, and the Muslim world.

960s　　Svyatoslav I of Kiev conquers the Khazars; over the next 50 years they are absorbed and assimilated into Kievan Rus.

988　　Vladimir I of Kiev converts to Christianity, after reportedly weighing the relative merits of Judaism, Islam and Christianity.

1200s-1400s　　Jews from Western Europe and Germany migrate to Poland and Lithuania in large numbers, both to escape religious persecution and to seek out the economic opportunities offered on the frontier.

1264	Poland's Boleslaw V the Pious issues the Statute of Kalisz, which grants the Jews in that country many freedoms and protections.
1300s	The Black Death in Western Europe results in the persecution and expulsion of many of the Jews living in the region, since they were blamed for the plague.
1334	Casimir III the Great of Poland reaffirms the Statute of Kalisz and allows many Jews to settle in Poland, with a promise of protection.
1388	The Grand Duke of Lithuania, Vytautas, issues a charter giving rights to the Jews in his kingdom.
1495–1505	Jews are expelled from Lithuania by a willful king, then shortly thereafter are allowed to return and reclaim the property they were forced to abandon.
1566	Jealous nobles in Lithuania push through an anti-Semitic Act whereby Jews are forbidden from wearing costly clothing and, further, "shall be distinguished by characteristic clothes; they shall wear yellow caps, and their wives kerchiefs of yellow linen, in order that all may be enabled to distinguish Jews from Christians."
1569	Poland and Lithuania are joined into a single commonwealth. Under this union, the Jews are granted significant autonomy and they participate in the settling of the southeastern frontier with Ukraine.
1648-1649	The Khmeltnytsky (Chmielnicki) Uprising by Cossacks, Tatars and peasants in Ukraine turns into a Ukrainian war of liberation from the Polish-Lithuanian Commonwealth. It results in the incorporation of Ukraine into the Tsardom of Muscovy. Thousands of Jews, who were serving as *arendators* managing the estates of Polish magnates in Ukraine, are massacred during the conflict.
1727	Catherine I (Peter I's wife, who ascended to the throne upon his death in 1725) issues a decree expelling all Jews from the Russian empire, including from Malorossiya (Ukraine), where they had lived for hundreds of years.
1742	Elizabeth of Russia attempts to expel all of Russia's Jews.
1772	After the First Partition of Poland, Catherine II ("the Great") issues a declaration confirming some rights for Jews in the annexed areas.

Brief Chronology of Jewish-Russian History

1791	Catherine the Great establishes the Pale of Settlement, an area in western Russia and newly annexed Poland where Jews are allowed to live. For the most part, they are not allowed to reside in the rest of Russia.
1804	Alexander I issues a statute allowing Jews to attain higher education and attend public schools, while at the same time severely restricting their occupations and land ownership in the villages.
1827	Nicholas I allows forcible conscription of Jews into military service. The Jewish community had to meet quotas and children were often kidnapped by special agents.
1835	Nicholas I further limits the areas where Jews are allowed to live.
1856–1863	Alexander II makes reforms giving Jews in the upper levels of Jewish society special privileges, including the right to live outside the Pale of Settlement.
1863	A failed Polish uprising results in retrenchment of Alexander's reforms.
1881	Revolutionaries assassinate Tsar Alexander II. He is succeeded by his son, Alexander III, who, abetted by his reactionary senior advisor Konstantin Pobedonostsev, attacks liberalism and allows free reign to anti-Jewish riots and pogroms throughout the Pale of Settlement that continue sporadically for the next 25 years.
1882	Alexander III imposes severe economic restrictions on the Jews. They are also, however, now allowed to leave Russia.
1881–1914	Over two million Jews leave Russia, most for the United States.
1889	Jews are only allowed to practice law with a special permit.
1903-1905	The anti-Semitic press and the government of Nicholas II support anti-Jewish riots and pogroms throughout Russia. Thousands of Jews are killed.
1913	During the trial of Mendel Beilis, the Russian Ministry of Justice attempts to prove that Jews use Christian blood in their religious rituals. The trial is met with intense international outrage and becomes a symbol of officially-sanctioned anti-Semitism in Russia. Beilis is acquitted by a jury and emigrates to Palestine, and later to the U.S.

Compiled by Noah Carnahan.

Bibliography

Авенариус В.П. *Бироновщина; Два регенства.* М., 1994.
Анисимов Е.В. *Анна Иоанновна.* М., 2002.
Анисимов Е.В. *Россия без Петра: 1725-1740.* Спб., 1994.
Афанасьев А.Н. *Народные русские сказки: В 3-х Т. Т.1-3.* М., 1984-1985.
Бейзер М. *Евреи в Петербурге.* Иерусалим, 1990.
Берхгольц Ф.В. *Дневник камер-юнкера Фридриха-Вильгельма Берхгольца* // Неистовый реформатор. М., 2000.
Берхин И. *Два еврейских врача при Московском дворе* // Восход. Т.III. 1888.
Беспятых Ю.Н. *Иностранные источники по истории России первой четверти XVIII века: Ч. Уитворт, Г. Грунд, Л. Эренмальм.* Спб., 1998.
Беспятых Ю.Н. *Петербург Анны Иоанновны в иностранных описаниях.* Спб., 1997.
Беспятых Ю.Н. *Петербург Петра I в иностранных описаниях.* Спб., 1991.
Бобе М. *Евреи в Латвии.* Рига, 2006.
Божерянинов И.Н. *Граф Егор Францевич Канкрин, его жизнь, литературные труды и двадцатилетняя деятельность управления Министерством финансов.* Спб., 1897.
Булгаков М.А. *Жизнь г-на де Мольера.* М., 1980.
Булгарин Ф.В. *Воспоминания.* М., 2001.
Булгарин Ф.В. *Иван Выжигин и его приложение Петр Иванович Выжигин.* М., 2002.
Быть евреем в России. Материалы по истории русского еврейства. 1880-1890 / Сост. И примеч. Н. Портновой. Иерусалим, 1999.
Вайскопф М. *Покрывало Моисея. Еврейская тема в эпоху романтизма.* М.; Иерусалим, 2008.
Вальдман Б. *Русско-еврейская журналистика (1860-1914): Литература и литературная критика.* Рига, 2008.
Венгеров С.А. *Критико-биографический словарь русских писателей и ученых. Т.1-6.* Спб., 1889-1904.
Вернадский Г.В. *Россия в Средние века.* Тверь; М., 1997.
Вигель Ф.Ф. *Записки.* М., 2000.
Вильбоа Ф. *Рассказы о подлинной смерти царя Петра I и о всешутейшем и всепьянейшем Соборе, учрежденном этим государем при дворе* // Вопросы истории. № 11, 1991.
Вихнович В.Л. *2000 лет вместе: Евреи России.* Спб., 2007.
Вокруг евреев. (Еврейский вопрос в России: Мемуарные и художественные хроники в изложении сочувствующих и негодующих) / Сост. М.Б. Авербух. Филадельфия, 2007.
Вяземский П.А. *Полн. собр. соч. Т.VII.* Спб., 1882.
Георги И.И. *Описание всех в Российском государстве обитающих народов, так же их житейских обрядов, вер, обыкновений, жилищ, одежд и прочих достопамятностей. Ч.1-3.* Спб., 1776-1777.

Гессен В.Ю. *К истории Санкт-петербургской еврейской религиозной общины от первых евреев до XX века.* Спб., 2000.
Гессен Ю.И. *Евреи в России: Очерки общественной, правовой и экономической жизни русских евреев.* Спб., 1906.
Гессен Ю.И. *Закон и жизнь.* Спб., 1911.
Гессен Ю.И. *История евреев в России.* Спб., 1914.
Гессен Ю.И. *История еврейского народа в России.* М.; Иерусалим, 1993.
Гинзбург С.М. *Из записок первого еврея-студента* (Л.И. Мандельштам, 1839-1840) // Пережитое. № 1 Спб., 1910.
Гинцбург Д.Г. *О русском стихотворении; опыт исследования ритмического строя стихотворений Лермонтова. Посмертное издание с портретом автора.* Спб., 1915.
Глинка Ф.Н. *Письма к другу.* М., 1990.
Гнедич Н.И. *Дон-Коррадо де Геррера, или Дух мщения и варварства испанцев.* М., 1803.
Голиков И.И. *Анекдоты, касающиеся до государя императора Петра Великаго...* М., 1798.
Голиков И.И. *Деяния Петра Великого, мудрого преобразователя России. Т.1.* М., 1837.
Головина В.Н. *Мемуары.* М., 2005.
Горшков А.И. *История русского литературного языка.* М., 1969.
Грачева И. *Из шутов – в графы* // Нева. № 6, 2005.
Греч Н.И. *Записки о моей жизни.* М., 2002.
Даймонт М.И. *Евреи, Бог и История.* Иерусалим, 1979.
Дело о сожжении отставного морского флота капитан-поручика Александра Возницына за отпадение в еврейскую веру и Бороха Лейбова за совращение его (1738 г.) / С предисл. и примеч. И.Ю. Маркона. Спб., 1910.
Дикий А. *Евреи в России и в СССР: Исторический очерк.* Новосибирск, 1994.
Дневник зверского избиения московских бояр в столице в 1682 году и избрание двух царей Петра и Иоанна // Рождение империи. М., 1999.
Долгоруков П.В. *Время Петра II и императрица Анна Иоанновна.* М., 1909.
Достоевский Ф.М. *Полн. собр. соч.: В 30-ти Т. Т.25.* Л., 1983.
Дудаков С.Ю. *История одного мифа: Очерки русской литературы XIX-XX веков.* М., 1993.
Дудаков С.Ю. *Парадоксы и причуды филосемитизма и антисемитизма в России: Очерки.* М., 2000.
Дудаков С.Ю. *Шафиров.* Иерусалим, 1989.
Евреи в России: XIX век. М., 2000.
Евреи в Российской империи XVIII-XIX веков. Сборник трудов еврейских историков. М.; Иерусалим, 1995.
Еврейская Энциклопедия: Свод знаний о еврействе и его культуре в прошлом и настоящем. Т. I-XVI. Спб., 1906-1913.
Екатерина II. *Записки императрицы Екатерины II.* М., 1989.
Елизарова М.М. *Община терапевтов* (Из истории ессейского общественно-религиозного движения I века н.э.) М., 1972.
Жихарев С.П. *Записки современника. Т.1-2.* Л., 1989.
Загоскин Н.П. *Очерки организации и происхождения служилого сословия допетровской Руси.* Казань, 1875.
Знаменитые россияне XVIII-XIX веков: Биографии и портреты. Спб., 1996.
Зорин А.Л., Рогов К.Ю., Рейтблат А.И. *Невахович* // Русские писатели 1800-1917: Биографический словарь. Т.4: М-П. М., 1999.
Иванов Вс.Н. *Императрица Фике: Исторические повести.* М., 1986.

Иосиф Волоцкий. *Просветитель, или Обличение ереси жидовствующих.* Казань, 1903.
История еврейства московского // www.russisk.org/article.
Каменский А.Б. *От Петра I до Павла I: Реформы в России XVIII века: Опыт целостного анализа.* М., 1999.
Каменский А.Б. *Российская империя в XVIII веке: Традиция и модернизация.* М., 1999.
Кантемир А.Д. *Реляции кн. А.Д. Кантемира из Лондона (1732-1733 г.).* М., 1892.
Карамзин Н.М. *История государства Российского. Кн.I-III.* Спб., 2000.
Карамзин Н.М. *Письма русского путешественника.* Л., 1984.
Кац А.С. *Евреи. Христианство. Россия: От пророков до генсеков.* М.; Красноярск, 2006.
Кацис Л.Ф. *Осип Мандельштам: Мускус иудейства.* Иерусалим; М., 2002.
Клейн Б. *Принадлежность к еврейству: Факты и версии* // www.kackad/com/article.asp
Клиер Дж. *Россия собирает своих евреев. Происхождение еврейского вопроса в России: 1772-1825.* М.: Иерусалим, 2000.
Князьков С. *Из прошлого земли русской. Время Петра Великого.* М., 1991.
Кожинов В.В. *История России и русского слова: Опыт беспристрастного исследования.* М., 1999.
Коллинс С. *Нынешнее состояние России, изложенное в письме к другу, живущему в Лондоне* // Утверждение династии. М., 1997.
Коняев Н. *Петр Первый и его птенцы* (из рассказов о русской литературе) www.zavtra.ru/cgi/veil/data/denlit/055/61.html
Корб И.Г. *Дневник путешествия в Московское государство* // Рождение империи. М., 1997.
Корнейчук Д. *Банкиры царского двора.* www.hrono.info/statii/2007/krn_bank.html
Корнилович А.О. *Нравы русских при Петре Великом.* Спб., 1901.
Корф М.А. *Жизнь графа Сперанского. Т.1.* Спб., 1861.
Котошихин Г.К. *О России в царствование Алексея Михайловича.* Спб., 1906.
Краткая Еврейская Энциклопедия. Т.1-11. Иерусалим, 1976-2005.
Крижанич Ю. *Русское государство в половине XVII века: Рукопись времен царя Алексея Михайловича.* М., 1859.
Купеческие дневники и мемуары конца XVIII – первой половины XIX века. М., 2007.
Курбский А.И. *Сказания князя Курбского.* Спб., 1868.
Курганов Е.Я. *Анекдот как жанр.* Спб., 1997.
Курганов Е.Я. *Литературный анекдот Пушкинской эпохи: Дис д-ра философии.* Хельсинки, 1995.
Курц Б.Г. *Сочинение Кильбургера о русской торговле в царствование Алексея Михайловича.* Киев, 1915.
Лажечников И.И. *Соч. Т.1-2* М., 1963.
Лахтин М.Ю. *Медицина и врачи в Московском государстве* (в допетровской Руси). М., 1906.
Лебедев Л. *Великороссия: Жизненный путь.* www.rusorthodon.com/books/lebedev/chapters
Левитина В. *Русский театр и евреи. Т.1-2.* Иерусалим, 1988.
Лизунов П.В. *Штиглицы – "некоронованные короли" российских финансов* // Вопросы истории. №10, 1999.
Линь Ш.Ж. де. *Портрет Екатерины II* // Екатерина II в воспоминаниях современников, оценках историков. М., 1988.
Лисаевич И. *На крыльях Меркурия: Из истории торгово-банковской жизни Петербурга.* Спб., 2004.

Лихачев Д.С. *Избранные работы в трех томах*. Т.1-3. Л., 1987.
Луппов С.П. *Книга в России в послепетровское время: 1725-1740*. Л., 1976.
Луппов С.П. *Книга в России первой четверти XVIII века*. Л., 1973.
Львов-Рогачевский В.Л. *Русско-еврейская литература*. Тель-Авив, 1972
Люблинский В.С. *Новые тексты переписки Вольтера*. Т.1-2. М., 1956-1970.
Мандельштам Л.И. *Еврейская семья: Драматическая повесть в трех отделениях*. Спб., 1872.
Мандельштам Л.И. *Стихотворения Л.И. Мандельштама*. М., 1840.
Мандельштам Л.И. *Учебник иудейской веры, для употребления в еврейских училищах*. Киев, 1870.
Мандельштам О.Э. *Времена года в жизни и в поэзии* (Избранные стихи). Иерусалим, 2007.
Мандельштам О.Э. *Соч.: В 2-х Т. Т.1-2*. М., 1990.
Манкиев А.И. *Ядро российской истории*. – 3-е изд. М., 1791.
Маркиш Д. *Еврей Петра Великого, или Хроника из жизни прохожих людей, 1689-1738*. Спб., 2001.
Мартынов С. *Финансы и банкирский промысел: Штиглиц, Гинцбурги, Поляковы, Рябушинские*. Спб., 1993.
Мейерберг А. *Путешествие в Московии* // Утверждение династии. М., 1997.
Мережковский Д.С. *Петр и Алексей* // Мережковский Д.С. Соч. Т.2. М., 1990.
Миллер А.И. *Империя Романовых и национализм*. М., 2006.
Молчанов Н.Н. *Петр I*. М., 2003.
Мордовцев Д.Л. *За чьи грехи? Великий Раскол*. М., 1990.
Нагибин Ю.М. *Шуты императрицы* // Нагибин Ю.М. Любовь вождей. М., 1994.
Нарежный В.Т. *Российсикий Жилблаз, или Похождения графа Гаврилы Симоновича Чистякова: Роман в шести частях*. М., 1938.
Неведомский М. *Зачинатели и продолжатели: Поминки, характеристики, очерки по русской литературе от Белинского до наших дней*. Пгд., 1919.
Немцы России: Энциклопедия. Т.1-3. М., 1999-2006.
Новиков В. *Три страницы*. www.nativregion.narod.ru/simple_page17.html
Олеарий А. *Описание путешествия в Московию*. Смоленск, 2003.
Орешкова С.Ф. *Русско-турецкие отношения в начале XVIII века*. М., 1971.
Пайпс Р. *Россия при старом режиме*. Кембридж, 1980.
Перетц В.Н., Перетц Л.Н. *Декабрист Григорий Абрамович Перетц: Биографический очерк. Документы*. Л., 1926.
Пештич С.Л. *Русская историография XVIII века*. Т.1-3. Л., 1961-1971.
Письма и донесения иезуитов о России конца XVII-начала XVIII века. Спб., 1904.
Письма русских писателей XVIII века. Л., 1980.
Платонов С.Ф. *Лекции по русской истории*. М., 1993.
Полонская И.М. и др. *Библиотека А.А. Матвеева: Каталог*. М., 1985.
Поляков Л. *История антисемитизма. Эпоха веры*. М.; Иерусалим, 1997.
Предпринимательство и предприниматели от истоково до начала XX века. М., 1997.
Проскурин О.А. *Поэзия Пушкина, или Подвижной палимпсест*. М., 1999.
Прохоров Г.М. *Памятники переводной русской литературы XIV-XV веков*. Л., 1987.
Пушкарева Н.Л. *Женищины Древней Руси*. М., 1993.
Пушкин А.С. *Полн. собр. соч. Т.1-10*. Л., 1977-1979.
Пыляев М.И. *Старая Москва: Рассказы из былой жизни первопрестольной столицы*. М., 1990.
Пыляев М.И. *Старый Петербург: Рассказы из былой жизни столицы*. Спб., 2004.
Пятковский А.П. *Государство в государстве: к истории еврейского вопроса в России и Западной Европе*. Спб., 1901.

Раковский Л.И. *Изумленный капитан. Исторический роман*. Л., 1938.
Ратнер Л. *На русской службе государевой*. www.hesed.ru/gazeta/archiv/2002/7/5/5.htm
Регесты и надписи: Свод материалов для истории евреев в России 80-1800 гг. Т.I-III. Спб., 1899-1913.
Резник С.Е. *Вместе или врозь: Заметки на полях книги А.И. Солженицына*. М., 2003.
Рогачевский А. "Верноподданный еврей": *Новые данные о Лейбе Неваховиче* // Вестник Еврейского университета в Москве. № 1. М.; Иерусалим, 1992.
Родионов А.М. *Хивинский поход* // www.kungrad.com/history/pohod/r
Розыскные дела о Федоре Шакловитом и его сообщниках. Т.1. Спб., 1884.
Русская летопись по Никоновскому списку. Ч.IV. Спб., 1790.
Русский биографический словарь. Т. I–XV. Спб., 1896-1918.
Савва В.В. *Московские цари и византийские василевсы: К вопросу о влиянии Византии на образование идеи царской власти московских государей*. Харьков, 1901.
Сафран Г. "Переписать еврея…": *Тема еврейской ассимиляции в Российской империи*. Спб., 2004.
Семевский М.И. *Историко-юридические акты XVI-XVII веков*. Спб., 1892.
Сементковский Р.И. *Е.Ф. Канкрин. Его жизнь и государственная деятельность*. Спб., 1893.
Серов Д.О. *Строители империи: Очерки государственной и криминальной деятельности сподвижников Петра I*. Новосибирск, 1996.
Синдаловский Н. *Санкт-Петербург. Действующие лица: Биографический словарь*. Спб., 2002.
Слезкин Ю. *Эра Меркурия: Евреи в современном мире*. М., 2007.
Слиозберг Г.Б. *Барон Г.О. Гинзбург: Его жизнь и деятельность*. Париж, 1933.
Слиозберг Г.Б. *Дела минувших дней: Записки русского еврея*. Т.1-3. Париж, 1933-1934.
Слободчикова Р.И. *Романовы. Нарышкины и их потомки*. Филадельфия, 2006.
Слова в дни памяти особо чтимых святых.
www.pravoslavie.uz/Vladika/Books/Slovo/II/Iosif3.htm
Соколов А.И. *Меншиков*. М., 1965.
Солженицын А.И. *Двести лет вместе. Т.1 (1795-1916)*. М., 2001.
Соловьев С.М. *История России с древнейших времен*. Кн.I-XVIII. М., 1988-1995.
Старикова Л.М. *Театральная жизнь в России в эпоху Анны Иоанновны*. М., 1995.
Стихотворная трагедия конца XVIII- начала XIX века. М.; Л., 1964.
Страленберг Ф.И. *Записки капитана Филиппа Иоганна Страленберга об истории и географии Российской империи Петра Великого: Северная и Восточная часть Европы и Азии*. Т. 1-2. М., 1985-1986.
Строев В.Н. *Бироновщина и Кабинет министров: Очерк внутренней политики императрицы Анны. Историческое исследование*. Т.1-2. Спб., 1909-1910.
Сумароков А.П. *Первый и главный стрелецкий бунт, бывший в Москве в 1682 году в месяце Майи*. Спб., 1768.
Татищев В.Н. *Избр. произв*. Л., 1979.
Тихомиров Л.А. *Тени прошлого*. М., 2000.
Толстой А.Н. *Петр Первый: Роман*. М., 1981.
Топоров В.Н. *На рубеже двух эпох: К новой русско-еврейской встрече (Л. Невахович и его окружение)* // Славяне и их соседи. Вып. 5. М., 1994.
Тредиаковский В.К. *Избр. произв*. Л., 1963.
Тройницкий С.Н. *Гербовед*. М., 2003.
Тростников В.Н. *Православная цивилизация: Исторические корни и отличительные черты*. М., 2004.
Фельдман Д.З. *Страницы истории евреев России XVIII-XIX веков: Опыт архивного исследования*. М., 2005.

Хотев П.И. *Книги с автографами лейб-медики А.Н.Р. Санчеса в фондах Библиотеки Российской Анкадемии наук.* Спб., 2003.
Чулков Н.П. *Происхождение Никиты Моисеевича Зотова* // Русский архив. №11-12, 1915.
Шаврыгин С.М. *Творчество А.А. Шаховского в историко-литературном процессе 1800-1840-х годов.* Спб., 1996.
Шубинский С.Н. *Исторические очерки и рассказы.* М., 1995.
Эдельман М. "Старик Державин нас заметил..." www.jew.spb.ru/ami/A235/A235-41.html
Юль Юст. *Записки датского посланника при Петре Великом* // Лавры Полтавы. М., 2001.
Янов А.Н. *Патриотизм и национализм в России 1825-1921.* М., 2002.
Янов А.Н. *Россия, у истоков трагедии: 1462-1584. Заметки о природе и происхождении русской государственности.* М., 2001.

Curtiss M.C. *A Forgotten Empress. Anna Ivanovna and Her Era. 1730-1740.* New York, 1974.
Dimont M. *Jews, God and History.* New York, 2004.
Fishman D. *Russia's First Modern Jews. The Jews of Shklov.* New York; London, 1995.
Hertz D. *Jewish High Society in Old Regime Berlin.* New Haven; London, 1988.
Jewish Apostasy in the Modern World. New York; London, 1987.
Israel J. *European Jewry in the Age of Mercantilism, 1550-1750.* London; Portland, 1998.
Klier J. I.S. *Aksakov and the Jewish Question, 1862-1886.* In *Евреи в России. История и культура. Сборник научных трудов.* St. Petersburg, 1998.
Lemos M. *Ribeiro Sanches; a sua vida I a sua obra.* Porta, 1911.
Lvov-Rogachevsky V. *A History of Russian Jewish Literature.* Michigan, 1979.
Montefiore S. *Prince of Princes: The Life of Potemkin.* New York, 2001.
Pipes, Richard *Russia Under the Old Regime.* New York, 1995.
Printer W.M. *Russian Rconomic Policy Under Nicholas I.* Ithaca; New York, 1967.
Rosman M.J. *Magnate-Jewish Relations in the Polish-Lithuanian Commonwealth during the 18th Century.* Cambridge, 1990.
Stanislawski M. *Tsar Nicholas I and the Jews: the Transformations of Jewish Society in Russia, 1825-1855.* Philadelphia, 1983.
Stanislawski M. *The Tsarist Mishneh Torah: A Study of the Cultural Politics of the Russian Haskalah.* In *American Academy of Jewish Research. Proceedings.* Vol.1. Jerusalem, 1983.
Stern S. *The Court Jew. A Contribution to the History of Absolutism in Europe.* New Brunswick; Oxford, 1985.
Weber F. C. *The Present State of Russia.* London, 1968.
Willemse D. *Antonio Ribeiro Sanches, eleve de Boerhaave – et son importance pour la Russie.* Leiden, 1966.
Zitser E. *The Transfigured Kingdom: Sacred Parody and Charismatic Authority at the Court of Peter the Great.* Ithaca, 2004.

Index

A

Abramovich, Roman 94
A Discourse Concerning the Just Causes of His Royal Majesty Peter I, Tsar and Sovereign of All Russia 78
Adventures in Czarist Russia 210
Afanasyev, Alexander 31
A History of the Jews 256
Akhmat, Khan 24
Aldanov, Mark 166
Aleichem, Sholom 226, 258
Alexander I, Tsar 112, 172, 178, 185, 197, 199, 209, 215
Alexander II, Tsar 220, 248, 259
Alexander III, Tsar, anti-Semitism of 257
Alexander the Great 35
Alexandra Pavlovna, Grand Duchess 204
Alexei and Dionysius 37
Alexei Petrovich, Tsarevich 110–111
Alexei, Tsar 10, 19, 45, 46, 59
Andrianova-Peretz, Varvara Pavlovna 182
Anisimov, Eugene 142
Anna Ioannovna, Tsaritsa 9, 12, 78, 82, 102–104, 114, 142, 144–154; anti-Semitism of 132; as Regent 104, 133
anti-Semitism 9, 18, 20, 28, 31, 81, 147, 165, 240–242, 257, 266, 269, 273; modern era 183
Antokolsky, Mark 256
apocalypse and 1492 39–41
Apothecary Department 53, 105
Apraksin, Alexei 102
Arakcheyev, Alexei 214
Aristotle 35
Arsenyev, Konstantin 255
Artsimovich, Viktor 260
Arzamas Society 193

Ash, Friedrich George 122–128
Ash, Ivan Fyodorovich 128
Ash, Pyotr Fyodorovich 128
Ash, Sholom 128
Ash, Yegor Fyodorovich 128
Ashkenazi Jews 122, 128
assignations 220
A Study of the Origins and Abolition of Serfdom or the Dependence of Farmers Primarily in Russia 217
Auer, Leopold 256
August II, King 77
autos da fé 37, 130, 241, 242

B

banyas 138
Basnin, Vasily 199
Battle of Kozhukovo 64
Battle of Poltava 77, 101, 123
Bauer, Rodion Khristianovich (Rudolf) 123
Bayezid II, Sultan 24
Beklemishev, Nikita 24
Benediktov, Vladimir 221
Berch, Carl 103
Bergholtz, Friedrich Wilhelm von 69, 89, 96, 124, 143
Berkov, Pavel 205
Bestuzheva Affair 113
Bestuzhev, Alexei 116, 125, 135
Bestuzhev, Mikhail 118
Betskoy, Ivan 137
Beyzer, Mikhail 268
Bibikov, Ivan 114
Biron, Ernst Johann von 12, 142-148, 150-152
Bironovshchina 142, 147–148
Black Hundreds 263, 267

Index

blood libel *97, 257*
Boborykin, Pyotr *255*
Bobrov, Semyon *192*
Boerhaave, Herman *131*
Bogolyubov, Alexei P. *249*
Bolotov, Andrei *146*
Book of Daniel *36*
Book of Enoch *36*
Bostunich, Grigory *241*
Botkin, Sergei *255*
Britain, Russia's relations with *119*
Bulgarin, Faddey *229*
Buturlin, Ivan *91*
Buturlin, Vasily *52*
Buzheninova, Avdotiya *104*

C

Cancrin, Georg von *10, 18, 20, 198, 212–223*
Casimir, King of Poland *24*
Cassian *40*
Cathedral of the Archangel *37*
Catherine I, Tsaritsa *82, 89, 99, 108, 142*; decree expelling Jews from living in Russia *131, 142*
Catherine II, Tsaritsa *137, 155–164, 165, 187, 204*; and settlement of Jews in Russia *156, 158*; and titles for Jews *128*; creates Pale of Settlement *164*; cured of pleurisy *133*; not predisposed against Jews *156*
Chancery of Secret Investigations *132*
Charles Leopold *78*
Charles V, King *141*
Charles VI, Emperor *109*
Charles XII, King of Sweden *101, 122*
Charter of the Rights, Freedoms, and Privileges of the Russian Nobility *205*
Chulkov, Yefim M. *208*
Church Council of 1490 *38*
Chwolson, Daniel *257, 267*
Clement XI, Pope *117*
Collins, Samuel *54*
Committee to Improve the Lives of Jews. *See Jewish Committee*
Constantinople *33*
Converted Misanthrope or the Lebedyan Fair 205
Cossacks *46–47*
Courland *78, 90-92, 144, 147, 150, 224*
Crimea *22-26, 33, 52, 59, 71, 114, 158, 160-162, 176-177, 197, 216, 248*
cryptography *127*

D

d'Acosta, Jan *94–104*
Dashkov, Dmitry *193*
Dashkova, Yekaterina *106*
Davydov, Abraham *150*
Davydov, Karl *256*
Dead Souls 210
Deborah, Or the Triumph of Faith 192
de Campredon, Jacques *89*
Decembrist Revolt *181*
Derzhavin, Gavrila, anti-Semitism of *168–173, 178*
de Saxe, Maurice *90*
Devier, Anton *18, 84–93, 95*
de Villebois, Francois Guillemotte *66*
Diplomatic Department *44–50, 108, 112*
Dmitry Ivanovich, Tsarevich *30, 40*
Dolgorukov, Ivan *203, 204, 209*
Dolgorukov, Pyotr *145*
Dolgorukov, Vasily *113*
Dolgoruky, Ivan *91*
Dubnov, Semyon *268*
Dudakov, Savely *63, 79, 163*
Dumas, Alexandre *210*
Dynin, David Ziskindovich *247*
Dynina, Rasya *247*

E

Economics of Human Society and the Financial Science of One Former Minister of Finance, The 222
Edelman, Mikhail *168*
education *250, 256, 269*
Elizabeth, Tsaritsa *9, 93, 114, 120, 125, 128*; anti-Semitism of *116, 135, 152–154, 156–164*; expulsion of Jews from Russia *153–154*
Elman, Misha *256*
Engelhardt, Yegor *219*
Engelhart, Nikolai *163*
Ens, Abraham *95*
Estates *15, 158*
Euler, Leonhard *135*
Ezra, Moses Ibn *266*

F

Feuchtwanger, Leon *104*
First Russian Fire Insurance Society *200*
Fishman, David *166*
folk tales *31*
For the Benefit of Russian Jews 233
Francisco, Diego *148*

Franz I, Emperor of Austria *128*
Friedrich I, King of Prussia *77*
Friedrich II, King of Prussia *161*
Friedrich Wilhelm, Duke of Courland *78*
Fyodor III, Tsar *57, 60, 81*

G

Gaden, Stephen (Daniel) von *10, 51–58*
Gagarin, Yuri *107*
Galich, Alexander *9*
Gates of Aristotle, The *35*
Gennady of Novgorod, Archbishop *37–41*
George I, King *117*
German Quarter *57*
Gessen, Yuly *168, 177, 179, 189*
Ginzburg Collection *238–242*
Ginzburg, David *239–240, 264–270*
Ginzburg, Evzel see Ginzburg, Joseph
Ginzburg, Horace *11, 253–270*
Ginzburg, Joseph *11, 238–270, 245–251*
Ginzburg, S.M. *233*
Giray, Khan Mengli I *22–26*
Giray, Murad *59*
Girshov, Berk (kidnapping of) *149*
Glinka, Fyodor *177*
Gluck, Johann Ernst *108*
Gnedich, Nikolai *229*
Gogol, Nikolai *210, 229*
Golden Horde *23*
Golikov, Ivan *61, 74, 96*
Golitsyn, Mikhail *102*
Golovin, Fyodor *77*
Golovina, Varvara *206*
Golovkin, Alexander *107*
Golovkin, Gavrilo *77*
Goncharov, Ivan *255*
Gorbachev, Mikhail *239*
Gorky, Maxim *270*
Gorshkov, Alexander *79*
Gostinaya sotnya *15*
Graetz, Henrich *256*
Grand Choral Synagogue, St. Petersburg *252, 261*
Grand Embassy *85*
Great Northern War *78*
Gretsch, Nikolai *180, 192, 207*
Grunstein, Peter *152*
Guryev, Dmitry A. *217*
Gustav IV Adolf, King *204*

H

Hablitz, Karl Ludwig von *161*
Ha-Me'assef *225, 231*
Hannibal, Ibrahim *95, 113*
Hasidic Jews *180, 185*
Haskalah *16, 17, 166, 175, 177, 184, 185, 189, 191, 224, 225, 250, 279*
Haven, Peder von *144*
Hebrew-Russian Dictionary *231*
Heifetz, Jascha *256*
Herder, Gottfried *194*
Hereditary Honorable Citizen *16*
heresy *32–41*
High Commission to Review Laws Pertaining to Jews *260*
Hirsh, Israel *141*
Hirsh, Moses *142*
Holy Roman Empire *46*
House of Ice *104*
Humboldt, Alexander von *219*
Huyssen, Heinrich von *108*

I

Ignatiev, Nikolai *258*
Inquisition *17, 84, 94, 129, 134-139, 242*
Inspector General, *125*
Ismaylov, Alexander *193*
Israelite Cavalry Regiment *163, 178*
Ivan the Young *27–31*
Ivan III, Grand Prince *12, 21–26, 27–31, 37*
Ivan IV, Tsar *26, 28, 41, 127*
Ivan VI, Tsar *104*
Ivanov, Almaz *10, 15, 19, 42–50, 55*
Ivanov, Vsevolod *29*
Izhorian Chancery *109*
Izmailovsky Regiment *204*
Izvolsky, Pyotr *269*

J

Jewish Cavalry Regiment *163*
Jewish Colonization Association *269*
Jewish Committee *169–170, 187*
Jewish Encyclopedia *268*
Jewish Family, The *234*
Jewish Historical Ethnographic Commission *256*
Jewish National and University Library *240, 244*
Jewish Statute of 1804 *172, 180*
Jews - colonies in Moscow and St. Petersburg *149*; conversion to Orthodoxy *49, 54, 63, 74, 111, 117*; conversion to Protestantism *180,*

190; court Jews *140–154;* elevated to Barons *128;* enemies of feudalism *141;* from Georgia *64;* granted full equality in rights *161;* higher education *227;* in courts of Europe *140–141;* in Crimea *22;* influence in Western European courts *22;* in Moscow *150;* in St. Petersburg *176, 185, 231;* Orthodox Church; *34–41;* refusing to convert *140–154, 146;* resettlement in Black Sea area *167;* settlement of southern Russia *158;* residency restrictions *171;* rights in Muscovy *21*
vocations: authors *79;* bankers *238–270;* diplomats *11, 23–26, 44–50, 59–70, 71–83, 90, 106–121, 112–121, 117–121;* doctors *27–31, 129–139;* entrepreneurs *43, 78, 197–202;* financiers *140–154, 165–173, 174–182, 197–202, 238–270;* government officials *191, 212–223, 224–237;* jesters *94–104, 203–211;* nobility *81, 191, 197, 246, 252, 254;* philanthropists *200, 238–270, 254–270;* physicians *10, 52;* police *11, 84–93;* postal director *77, 122–128;* purveyors to military *162, 156, 169, 191, 216, 252;* rights activists *165–173, 178, 251;* royal tutor *112–121;* scholars *266–267;* teachers *60;* traders *176–182;* translators *75;* writers *183–195, 205–211, 224–237*
Josel of Rosheim *141*
Joseph of Volotsk *40*
Judaizers *32–41*
Judeophobia *87*

K
Kaffa *22*
Kakhetia *10*
Kamensky, Alexander *142*
Kankrin, Yegor Frantsevich *212. See Cancrin, George von*
Kantemir, Antiochus *120*
Kapnist, Vasily *155*
Karamzin, Nikolai *31, 186, 189*
Karatygina, Alexandra *192*
Karl Friedrich, Duke of Holstein *91, 143-144*
Katsnelson, Lev *268*
Kavelin, Konstantin *255*
Kazan *23*
Khazars *33*
Khmelnytsky, Bohdan *10, 45, 47, 53, 272*
Khvostov, Dmitry *209*
Kiev *32*
Kitai Gorod *43*
Klein, Boris *196*
Klier, John *189*

Kochubey, Viktor *172, 187*
Kokos, Hosea *21–26*
Kol Shav'ath Bath Yehudah. See Lament of the Daughter of Judah
Koni, Anatoly *255*
Konyayev, Nikolai *87*
Kopiev, Alexei Danilovich *10, 203*
Kornilovich, Alexander *81*
Kościuszko Uprising *163*
Kramskoy, Ivan *256*
Krauss, Henrik Gottlieb *123*
Krizhanich, Yuri *49*
Krylov, Ivan *210*
Kurakin, Alexei *167*
Kurakin, Boris *108, 117*
Kurbsky, Prince Andrei *28*
Kurganov, Efim *205*
Kuritsyn, Fyodor *25, 37*
Kuritsyn, Ivan *37*
Kutaysov, Ivan *176, 177*
Kutuzov, Mikhail *216*

L
Lakier, Alexander *50*
Lakosta, Jan. *See d'Acosta, Jan*
Lament of the Daughter of Judah 169–170, 179, 187–188
Lazhechnikov, Ivan *21, 28, 147, 154, 229*
Lebed, Alexander *94*
Lebedev, Lev *179*
Lefort, Franz *67, 86*
Lehmann, Behrend *141*
Leibov, Baruch *10, 96, 132, 150*
Leon of Venice *12, 27–31*
Levin, Hirschel *175*
Levin, Mendel *175, 184*
Levinsohn, Isaac Bar *250*
Lev, Mendel *156*
Lifeguards *204*
Likhachyov, Dmitry *35, 41*
Lilienthal, Max *228, 250*
Lipman, Levy *12, 140–154*
Löbel, Hirshel *175*
Locke, John *189*
London - first Orthodox church *117*
Lopatochnik *36*
Lopukhina, Yevdokia *110*
Loris-Melikov, Mikhail *257*
lubok 62
Lunacharsky, Anatoly *239*
Luppov, Sergei *76*
Lyon, Hart *175*

M

mail - monitoring and censorship of *126*
Malorossiya - banning of Jews from *150*
Mandelstam, Benjamin *236*
Mandelstam, Leon Iosifovich *224–237, 250*
Mandelstam, Osip *224, 236*
Maria Theresa, Empress *161*
Markish, David *72, 85, 96, 110*
Markon, Isaac *268*
Markovich, Yakov *153*
Markov, Nikolai *241*
Marranos *9, 11, 17, 84, 94, 97, 129, 130, 132*
Marshak, Samuil *270*
Maskil *17*
maskilim *16, 175, 184-5, 228, 233, 250*
Matveyev, Andrei Artamonovich *127*
Matveyev, Artamon Sergeyevich *51–58*
Mavrin, Semyon *113*
May Laws restricting Jewish rights *258*
Mechnikov, Ilya *195*
Mechnikov, Lev *195*
Medvedev, Dmitry *245*
Mehmed II, Sultan *33*
Mendelssohn, Moses *16, 175, 185, 227*
Menshikov, Alexander *73, 81, 86–93, 102, 109, 114, 141, 144;* exile and death *92*
Mikhailovsky Castle *208*
Mikhail, Tsar *42–50*
military conscription *252, 260, 273*
Miloslavsky family *56-7, 60*
Milyutin, Yuri *269*
Ministry of Education *232*
Ministry of Internal Affairs *11*
Minor, The *205*
Minsky, Nikolai M. *249*
Misnagdim *17, 181, 185, 250*
Molchanov, Nikolai *110*
Molière, Jean Baptiste *100*
monetary reform *220*
Montefiore, Simon Sebag *159*
Mordovtsev, Daniil *46*
Moscow State University *120, 227*
Most Drunken Synod of Fools and Jesters *65–70, 99*
Muravyov-Apostol, Sergei *217*
Muravyova, Yekaterina *217*

N

Nagibin, Yuri *104*
Napoleon *180, 197*
Naryshkin family *51*
Naryshkin, Alexander *91*
Naryshkina, Maria *192*
Nash Sovremennik 238–242
Neledinsky, Yury *114*
Nenets. See Samoyed
Nesselrode, Karl *45, 199*
Netanyahu, Benjamin *245*
Neubauer, Adolf *265*
Nevakhovich, Alexander *195*
Nevakhovich, Lev *11, 169–170, 178, 183–195, 228, 250*
Nevakhovich, Mikhail *195*
Nicholas II, Tsar *255;* anti-Semitism of *263*
Nicholas I, Tsar *45, 200, 221, 246*
Nil Sorsky *38–41*
Noach, Judah Leib (Löb) ben. See Nevakhovich, Lev
Northern War *125*
Notkin, Nota *162, 165–173*
Novgorod *32–41*
Novoliltsev, Nikolai *191*

O

Oden, King of the Scythians 193
Okhotsk *93*
Olearius, Adam *42*
Olelkovich, Mikhail *32*
Oppenheimer, Samuel *140*
Order of St. Alexander Nevsky *18, 103–104, 115, 120*
Order of St. Andrew *123, 220*
Order of St. Anna *18, 216*
Order of St. Benedetto *103–104*
Order of St. Stanislaus *193*
Order of St. Vladimir *193*
Oreshkova, Svetlana *72*
Orlov, Alexei *106, 111*
Orthodox Church *34;* and possible merger with Anglican Church *118*
Osterman, Andrei *119*
Osterman, Heinrich *214*
Ostrovsky, Alexander *149*
otkupshchik 20, 150, 176, 180, 214, 247; end of practice *248*
Ottoman Empire *11*

Index

P

Pahlen, Konstantin 260
Pale of Settlement 164, 251, 257; rights granted to live outside 252
Pamyat nationalists 243–244
Passages Regarding the Military Art from the Perspective of Military Philosophy 215
Patriarch Nikon 49
Patronymic 18
Paul, Tsar 206–211
Pechersk Monastery 26
Peretz, Abraham 12, 174–182, 184, 197, 214, 216, 250
Peretz, Alexander 181
Peretz, Grigory 181
Peretz, Vladimir Nikolayevich 181
Peter I, Tsar 10, 19, 20, 60–70, 85, 94, 122, 143; and Dutch Jews seeking asylum 95; anti-Semitism of 95, 109, 158
Peter II, Tsar 144
Peter III, Tsar 10, 112, 115
Petitions, Department of 59
Petrograd Artel 200
Phull, Karl Ludwig von 215
Pikul, Valentin 103, 132, 148
Pipes, Richard 161
Pirogov, Nikolai 234
Plehve, Vyacheslav von 260
Poland, war with (1654) 48
Poland, First Partition of 159
Polish-Lithuanian Commonwealth 45, 165
Polotsky, Simeon 61
Polyakov, Lev 31
Portugal 129, 136; Jews in 94
post office 11
Potemkin, Grigory 12, 165, 175–182; patron of Jews 155–164; Zionism 163
Potemkin, Nikolai 159
Pototsky, Nikolai 52
Prikaz 14
Prokopovich, Feofan 71
Proskurin, Oleg 186
Psalter of Fyodor Zhidovin 36
publishing 256
Pushkareva, Natalia 29, 41
Pushkin, Alexander 95, 147, 154, 172, 221, 224
Pushkin, Sergei 204
Putin, Vladimir 245
Pyatkovsky, Alexander 141
Pypin, Alexander 255

R

Rabbinical Commission 230
Rabinovich, Hirsch 265
Rakovsky, Leonty 146
Razumovsky, Kirill 137
Reznik, Semyon 170
Rodionov, Alexander 102
Rönne, Karl Ewald von 122
Rosen, Victor 265
Roth, Abraham 141
Rubinstein, Anton 256
Rumyantsev, Alexander 110
Rumyantsev Museum 240
Russian-Hebrew Dictionary 231
Russian Orthodox Church in London 117
Russian State Library 238
Russo-Turkish War 165

S

Sachs, Senior 250, 264
Saltykov-Shchedrin, Mikhail 255
Samoyed 99–104
Sanchez, Antonio Nunes Ribeiro 94, 129–139
Saray 26
Sarmento, Jacob de Castro 131
Savva, Vladimir 28
Schick, Rabbi Baruch 175, 184
Schneersohn, Menachem Mendel 230
School of Eastern Studies 257
Schulman, Naftali Hirtz 184
Secretum Secretorum 35
Sementkovsky, Rostislav 222
Semevsky, Mikhail 43
Serov, Dmitry 75, 117
Shafirov, Mikhail 81
Shafirov, Pyotr 11, 18, 20, 71–83, 87, 95, 105, 108, 111, 127, 203
Shakhovskoy, Alexander 192
Sheremetev, Boris 69
Shiffman, Daniel 189
Shishkov, Alexander 192
Shklov 165–173, 175, 184
Shklover, Natan. See Notkin, Nota
Shlisselburg Fortress 65
shtadlan 19, 177, 249, 263
Shubinsky, Sergei 97
Shulman, Naphtali Herz 175
Shuvalov, Ivan 120, 137
Shuvalova, Marva 152
Shvenon, Samuel 156
Six Wings 35
Skornyakov-Pisarev, Grigory 91

Sliozberg, Heinrich 249, 262, 268
Society for Jewish Scholarly Publications 268
Society for the Promotion of Agriculture
   among the Jews of Russia 269
Society to Promote Education among the Jews
   of Russia 250, 256, 269
Sokolov, A.I. 84
Solovyov, Sergei 57, 64, 81
Solovyov, Vladimir 255
Solzhenitsyn, Aleksandr 142, 150, 161
Sonka-Bogatyrka 31
Sophia Paleologue 27–31, 40
Sophia, Regent 19, 51, 60, 64
Sorokin, Pitirim 222
Spasovich, Vladimir 255
Speransky, Mikhail 176; Judeophilia of 178
St. Andrew the First-Called 17
Stanislawski, Michael 222
Stasov, Vladimir 255, 266, 270
Stasyulevich, Mikhail 255
Stieglitz & Co. 198
Stieglitz, Alexander 202, 248
Stieglitz, Ludwig 15, 197–202, 216
Stieglitz, Nicholas 162, 197–202, 216
stolnik 105
St. Petersburg Postal Authority 123
St. Petersburg's Courses in Eastern Studies 268
Strahlenberg, Philip Johan von 100
Streltsy 10, 12, 19, 20, 51, 52, 53, 55, 56, 57, 58, 64, 76
Streltsy Uprising 19, 51, 53, 76
strigolnik 36
Suliots or the Spartiates of the Eighteenth Century: A Historical Tale in Five Acts 191
Sumarokov, Alexander 132
Suvorin, Alexei 240
Sweden, war with 77

T

Table of Ranks 20
Tale of Ivan Tsarevich, The 31
Taubert, Ivan 127
Taurida 160
tax farming. See *otkupshchik*
Temkin, Rabbi Vladimir 261
Textbook of the Jewish Faith 232
thieving at court 73
Tikhomirov, Lev 149
Times of the Year in Life and Poetry, The 237
Tolly, Mikhail Barclay de 215
Tolstoy, Alexei 62
Tolstoy, Ivan 269

Tolstoy, Pyotr 91, 107, 110
Toporov, Vladimir 194
Treasury Department 44–50
Treaty of Bakhchisarai 59–70
Treaty of Nemirov 82
Treaty of Nystad 78
Treaty of Rasht 82
Tredyakovsky, Vasily 104
Trostnikov, Victor 34
Turgenev, Ivan 249, 255
Turkey, war with (1711) 71–72
Tverskaya, Maria Borisovna 29

U

Ukhtomsky, Esper 269
Union of Zborov 49
Ushakov, Andrei 91, 132
Uspensky Cathedral 37
Uvarov, Sergei 227, 250

V

Vasily, Grand Prince 31, 40
Velikhov, Yevgeny 239
Vernadsky, George 21, 28, 31, 40
Verse of L.I. Mandelstam, The 228
Veselovsky family 105–121
Veselovsky, Abraham 19, 95, 106–112
Veselovsky, Alexander Nikolayevich 121
Veselovsky, Boris Borisovich 121
Veselovsky, Fyodor 18, 117–121
Veselovsky, Isaac 20, 95, 112–121
Veselovsky, Nikolai Ivanovich 121
Veselovsky, Stepan Borisovich 121
Vigel, Philip 210
Vimeni, King of the Samoyed 100–101
Vinaver, Maxim 259
Vishnitser, Mark 268
Volkonskaya, Anna 113
Volkonsky, Nikita 102
Voloshanka, Yelena 37
Volsky. See *Gagarin, Yuri*
Volynsky, Artemy 131
Vorontsov, Mikhail 116, 137
Voznitsyn, Alexander 132, 150
Vronchenko, Fyodor P. 247
Vyazemsky, Pyotr 203, 208, 221

W

War with France (1812) *180, 216, 247*
Weber, Christian Friedrich *101*
We Don't Even Need What's Ours *205*
Wertheimer, Samson *141*
Wolf, Levin *156*
World Wealth, National Wealth, and State Economy *217*

Y

Yanov, Alexander *37*
Yelena Prekrasnaya *31*
Yelizarova, M.M. *36*
Yid, abolished in state documents by Catherine *155–164*
Yudin, Vasily *10, 55*
Yuryev Monastery *40*

Z

Zachariah *32–41*
Zagoskin, Nikolai *43*
Zalman, Elijah ben Solomon *175*
Zalman, Schneur *185*
Zaporozhian Cossacks *46*
Zarzovsky, Abraham *268*
Zeitlin, Joshua *162, 175, 178, 179, 181, 250*
Zhidovin, Ivan Vasilyevich *10, 55*
Zhidovin, V.S. *55*
Zhukov, Dmitry *48*
Zichy, Mihály von *256*
Zionism *12, 262*
Zlatopolsky, Hilel S. *240*
Zlobin, Stepan *49*
Zorich, Semyon Gavrilovich *165–173*
Zosimus, Metropolitan *38–41*
Zotov, Nikita *10, 19, 59–70, 165-167, 177*
Zubov, Platon *204*

About the Author

Lev Berdnikov, a native of Moscow, earned his Ph.D. in eighteenth-century literature. He has conducted extensive primary source research into this period of Russian history and others, including during his tenure as a senior researcher at what was then the Lenin Library. He is well known in Russia as a historian with a gift for extracting fascinating but little-known stories from dusty archives and forgotten sources.

The author of six books and over 400 essays and articles, Berdinkov received the Gorky Literary Prize for his 2009 book *Clowns and Jesters* (*Шуты и скоморохи*), and in 2010 was honored by the Bulat Okudzhava Cultural Fund for the Americas. *Jews in Service to the Tsar* is the first of Berdnikov's books to be translated into English. It has been called "a weighty document of historical truth" that is "beautifully written," a book composed with "calm impartiality."

Berdnikov has lived in Los Angeles since 1990. He is a member of the Moscow Union of Writers and serves on the editorial committee of the Danish journal *New Shore* (*Новый берег*).

About the Translator

Nora Seligman Favorov is an accomplished Russian to English translator. Among her recent published translations is *Master of the House: Stalin and His Inner Circle* by Oleg Khlevniuk (Yale UP: 2008). She is associate editor of *SlavFile*, a newsletter for Slavic translators and interpreters, and a frequent translator and contributor to *Russian Life* magazine and *Chtenia*, a literary journal of translations from Russian. She lives in Chapel Hill, NC.

www.ingramcontent.com/pod-product-compliance
Lightning Source LLC
Chambersburg PA
CBHW071335080526
44587CB00017B/2843